and Beyond

Facilitated Positional Release

A Quick and Accurate
Manual Medicine Method

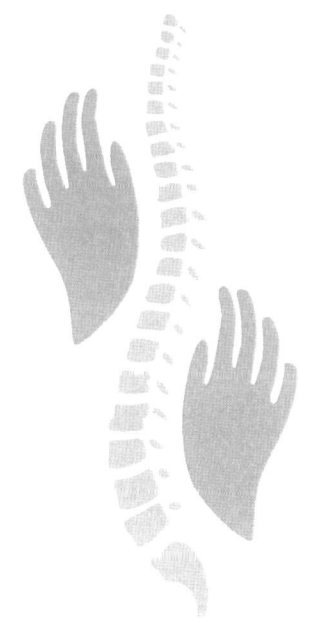

Stanley Schiowitz D.O., FAAO
Ellen P. Ellis D.O.

Preface

Dr. Stanley Schiowitz
1922 - 2011

A precocious child, Stanley Schiowitz was accelerated through the educational system; by age twenty-one, he had become a licensed practicing physician. Due to his exceptional diagnostic skills and his unparalleled treatment abilities, Dr. Schiowitz' reputation among both patients and colleagues grew quickly. It was clear that he had enormous intellect, boundless energy, and what would now be termed an innate ability to multi-task.

In 1977, the newly-opened New York College of Osteopathic Medicine (NYCOM - now known as the NYIT College of Osteopathic Medicine) asked Dr. Schiowitz to develop its Department of Osteopathic Manipulative Medicine. This allowed him to pass on his well-honed skills to upcoming generations of Osteopathic physicians. Over the next few decades, in addition to treating patients, teaching students, and developing fellowships in Osteopathic manipulation, Dr. Schiowitz perfected many of the successful manual medicine techniques that he had developed. He named these new treatment procedures "Facilitated Positional Release" (FPR).

In 1991, Dr. Schiowitz co-edited "An Osteopathic Approach to Diagnosis and Treatment" which is now the primary textbook at many Osteopathic schools. In 1992, he became Dean for Medical Affairs of NYCOM, and in 1995 he assumed the additional position of Dean of the School of Allied Health and Life Science at the New York Institute of Technology. Upon his retirement from NYCOM, in 2002, Dr. Schiowitz became Dean Emeritus.

Over the course of his career, Dr. Schiowitz received many professional awards. These include the Andrew Taylor Still Medallion of Honor from the American Academy of Osteopathy, the Dale Dodson, D.O. Award from the American Association of Osteopathic Manipulative Medicine, the Mentor Hall of Fame Award from the American Osteopathic Association, the Great Pioneer in Osteopathic Medicine Award from the American Osteopathic Association. Finally, in 2007, he received the Distinguished Service Certificate—the highest award given out by the American Osteopathic Association.

From the day he graduated from the Philadelphia College of Osteopathy in 1944, until his last days in 2011, Dr. Schiowitz embodied the underlying tenets of Osteopathy and its holistic medical approach to all patients. By combining his training from an Osteopathic school with his apprenticeship in family medicine, he was able to bridge two schools of thought: the allopathic approach to disease, and the Osteopathic approach to healing. This enabled him to use the largest possible armamentarium to treat his patients.

Dr. Schiowitz always believed that true wisdom only exists if it is put to use. During his retirement years, this philosophy led him to travel widely to lecture and to run hands-on FPR seminars. Dr. Schiowitz' students repeatedly asked him to put his techniques and philosophy into writing; that is how this book began. Dr. Schiowitz and I met weekly to work on the book, by meeting with students and patients, traveling to seminars, and refining and compiling each individual technique. As both his daughter and his long-time colleague,

I feel particularly fortunate to have worked so closely with him on this project.

Dr. Schiowitz was personal physician, teacher, mentor, and friend to many people. Unfortunately, he passed away before this book was published. Although no book can capture the essence of a man, I hope that this book will allow you to share in Dr. Schiowitz's vast wisdom, experience, and understanding of the human body. With his teachings, his legacy of healing will be passed on.

Ellen Ellis, D.O.

This book is dedicated to all our patients, students, and family members, without whom it could not have been written.

Disclaimer

The information is provided "as is" and without warranties of any kind either express or implied. To the fullest extent permissible pursuant to applicable law, we disclaim all warranties, express or implied, including, but not limited to, implied warranties of merchantability and fitness for a particular purpose.

This book is not intended as a substitute for the medical advice of physicians. The reader should regularly consult a physician in matters relating to his/her health and particularly with respect to any symptoms that may require diagnosis or medical attention.

Application of this information in a particular situation remains the professional responsibility of the practitioner; the clinical treatments described and recommended may not be considered absolute and universal recommendations.

Neither the publisher nor the Authors assume any responsibility for any loss or injury and/or damage to persons or property arising out of or related to any use of the material contained in this book. It is the responsibility of the treating practitioner, relying on independent expertise and knowledge of the patient, to determine the best treatment and method of application for the patient.

Copyrighted Material

Text and Illustrations copyright ©2016 by Decamus LLC

All rights reserved. This book is protected by copyright. No part of this publication may be reproduced or transmitted in any form or by any means, electronic or mechanical, including photocopying, scanned-in, or other electronic copies, recording, or utilized by any information storage and retrieval systems, without written permission from the copyright owner, except for brief quotations embodied in critical articles and reviews.

ISBN: 978-1791826703

To request permission, please contact:
Decamus at fprandbeyond@gmail.com, or www.fprandbeyond.com.

Acknowledgements

Many people helped make this book a reality. Thanks to all of the patients and students who allowed Dr. Schiowitz to learn from them; the New York College of Osteopathic Medicine (now called the NYIT College of Osteopathic Medicine) faculty and staff members, who worked so closely with him over the years; and the many Osteopathic colleagues who encouraged and supported him throughout this endeavor. A special thanks to the NYIT College of Osteopathic Medicine for granting permission for the use of Dr. Schiowitz's photos taken by NYITCOM's media department.

Thanks to Pilates on Fifth in New York City for so generously lending their studio for photographs and videos; Kurt Gorrell for modeling for the photographs and videos; Evan Benvenisti for his layout and artistic designs, including the book's cover; Debbie Klaber for donating so much of her time towards this effort (including by volunteering as "the body"); Adriana Alter for proofreading and assisting in editing; Justine Ellis for editing, photography and videography, and constant encouragement and support; friends (that includes you, Howard Flaxbaum) and family members (especially Josh Schiowitz) who boosted morale and encouraged us to forge ahead. And, lastly, a special thanks to Keith Ellis, who was always there, as a friend, support system, sounding board, and whatever else was needed.

Table of Contents

PREFACE i

Chapter One
INTRODUCTION

WHY THIS BOOK IS NEEDED 3
PHILOSOPHY 4
THE BIO-MECHANICAL MODEL 5
MY PERSONAL PHILOSOPHY 6
TERMINOLOGY 7
   Functional Spinal Unit 7
MOTION PATTERNS OF THE THORACIC AND LUMBAR VERTEBRA
ON THE VERTEBRA BELOW IT 7
   Flexion 7
   Extension 7
   Lateral Flexion 7
   Rotation 8
REGIONAL BODY MOTION DESCRIPTIONS 9
   Forward Bending 9
   Backward Bending 9
   Sidebending 10
   Rotation 10
MUSCLE TERMINOLOGY 11
   Superficial muscles 11
   Deep muscles 11
PHYSICAL RULES OF MOTION 11
SOMATIC DYSFUNCTION 12
PHYSICIAN'S EFFICIENCY OF EFFORT 12
   Exercise for the Upper Back 13
   Exercise for the Lower Back 14
WHAT IS FACILITATED POSITIONAL RELEASE (FPR)? 15
   How is FPR applied? 15
   Neutral Position of the Spine 16
GOING BEYOND 17
HOW DOES FPR WORK? 18

Chapter Two
THE CERVICAL REGION

Technique 1
Diagnosis and Treatment of a Posterior Cervical Hypertonic Superficial Muscle 20

Technique 2
Diagnosis of a Cervical Type II Somatic Dysfunction 23

NAMING A SOMATIC DYSFUNCTION 24

Technique 3
Treatment of a Type II Cervical Somatic Dysfunction 25

Technique 4
Treatment of an Anterior Cervical Hypertonic Muscle or Tender Point 27

Technique 5
Treatment of a Hypertonic Stenocleidomastoid Muscle 28

Technique 6
A "Shotgun Technique" to Treat All the Superficial Muscles
of the Posterior Cervical Region at Once 29

Technique 7
Combination Technique for the Diagnosis and Treatment of a Type II Somatic Dysfunction ... 31

Technique 8
Treatment of Chronic Restriction of Regional Motion of the Neck 34

Technique 9
Use of Spinal Vector Forces in the Treatment of Restriction of Motion in the Cervical Spine ... 37

Technique 10
Use of Spinal Vector Forces to Diagnose and Treat Dysfunctions of C3 through C7 39

Technique 11
Treatment of Acute Posterior Hypertonic Neck Muscles 41

Technique 12
Treatment of a Type II Somatic Dysfunction Locked in Extension 43

MOTION OF THE OCCIPITOATLANTAL ARTICULATION 44

Technique 13
Method for Diagnosing Occipitoatlantal Somatic Dysfunctions 45

Technique 14
Treatment of an Occipitoatlantal Somatic Dysfunction 46

Technique 15
Treatment of a Stubborn Occipitoatlantal Somatic Dysfunction 48

Technique 16
Traction Treatment of a Stubborn Occipitoatlantal Somatic Dysfunction 50

CERVICAL HERNIATED DISC...51
Technique 17
Treatment of Cervical Pain with Radiating Nerve Pain down the arm Secondary to Cervical Discogenic Changes or from the Narrowing of the Cervical Disc Space caused primarily by Degenerative Changes 51

POSTERIOR CERVICAL SYMPATHETIC SYNDROME AKA BARRE-LIEOU SYNDROME 54
Technique 18
Treatment for a Posterior Cervical Sympathetic Syndrome 55

Chapter Three
THE THORACIC REGION

TECHNIQUES ON PATIENTS IN THE PRONE POSITION 58
Technique 1
Treatment of Superficial Hypertonic Muscles or Tender Points in the Thoracic and Upper Lumbar Region...58

Technique 2
A Simple Method to Diagnose a Type II Thoracic or Lumbar Somatic Dysfunction 61

TECHNIQUES ON PATIENTS IN THE SEATED POSITION...............62
Technique 3
A Simple and Speedy Scanning Technique for Diagnosing Gross Deformities and Somatic Dysfunctions of the Thoracic and Lumbar Spine 62

Technique 4
Diagnosing a Somatic Dysfunction 65

Technique 5
Treatment of a Type II Somatic Dysfunction in the Thoracic and Upper Lumbar Area....66

Technique 6
Use of Spinal Vector Forces to Treat a Severely Locked Vertebra in the Thoracic and Lumbar Area...68

Technique 7
Chronic Localized Flattening of Two or More Segments in the Thoracic Spine 70

Technique 8
Treatment of an "S" Shaped Scoliosis of the Thoracic and Lumbar Spine...............72

Technique 9
Treatment of Superficial Tender Points on the Anterior Thoracic Wall 75

Technique 10
Treatment of a Tender Point on the Left Lateral Chest Wall 76

TECHNIQUES ON PATIENTS IN THE SUPINE POSITION 78
Technique 11
Treatment of a Tender Point on the Anterior Upper Chest Wall...................78

TECHNIQUES TO TREAT RIB AND CLAVICULAR DYSFUNCTIONS 79

Technique 12
Treatment of a Tender Point on a Lower Rib 79

DYSFUNCTIONS OF THE RIBS 80

Technique 13
A Simple Method for Diagnosing Posterior Rib Restrictions 81

Technique 14
Treatment of Posterior Restriction of Motion of the First Rib 82

Technique 15
Treatment of Posterior Rib Restrictions 83

Technique 16
Treatment of an Anteriorly Displaced Rib at its Sternochondral End 85

Technique 17
Treatment of a Depressed Rib at its Sternochondral End 86

Technique 18
Treatment of an Anteriorly Displaced Sternoclavicular Articulation 87

Technique 19
Treatment of a Posterior Sternoclavicular Displacement 89

Technique 20
Normalizing Rotation Motion of the Clavicle on the Acromion 90

Chapter Four
THE LUMBAR AND SACRAL REGION

A QUICK SCAN TO EVALUATE LUMBAR, ILIAC AND FEMORAL MOTION .. 92

Technique 1
Treatment of Hypertonic Muscles or Tender Points in the Lower Lumbar Area 93

Technique 2
Treatment of a Lumbar Flexion Type II Somatic Dysfunction 95

Technique 3
Treatment of a Lumbar Extension Type II Somatic Dysfunction 97

ALTERNATIVE WAYS TO CREATE A FIRST CLASS LEVER AND FULCRUM ... 98

Technique 4
Treatment of a Lumbar Flexion Type II Somatic Dysfunction 99

Technique 5
Treatment of a Lumbar Extension Type II Somatic Dysfunction 101

Technique 6
Treatment of Lumbar Nerve Root Pain 102

Technique 7
Diagnosis and Treatment of an Increased Lumbosacral Angle 104

An Exercise to Relieve Lordosis and Accompanying Pain in the Lumbar Region... 108

TECHNIQUES FOR SACROILIAC AND ILIOSACRAL DYSFUNCTIONS ... 109

Technique 8
Diagnosis of Restriction of Motion at the Sacroiliac Articulation.................. 110

Technique 9
Treatment of Restriction of Motion at the Sacroiliac Articulation 111

Technique 10
Treatment to Increase Motion of a Severely Restricted Sacroiliac Articulation.......... 113

Technique 11
Diagnosis and Treatment of a Severely Locked Sacrum Creating a Chronic "Low Back Syndrome"................. 115

TESTS FOR ILIOSACRAL DYSFUNCTIONS AND FUNCTIONAL LEG LENGTH DIFFERENCES 118

Test 1 *Standing Flexion Test*............... 118

Test 2 *Measuring Leg Length Differences* 118

Test 3 *A Scanning Technique to Determine Anatomical versus Functional Leg Length Differences*................. 119

Technique 12
Treatment of a Functional Short Leg due to an Iliosacral Dysfunction............... 120

Technique 13
Treatment of a Functional Long Leg due to an Iliosacral Dysfunction 121

PELVIC TENDER POINTS 122

Technique 14
Diagnosis and Treatment of a Piriformis Hypertonic Muscle or Tender Point.......... 122

Technique 15
Diagnosis and Treatment of a Gluteus Maximus Hypertonic Muscle or Tender Point 123

Technique 16
Diagnosis and Treatment of a Tensor Fascia Lata Hypertonic Muscle or Tender Point.... 124

ILIOPSOAS MUSCLE DYSFUNCTION.................. 125

Technique 17
Diagnosis of a Chronic Iliopsoas Hypertonicity........................ 125

Technique 18
Treatment of a Chronic Hypertonic Iliopsoas Muscle 126

Technique 19
A Stretching Exercise to Normalize Hypertonicity of the Iliopsoas Muscle............. 127

DIAGNOSIS OF THE ACUTE ILIOPSOAS DYSFUNCTION 128

Technique 20
Treatment of an Acute Iliopsoas Dysfunction caused by Lumbar Dysfunctions 129

A QUICK MOBILIZATION TECHNIQUE FOR THE ENTIRE
THORACOLUMBAR AREA... 131

Chapter Five
THE EXTREMITIES

APPROACH TO THE EXTREMITIES 138

CATEGORY 1
Hypertonic Muscles or Tender Points................................. 138

An Overall Approach to Treatment of Hypertonic Muscle Dysfunctions in the Extremities... 139

A Scanning Test for Upper Extremity Motion 140

Technique 1
Treatment of Hypertonic Muscles or Tender Points at the Shoulder Joint and its Surrounding Region 141

Helpful Pointers 142

Technique 2
Treatment of Hypertonic Muscles or Tender Points at the Elbow Joint and its Surrounding Region 143

Technique 3
Treatment of Hypertonic Muscles or Tender Points at the Wrist Joint and its Surrounding Region 144

Technique 4
Treatment of Hypertonic Muscles or Tender Points at the Hip Joint and its Surrounding Region 145

Technique 5
Treatment of Hypertonic Muscles or Tender Points at the Knee Joint and its Surrounding Region 146

Technique 6
Treatment of Hypertonic Muscles or Tender Points at the Ankle Joint and its Surrounding Region 147

Technique 7
Treatment of Hypertonic Muscles or Tender Points at the Plantar Region of the Foot..... 148

Technique 8
Treatment of Hypertonic Muscles or Tender Points in the Middle of a Muscle........... 149

CATEGORY 2
Motion Restrictions of the Large Joint Articulations 150

BIOMECHANICAL RULES OF MOTION IN THE EXTREMITIES........ 150

Technique 9
Treatment to Increase Motion at the Glenohumeral Articulation................. 151

Technique 10
Treatment to Increase Motion at the Elbow Articulation........................ 152

Technique 11
Treatment to Increase Motion at the Femoroacetabular Articulation 153

Technique 12
Treatment to Increase Motion at the Tibiofemoral Articulation.................. 154

Technique 13
Treatment to Increase Motion of the Ankle and Foot........................... 155

CATEGORY 3
Motion Restrictions of the Small Joint Articulations........................... 156

Technique 14
Diagnosis and Treatment to Relieve Restrictions
at the Humeral-Olecranon Articulation 157

Technique 15
Treatment to Relieve Restrictions of the Radial Head 158

Technique 16
Treatment of Restriction of Motion at a Metacarpal Bone....................... 159

Technique 17
Treatment to Relieve Restrictions at the Fibula Head 160

Technique 18
Treatment to Relieve Restrictions of the Cuboid Bone 161

Technique 19
Outline for the General Treatment of an
Extremity Articulation Somatic Dysfunction 162

COMMONLY FOUND SYNDROMES AND THEIR TREATMENT 163

Syndrome 1
Carpal Tunnel Syndrome 163

Syndrome 2
Treatment for Restriction of Shoulder Motion................................. 164

An Exercise to Increase Shoulder Joint Motion................................ 165

Syndrome 3
Thoracic Outlet Syndrome 166

Diagnosing Thoracic Outlet Syndrome 167

Treatment for Thoracic Outlet Syndrome 168

An Exercise to Improve Posture in the Cervical and Upper Thoracic Region ... 170

Chapter Six
THE FOOT

BASIC STRUCTURE AND BIOMECHANICS OF THE FOOT 172
A Test For Medial Longitudinal Arch Function 173
An Exercise for Strengthening of the Medial Longitudinal Arch 175
CALCANEAL VALGUS 176
  A Test for Calcaneal Valgus 176
  Treatment for Calcaneal Valgus 177
INTRODUCTION TO SHOES 178
LAST 178
MEASURING SHOE SIZE 179
ANTERIOR TRANSVERSE ARCH OF THE FOOT 179
  Treatment for a Dropped Anterior Transverse Metatarsal Arch 180
  Exercises for a Dropped Anterior Transverse Metatarsal Arch 181
  Shotgun Technique to Restore Motion of the Metatarsals 183
  Shoe Modifications to Relieve Pain at the Metatarsals 184
  Treatment Of Pes Cavus (High Arch) 184
PLANTAR FASCIITIS 185
CONDITIONS FOUND IN PEDIATRIC PATIENTS 186
  Flat Feet 186
  Pronation of the Foot 186
  Metatarsus Varus 186
  Calcaneal Valgus 186
  Calcaneal Varus 186

Chapter Seven
AN APPROACH TO GAIT ANALYSIS

GAIT ANALYSIS 188
BIOMECHANICS OF GAIT 188
OBSERVING THE PATIENT'S GAIT 192
DYSFUNCTIONAL GAIT PATTERNS 193
  The Psoatic Gait 193
  Erector Spinae Gait 193
  Antalgic Gait 193

Gluteus Medius Gait 194
Gluteus Maximus Gait. 194
Plantar Flexion Deficiency 194
Hiking up of the Pelvis. 194
Dysfunction of the Foot Tripod Action. 194

GAIT PATTERNS OF SOME COMMON NEUROLOGICAL PROBLEMS 195
Hemiplegic Gait 195
High Steppage Gait with the Toe touching first (Foot Drop) 195
High Steppage Gait with the Heel touching first (Ataxic Gait) 195
Shuffling Gait. 195
Scissors Gait 195
Waddling Gait 195

Chapter One
INTRODUCTION

Dr. Stanley Schiowitz, D.O., FAAO

WHY THIS BOOK IS NEEDED

When I graduated from the Philadelphia College of Osteopathy in 1944, I opened up a solo family practice in Brooklyn, New York. Over the next thirty years, I combined general medicine with osteopathic manipulative treatment in the daily care of my patients.
To balance my busy practice, to keep up with my studies, to stay involved in my professional organizations and to have time left for my family, I needed to develop a quick and accurate method of administering manipulative techniques. Over time, I began to work out fast and efficient manipulative diagnostic and treatment methods that expended minimal effort. These techniques freed me up to attend to the general practice and manipulative medicine needs of my patients — all during the same visit.

In 1977, I was asked to create the Osteopathic Manipulative Medicine department at the newly opened New York College of Osteopathic Medicine (NYCOM) of the New York Institute of Technology (now known as the NYIT College of Osteopathic Medicine). Over the next fifteen years, I developed the curriculum for the osteopathic manipulative department, taught the faculty and students at NYCOM, and continued to treat patients. In 1992, I became Dean of the New York College of Osteopathic Medicine, and served in that capacity until my retirement in 2002. During my years at NYCOM, I refined the diagnostic and treatment methods I had developed earlier in my career. The techniques that emerged from this period could easily be used by any practitioner, regardless of previous experience or specialty. I eventually formalized these methods into a system called "Facilitated Positional Release" (FPR).

For many years, I have taught FPR to practitioners from all over the world. The students, faculty, and manual medicine practitioners whom I encountered during my travels embraced the FPR techniques eagerly. Regardless of the individual student's initial level, he or she easily learned the methods. This reception and rapid adoption of FPR reinforced what I knew from the very first day I was introduced to Osteopathy: Osteopathic manipulation is an important and integral part of the complete care of every patient.

After so many of years of witnessing the positive results of manual medicine, I believe even more strongly in the importance of manipulative medicine. My hope is that physicians and practitioners of manual medicine will embrace the philosophy outlined in this book and will begin to incorporate these fast and efficient techniques into their busy medical practices. Once you have grasped the FPR methods and begun to practice them on your own, I trust that you will be able to adapt them independently to your patients' needs.

Dr. Stanley Schiowitz, D.O., FAAO

PHILOSOPHY

"Find It, Fix It and Leave It Alone"

Dr. Andrew Taylor Still, the founder of Osteopathy, is credited with coining the maxim "Find It, Fix It, and Leave It Alone." This statement was presented to me as a truism when I first started my studies at the Philadelphia College of Osteopathic Medicine in 1941. Regardless of the attribution's accuracy, I feel that this philosophy should always be followed in the practice of manipulative medicine. Simply put, it is our job as osteopathic physicians or manual medicine practitioners to find out what is wrong with the mechanical system, fix it, and then let the body respond.

What does the word "IT" signify? "IT" refers to a malfunctioning anatomical unit, which used to be called the "Osteopathic Lesion." The "Osteopathic Lesion," now called a "Somatic Dysfunction," is defined as a limitation of motion of an articulation within its parameters of normal physiological motion.

If manipulative treatment is being applied towards the normalization of the dysfunction (IT), the treatment must be directed towards the restoration of the normal parameters of physiological motion of the involved articulation.

What does this statement really mean? It implies that the osteopathic physician or manual medicine practitioner, who is utilizing manipulative treatment on a somatic dysfunction, is not directly treating the autonomic nervous system or the patient's headache. Rather, the physician or practitioner is specifically trying to normalize the somatic dysfunction, with the expectation that this will assist the body in its restoration of the patient's health. Once you accept this explanation, the practice of manipulative treatment becomes simple.

You find "IT" (diagnosis), you fix "IT" with manipulative techniques, and then you leave "IT" alone. The "leave 'IT' alone" part refers to the use of further manipulation to the area at that time; it does not refer to additional recommendations needed to assist in the maintenance of the restored health such as rest, exercise, or medication.

If you review the methods of applying manipulative treatments with which you are familiar, you will realize that most of them, if not all of them, fit the above description.

THE BIO-MECHANICAL MODEL

A.T. Still often described man as a perfect machine. This concept, later termed the "Bio-Mechanical Model," was derived from Still's engineering background and mechanical skills. When I was a medical student, this model was used to demonstrate the principles of osteopathic manipulative treatment, and it taught me to see the human body as a highly complex machine. Once I acknowledged this concept, it became clear that every system of the body, including the musculoskeletal system, is part of this machine and therefore obeys the bio-mechanical principles that govern the entire body. These principles are:

1 All parts of the body are interconnected in some fashion.

2 A dysfunction in any one part or system of the body can affect the function of any other part or system of the body.

3 In performing its functions, the body obeys specific physiological and bio-mechanical rules.

By applying these principles to the musculoskeletal system, we can see that any dysfunction of the musculoskeletal system can affect any other part of the musculoskeletal system, as well as any other system of the body. In addition, the musculoskeletal system obeys the same specific physiological and bio-mechanical rules as do all other systems of the body.

MY PERSONAL PHILOSOPHY

My personal philosophy has developed over my many years of treating patients and teaching students. During this time, I noticed that, on many occasions, neither students nor practitioners listened to their fingers. They studied a technique or pattern, and then told their fingers what to feel, rather than allowing their fingers to guide them in what to think. I have also observed that many students and practitioners memorize techniques without understanding what a particular technique is meant to achieve. Without this understanding, it becomes very difficult to adjust a particular method to a patient's needs.

These observations have led me to emphasize two concepts that I believe are essential to becoming a skillful practitioner. First, you must learn to feel and think through your fingers. Trust your hands and treat what your hands feel, not what you have been told you should be finding or what you think you should be feeling. When you get to the point where you are thinking through your fingers, you can then rely on your hands to guide you through the diagnosis and treatment of your patients. Second, understand what goals you are trying to achieve with your chosen treatment, and make sure you convey these objectives to your patient. This will ensure that both you and your patient have realistic expectations of the treatment's course and outcome.

TERMINOLOGY

To avoid any confusion, I have included my bio-mechanical definitions for the terms in this book. If there are any exceptions to these definitions, or if a technique requires any additional explanations on a specific bio-mechanical principle, I will include it at that time.

MOTION PATTERNS OF THE THORACIC AND LUMBAR VERTEBRA ON THE VERTEBRA BELOW IT

In all cases below we are referring to the motion of a "Functional Spinal Unit."

A Functional Spinal Unit

A "Functional Spinal Unit" consists of two contiguous vertebrae, and their intervertebral disc and connecting ligaments and muscles.

Flexion

"Flexion" is a rotary motion in which the anterior portion of the upper vertebra approximates the anterior portion of the vertebra underneath it, coupled with a forward translatory slide in the sagittal plane.

When T3 flexes on T4, the anterior portion of T3 rotates downwards towards the upper portion of T4, coupled with the motion of the T3 vertebra sliding forward on T4.

Extension

"Extension" is a rotary motion in which the posterior portion of the upper vertebra approximates the posterior portion of the vertebra underneath it, coupled with a dorsal translatory slide in the sagittal plane.

When T3 extends on T4, the posterior portion of T3 rotates downwards towards the posterior portion of T4, coupled with the motion of the T3 vertebra sliding posteriorly on T4.

Lateral Flexion (left or right)

"Lateral Flexion" is a rotary motion in which one side of the upper vertebral body approximates the same side of the vertebra beneath it, coupled with a contralateral translatory slide in the frontal plane. We name the motion for the side towards which it flexes.

When T3 laterally flexes to its right on T4, the right side of T3 rotates downwards towards the right side of T4, coupled with the motion of the T3 vertebra sliding towards the left, in relation to T4.

> **Note:** *In osteopathic literature the description of a vertebral Type II Somatic Dysfunction uses the term "sidebending" rather than "lateral flexion." To avoid any confusion, throughout this book we will follow the familiar osteopathic notation style of using "sidebending," not "lateral flexion," when naming a lesion.*

Rotation

"Rotation of a vertebra" refers to the direction of motion of the anterior surface of the vertebra, either to the right or left in the horizontal plane. Rotation is accompanied by the coupled translatory motion of the upper vertebra approaching the one beneath it. As rotation occurs, the intervening vertebral disc is compressed; when the vertebra rotates back to the midline, the compressed disc returns to its normal size.

Rotation of T3 to the right describes the motion of the anterior surface of the vertebra of T3 rotating to its right side. The rotation motion is accompanied by a coupled motion of the T3 vertebra approximating the T4 vertebra.

> **Note:** *The typical cervical vertebra from C3 through C7 obeys all the above laws. It's motion varies from other vertebra when describing the coupled motion of lateral flexion and rotation. At the level of C3 through C7, lateral flexion and rotation are always towards the same side.*

When looking at the patient's spine from behind, we cannot see or feel the motions of the vertebral bodies. Instead, we see and feel the motions of the spinous process and the transverse processes. When T3 rotates to the right, we see and feel the spinous process of T3 rotate to the left in relation to the spinous process of T4, as well as the right transverse process of T3 becoming more prominent as it rotates in a posterior direction.

REGIONAL BODY MOTION DESCRIPTIONS

Forward bending

This term describes bending the top portion of an area of the body forward to approximate a lower part of the body. For example: If you bend your neck forward so that your chin approximates your chest wall, this would be forward bending of your cervical region. [Fig. 1.1]

Backward bending

This term describes bending the top portion of an area of the body back to approximate the portion below it. For example: If you bend your head backwards so that the back of the head approximates the posterior aspect of your neck, this would be backward bending of your cervical region. [Fig. 1.2]

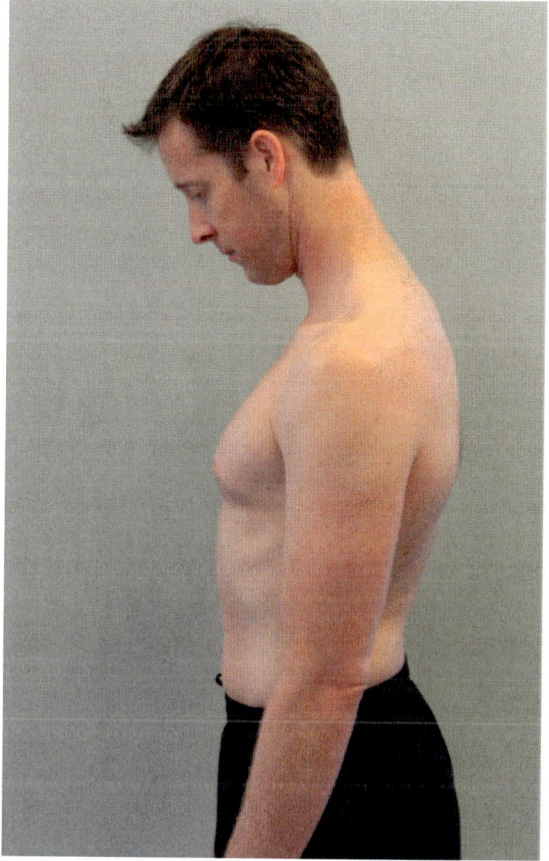

Figure 1.1
Forward Bending of the Cervical Region.

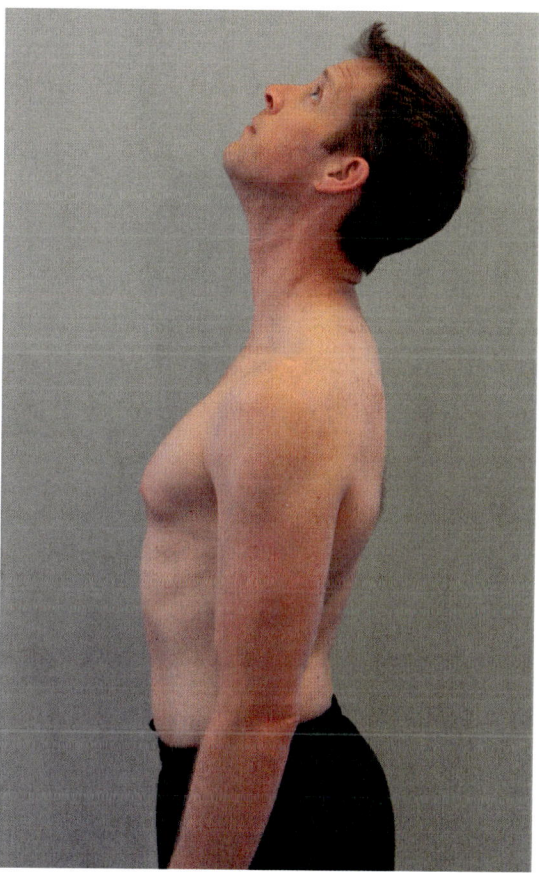

Figure 1.2
Backward Bending of the Cervical Region.

Sidebending (left or right)

This term describes motion of the body towards the right or left. For example: If you stand up straight and slide your right hand down the right side of your body towards your right foot, this would be sidebending to the right. [Fig. 1.3]

Rotation (Left of Right)

This term describes rotary motion of the body to the right or to the left side.
For example: If you turn your entire upper torso so it is facing towards the left side, this would be rotation left.
[Fig. 1.4]

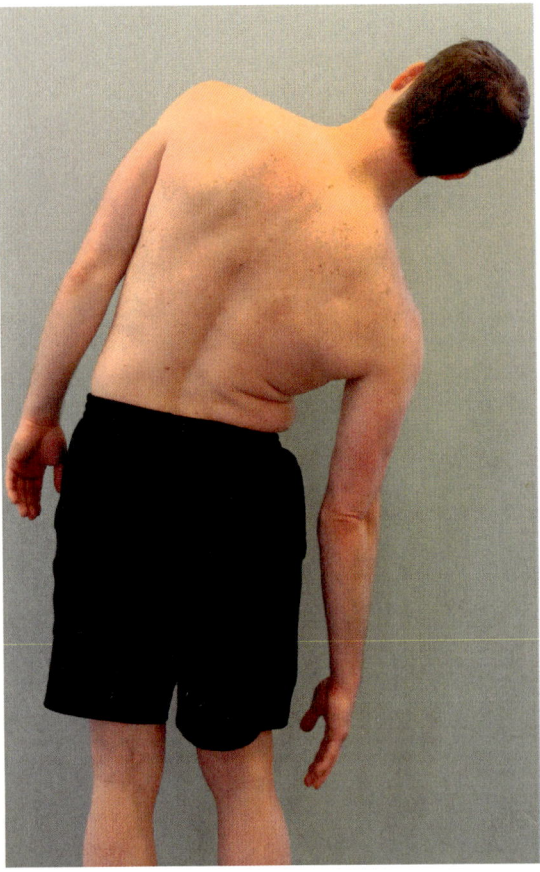

Figure 1.3
Sidebending to the Right.

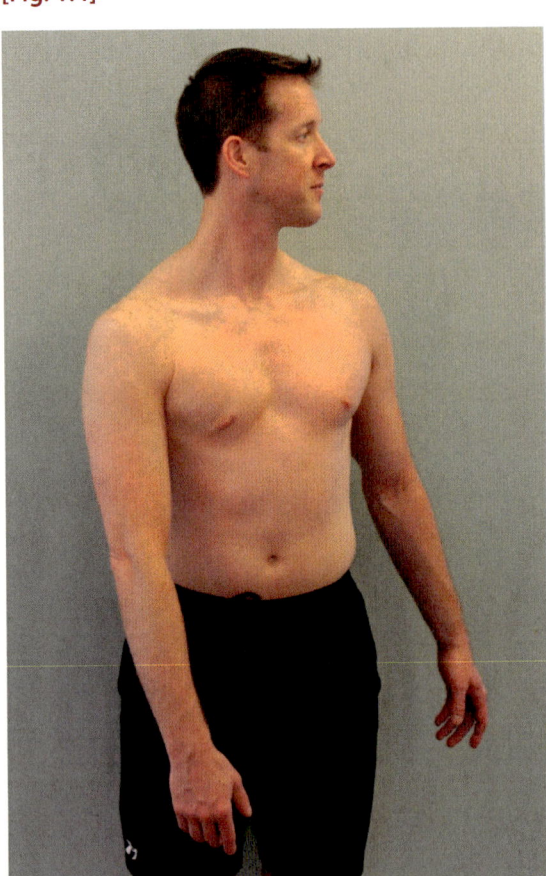

Figure 1.4
Rotation to the Left.

Note: *Be aware that both "sidebending" and "rotation" describe motion of both an individual vertebra and of a region of the body.*

FREEDOM OF MOTION

Freedom of motion occurs in three planes. Flexion and extension occur in the sagittal plane; lateral flexion, right or left, occurs in the frontal plane; and rotation, right or left, occurs in the horizontal plane.

MUSCLE TERMINOLOGY

Superficial muscles

These are the easily palpable muscles just below the skin. Their primary function is to create regional motion at the portion of the body to which they are attached.

If the muscle is at the back of the torso, the attached muscles' freedom of motion is backward bending, and sidebending towards the muscle. If the muscle is at the front of the torso, its freedom of motion is usually forward bending, and rotation of the torso towards the muscle.

Deep muscles

These are the very small muscles that are attached to the vertebra and cannot be palpated. They create and control the small motions of each vertebra's movement in relation to the vertebra below it.

The deep muscles' freedom of motion is in all three planes: frontal, sagittal, and horizontal. When a Type II Somatic Dysfunction is diagnosed, it is named to describe the deep muscles' freedom of motion at that Functional Spinal Unit.

PHYSICAL RULES OF MOTION

1. When a body placed in motion meets a barrier in that plane of motion, the body will try to move around the barrier into its freedom of motion.

2. Lateral flexion and rotation motion of the vertebrae are always coupled motions. If you apply a lateral flexion motion to a vertebra, the lateral flexion motion will always be accompanied by its rotary motion. Depending on the vertebra involved, this can be either in the same direction or in the contralateral direction of the lateral flexion.

For example: If you try to flex T4 on T5 and there is a barrier to flexion, then T4 will move around this barrier and attempt to move into a direction that is free, which in this case would be either, right or left lateral flexion accompanied by right or left rotation.

SOMATIC DYSFUNCTION

(Previously referred to as an Osteopathic Lesion)

In this textbook, a Somatic Dysfunction is defined as a limitation of motion of a Functional Spinal Unit within its parameters of normal physiological motion.

TYPE II SOMATIC DYSFUNCTION

A Type II Somatic Dysfunction is present when the motion of one vertebra, in relation to the one below it, has developed barriers to motion in all three primary planes of the body: frontal, sagittal, and horizontal.

A Type II Somatic Dysfunction is named by describing its freedom of motion. For example: If T3 vertebra's freedom of motion were in flexion, sidebending, and rotation to the left, then the name of the Somatic Dysfunction would be T3 Flexion, Sidebent left, Rotated left (T3 F SL RL). In other words, T3 is restricted in motion on T4 in extension, right lateral flexion, and rotation to the right.

PHYSICIAN'S EFFICIENCY OF EFFORT

Many practitioners who attend my programs complain that they are exhausted and more prone to develop back problems after treating several patients a day. These difficulties deter them from incorporating manipulative medicine into their practices. They then ask me, "How did you find the time and energy to treat as many as sixty patients a day?" The answer is "Organization of time, coupled with efficiency of effort."

Below are some suggestions for reducing wear and tear on the practitioner:

1. Purchase a table whose height can be adjusted, as well as a wheeled stool or chair that can be rolled easily.

2. Whenever you perform a technique which requires force, rely on your body weight rather than your muscle power.

3. When you apply force, use your larger muscles rather than your smaller ones; for example, use your lower back or upper thigh muscles rather than your arm muscles.

4. Whenever possible, sit rather than stand while you apply manipulative techniques.

5. Whenever possible, train and use assistants to explain and review any exercise, diet, or medications prescribed.

6. Care for your own back by performing the following daily exercises.

Exercises for the Back

Exercise for the Upper Back

Step 1
Either sit or stand in front of a mirror and place an opened tissue box on your head, with the open side facing down. [Fig. 1.5]

Step 2
Bring your chin straight back without flexing or extending your head; if you tilt your head, the tissue box will fall off. You should feel a straightening of the normal cervical lordosis and the upper thoracic kyphosis. Hold this position for ten to fifteen seconds and then release. [Fig. 1.6]

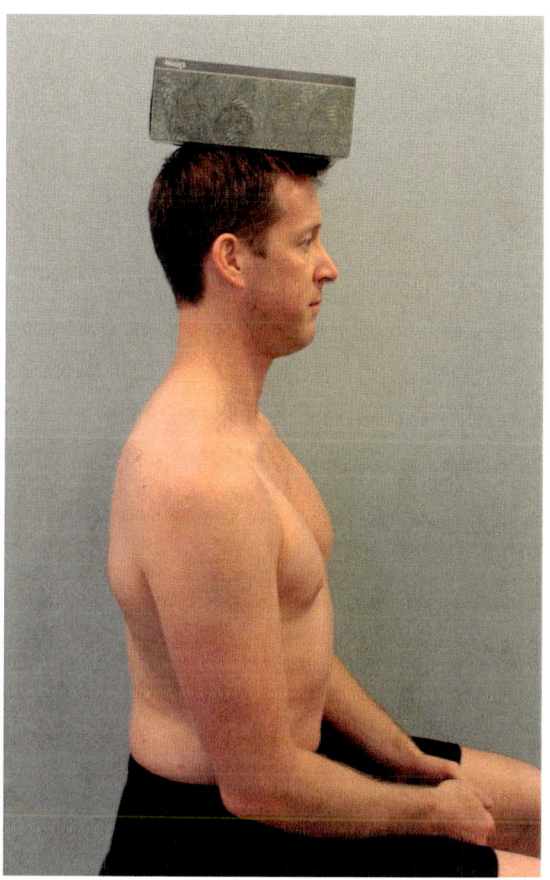

Figure 1.5
Exercise for the Upper Back - Step 1.

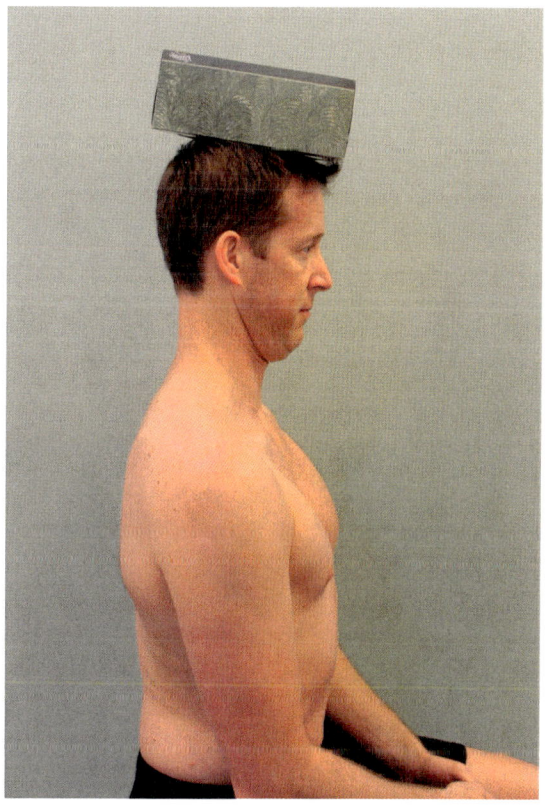

Figure 1.6
Exercise for the Upper Back - Step 2.

Step 3
Repeat this exercise two to three times and perform it several times during the day. With time you will no longer need to look in the mirror or place the tissue box on your head to perform the exercise.

Excercise for the Lower Back

Step 1

Stand with your feet about six to ten inches apart. Imagine trying to squeeze a pencil between your buttocks. Continue squeezing and at the same time contract your abdominal muscles as firmly as you can.

Step 2

Hold this position and rotate your upper thighs towards the midline, but do not move your feet. You will notice a flattening of your lumbar lordosis and a relief of any strain in your lower back. Maintain this position for ten to fifteen seconds.

Step 3

Repeat this exercise at least three times. Perform it several times during the day.

I recommend practicing these exercises daily, so that you will eventually be able to perform them just about anywhere and at any time during the day, including while talking on the phone or even while treating patients.

WHAT IS FACILITATED POSITIONAL RELEASE (FPR)?

Facilitated Positional Release is a non-traumatic, highly effective system of manual medicine. FPR can easily be used to normalize hypertonic voluntary muscles.

Note that I didn't mention Somatic Dysfunctions when describing Facilitated Positional Release. This is because, when using FPR, you are treating hypertonic muscles; if these hypertonic muscles are involved in the development of Somatic Dysfunctions, then normalization of the muscles will indirectly affect the involved Somatic Dysfunctions.

WHEN IS IT APPROPRIATE TO USE FPR?

FPR can be used to normalize hypertonic muscles in any part of the musculoskeletal system. This includes the large superficial muscles, the small deep muscles, and the small group of muscle fibers that cause point tenderness and are called "tender points."

HOW IS FPR APPLIED?

1. The muscle or muscle fibers involved are placed at rest.
2. If the muscle to be treated is attached to an articulation, then that articulation must not be in the closed pack position. An articulation is considered to be in the closed pack position when no more motion can occur at the articulation and the articulation is locked.
3. The articulation, extremity, or Functional Spinal Unit is then placed into its neutral position.
4. The area to be treated is monitored, and a mild compressive force is applied to shorten the muscle fibers.
5. While the practitioner maintains the compression, the muscle fibers are moved through their freedom of motion.
6. An immediate softening and normalization of the muscle fibers or tender points will occur.

The goal in treatment is to normalize motion. Treatment with FPR will restore the hypertonic muscle fibers to their normal motion and tone and indirectly normalize a Type II Somatic Dysfunction.

WHAT IS MEANT BY THE NEUTRAL POSITION OF THE SPINE?

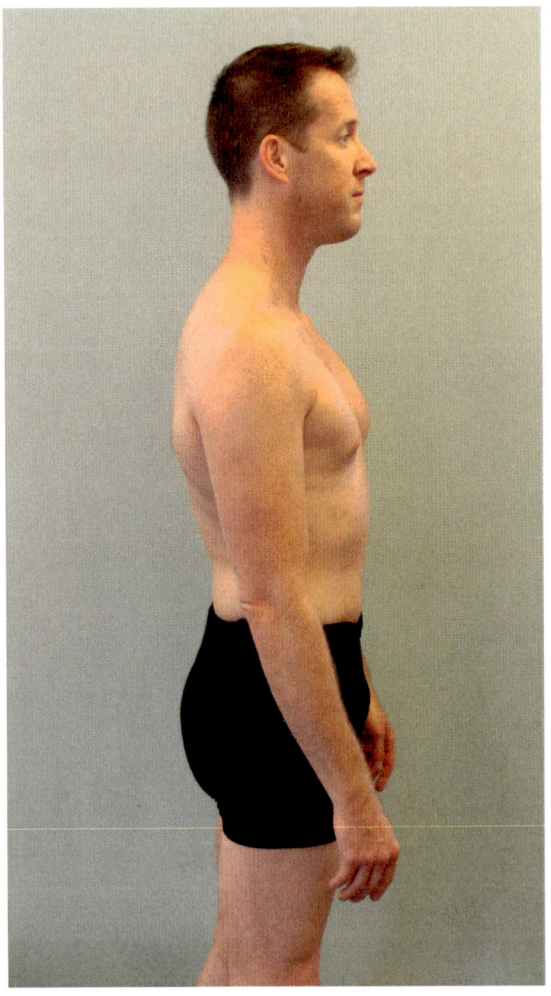

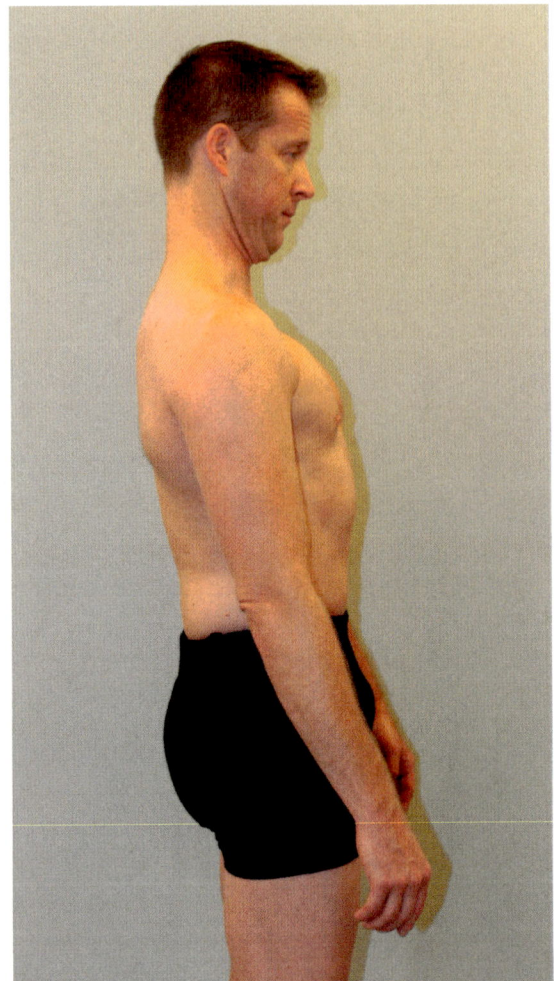

Figure 1.7
Normal Curvatures of the Spine.

When the spine is observed from the side, in its upright position, the normal spinal curvatures will consist of a lordosis in the cervical and lumbar regions and a kyphosis in the thoracic region. When the spine is in its upright position no individual vertebra will be in the neutral position in relation to the vertebra above or below it. [Fig. 1.7]

Figure 1.8
Neutral Position of the Spine

The spine is in its neutral position when each vertebra, or its Functional Spinal Unit, is directly aligned with the one below it. [Fig. 1.8]

Placing an area to be treated in its neutral position is important because, in this position, the articular facets are disengaged and have complete freedom of movement. This freedom of motion allows you to utilize very small motions while working on a patient. It will also increase your accuracy and ability to treat difficult cases.

GOING BEYOND

There will be times when a dysfunction will not respond to the basic application of FPR techniques. In such cases, I recommend adding traction, jiggling and/or isometric contractions.

1. Traction: Adding traction to an articulation will separate the articulation and allow you to introduce other procedures to increase specific motions of that articulation.

2. Jiggling: Applying multiple, low amplitude thrusts through the ease of motion(s) of an articulation will assist in increasing the motion of the articulation.

3. Isometric contractions: Adding isometric contractions to the muscles involved may help restore their normal tone.

HOW DOES FPR WORK?

The theory behind FPR is that a negative muscle spindle reflex is initiated, and will restore the muscle's normal resting tone. What do I mean by this?

FPR is based on the following concept: placing the muscle fibers involved into their shortened positions of freedom of motion will stop the firing of nerve impulses that keep the muscle shortened and allow the muscle to relax.

A familiar test performed on a patient is eliciting a patella reflex. This test, which is usually performed on a seated patient, relies on creating a simple muscle spindle reflex. The test begins when you strike the patient's patella ligament with a reflex hammer. Note that this entire process takes less than a second.

1 The initial blow pulls and stretches the quadricep's tendon and the muscle to which it is attached.

2 When the muscle spindles within the muscle fibers are stretched, they send an afferent impulse to the spinal cord, signaling that the muscle is being stretched and needs to be shortened.

3 The spinal cord immediately responds with an efferent impulse to the muscle spindles, which shortens the stretched muscle fibers.

4 As the muscle contracts and shortens, the knee joint extends.

5 When the muscle has shortened, a second afferent message is sent by the muscle spindle to the spinal cord, signaling that the efferent impulses should be turned off.

6 The spinal cord responds with a second efferent message to the muscle spindles, signaling them to stop shortening the muscle fibers. This will return the muscle to its resting state, and the knee to a flexed position.

If the muscle does not properly receive the second efferent message telling it to stop the shortening, the muscle spindles and their respective muscle fibers will stay in a constant state of hypertonicity and shortened position. To correct this, a separate signal needs to be sent to the muscle fibers to turn off the hypertonicity.

At this point, the negative muscle spindle reflex comes into play. A negative muscle spindle reflex is the inhibition of the muscle spindle reflex that is causing the shortening. So, if the muscle fibers are in a constant hypertonic state, further shortening of the muscle's fibers will trigger a negative muscle spindle reflex. This reflex will turn off the message that is keeping the muscles in a hypertonic state, thereby restoring them to their normal state of rest.

I must add a disclaimer at this point. I am certain that, some day, we will be able to explain this phenomenon better. In the meantime, this is the best explanation we have. What is certain, however, is that the techniques work.

Chapter Two

THE CERVICAL REGION

Technique 1
Diagnosis and Treatment of a Posterior Cervical Hypertonic Superficial Muscle

Patient position
Ask the patient to lie in the supine position.

Practitioner position
Sit at the head of the table with a pillow on your lap.

Procedure:

Step 1
Ask the patient to slide back until his cervical spine and the middle portion of his trapezius muscle are off the table and resting comfortably on the pillow on your lap. This position will allow for relaxation of the cervical area and freedom of motion of the involved muscles.

Step 2
Beginning at the suboccipital area, place the index or middle finger of each hand lateral to the sides of the spinous processes. [Fig. 2.1]

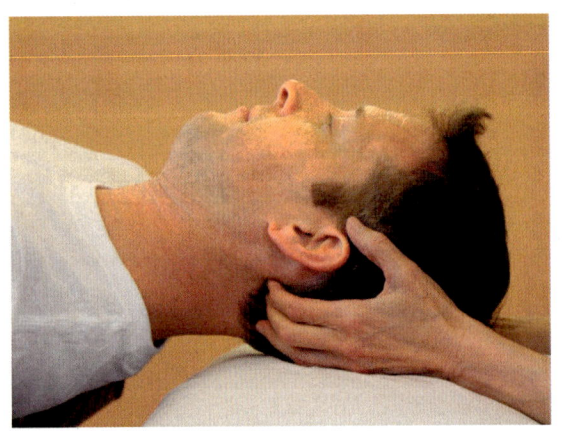

Figure 2.1
Superficial Muscle Palpation.

Step 3
Slide your fingers slowly down the superficial muscles and monitor for any tender, boggy, or ropy area in the muscles. Stop when you find any hypertonic muscles.

> *Note:* *The force with which you palpate for hypertonic muscles should be very slight. This ensures that you are palpating right beneath the skin and superficial fat layer, not the deeper tissue around the vertebrae.*

Step 4
In this example, we will treat a right-sided hypertonic superficial muscle. First, you need to change your hand position. Slide your left hand under the patient's neck with your palm up and your fingers pointing towards the patient's right side. This hand will support the patient's neck and help him relax.

Step 5
Place one finger of your left hand on the right-sided hypertonic muscle. This will be your monitoring finger.

Step 6
Use your right hand to grasp the top portion (not the anterior portion) of the patient's head. Below are several hand placements I suggest. Choose whichever position provides you with maximum control and support of the patient's head.

6.1 Wrap your fingers over the patient's forehead and place your thumb on the back of his head. The top of his head should be resting in the palm of your hand. [Fig. 2.2]

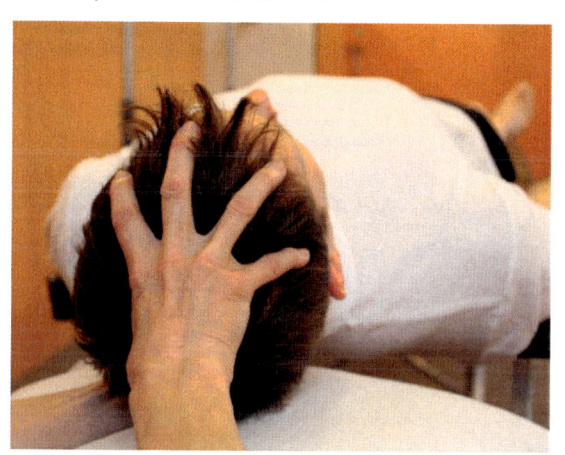

Figure 2.2
Hand Position #1.

6.2 Place your fingers on one side of the patient's head, and your thumb on the other side. Rest the patient's head in the palm of your hand. [Fig. 2.3]

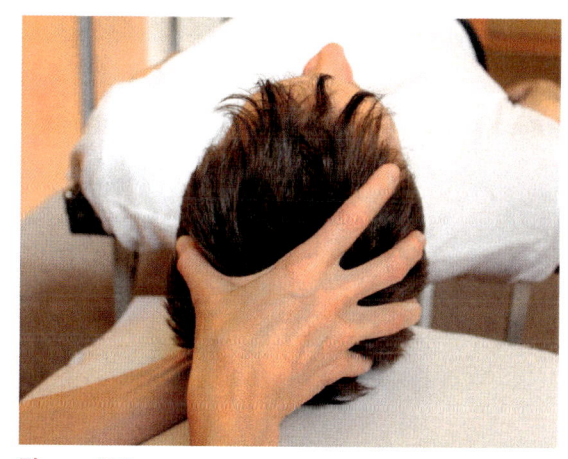

Figure 2.3
Hand Position #2.

6.3 Cup your hand and fingers under the patient's head so that its weight is in the palm of your hand. [Fig. 2.4]

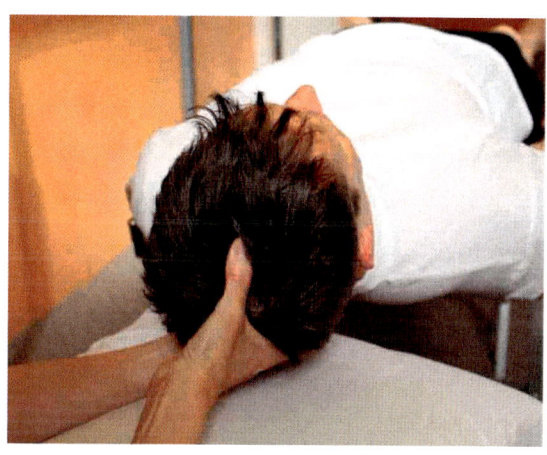

Figure 2.4
Hand Position #3.

Step 7

With your right hand, bend the patient's neck forward. Stop when you feel motion at your left monitoring finger. This will be the neutral position.

Step 8

With your right hand, apply a slight compressive force to the top of the patient's head. Stop when you feel the motion at your monitoring finger. Use no more than two to three ounces of force.

Step 9

Maintain the compression and place the muscle into its freedom of motion, which, in this case, is backward bending followed by sidebending to the right. Rotation is not necessary, since it is a coupled motion. Your monitoring finger will feel an immediate relaxation of the muscle fibers. **[Fig. 2.5]**

> ***Note:*** *To treat a left -sided hypertonic muscle, reverse your hand placement.*

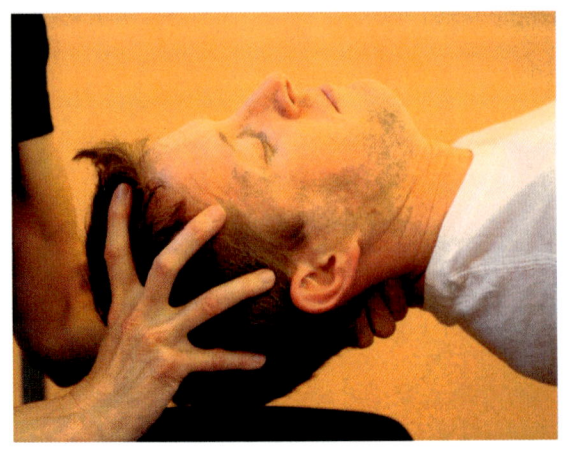

Figure 2.5
Final position for Treatment of Superficial Muscles.

Common Pitfalls While Treating Patients

1 A common mistake is to move the neck beyond the monitoring finger, particularly when trying to place the region in the neutral position or when trying to localize the treatment (e.g., sidebending or compression). To avoid this error, think in terms of small but exact motions. Whenever you forward bend or backbend any portion of the spine, imagine that you are moving one vertebra at a time. Think, " I am flexing the occiput upon C1, next I am flexing C1 upon C2, etc.," until you reach the monitoring finger.

2 Many other methods of treatment involve long waiting periods before results can be felt. However, with FPR techniques, the results are immediate; they might take effect in only milliseconds. There will be times when the change happens so quickly that you may miss it.

Technique 2
Diagnosis of a Cervical Type II Somatic Dysfunction

Patient position
Ask the patient to lie in the supine position.

Practitioner position
Sit at the head of the table with a pillow on your lap.

Procedure

Step 1
Ask the patient to slide back until his cervical spine and the middle portion of his trapezius muscle are off the table and resting comfortably on the pillow on your lap. You may also perform this technique with the patient's head on the table.

Step 2
Cup both hands under the patient's head, and use the heels of your hands to support it. Starting at the occiput, place one or two fingers of each hand lateral to the patient's cervical spinous processes, and press slightly deeper than you would for a superficial muscle. If the patient has a wide or heavy neck, rest your chest or abdomen against his head to help support its weight. You may want to place a towel or small pillow between the patient's head and your chest wall. [Fig. 2.6]

Step 3
Slowly slide your fingers down the posterior cervical region and note if any articulations are rotated to the right or left side. If one side feels more prominent than the other, then you will need to determine if the posterior facet you are feeling is a Type II Somatic Dysfunction, part of a group curve, or an anatomical change in the bony structure.

Step 4
With your fingers still on the posterior aspects of both articular processes, slowly forward bend the patient's head until you feel motion at your monitoring fingers. This is the neutral position for that vertebra. If you are using your chest wall for support, sit up straight to introduce forward bending and flexion.

Step 5
Maintaining the neutral position, use your monitoring finger as a fulcrum over which to flex and extend the vertebra. Apply very small motions (no more than one to two degrees). If you are using your chest wall as support, sit up taller to create flexion and slouch slightly to create extension.

Interpreting the results
If a Type II Somatic Dysfunction is present, the posterior articular facet will become more pronounced when either flexion or an extension motion is introduced.

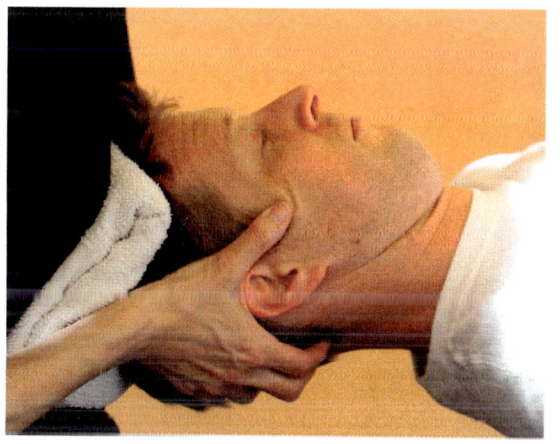

Figure 2.6
Chest support of the Head.

NAMING A SOMATIC DYSFUNCTION

In the region of C3 through C7, the motion of rotation and sidebending is always coupled in the same direction. If the vertebra is rotated right, it must also be sidebent to the right. To name a lesion, you must test whether the vertebra with the prominent posterior articular facet changes with either flexion or extension. Let's look at an example: If C4's articular facet is more pronounced on the right side and becomes more pronounced when you add flexion, then your diagnosis is C4 Extension, Sidebent right, Rotated right (C4 E SR RR). You name the lesion according to the involved vertebra's freedom of motion. When you add flexion to C4, it hits a barrier. The vertebra moves away from the barrier and into its freedom of motion, which, in this case, is extension, sidebending right, and rotation right.

***Note:** Treatment with FPR involves placing the dysfunction into its freedom of motion.*

Technique 3
Treatment of a Type II Cervical Somatic Dysfunction

Example
C4 Extension, Sidebent right, Rotated right (C4 E SR RR).

Patient position
Ask the patient to lie in the supine position.

Practitioner position
Sit at the head of the table with a pillow on your lap.

Procedure

Step 1
Ask the patient to slide back until his cervical spine and the middle portion of his trapezius muscle are off the table and resting comfortably on the pillow on your lap.

Step 2
Slide your left hand under the patient's neck so that your fingers aim towards the right posterior articular facets.

Step 3
Place one finger of your left hand (monitoring finger) on the right articular process of C4.

Step 4
Grasp the top of the patient's head with your right hand. You may use either of the hand positions described in Techniques 1 and 2. Alternatively, you can use your chest wall to support the patient's head. Gradually forward bend the patient's cervical spine until you feel motion at the monitoring finger. C4 is now in its neutral position.

Step 5
With your right hand or chest wall, mildly compress the top of the patient's head until you feel the motion at the monitoring finger.

Step 6
Maintain the compressive force and introduce a slight extension motion of C4 upon C5.

Step 7
With your left monitoring finger, pull the right articular process of C4 towards the left side. This will create a translatory force of right lateral flexion and rotation of C4 on C5. You will feel an immediate release of the C4 posterior articular process and a normalization of the relationship of C4 on C5.

Common Pitfalls While Treating Patients

1 The region to be treated wasn't in neutral.

2 The sidebending, flexion, extension, or compression motions went beyond the monitoring finger. Remember to always "think through your fingers" and to use small but exact motions.

3 The original diagnosis of flexion or extension was incorrect. To fix this, just reverse the direction from flexion to extension, or from extension to flexion, and continue with the treatment.

4 Even though you have created the small motions needed, the area to be treated has still been bypassed. This may be caused by a locking of one vertebra on another. To correct this, you need to unlock the vertebra before continuing with the treatment. This technique will be described later on in this chapter.

Technique 4
Treatment of an Anterior Cervical Hypertonic Muscle or Tender Point

Example
Right anterior hypertonic muscle.

Patient position Ask the patient to lie in the supine position.

Practitioner position Sit by the patient's head.

Procedure

Step 1
Place one finger of your right hand (monitoring finger) on the area to be treated.

Step 2
Grasp the top of the patient's head with your left hand. Alternatively, you can slide your left hand underneath the patient's head with your palm facing up, your fingers aimed towards the patient's neck, and your thumb resting on top of the head.

Step 3
Forward bend the patient's neck until you feel motion at the monitoring finger. [Fig. 2.7]

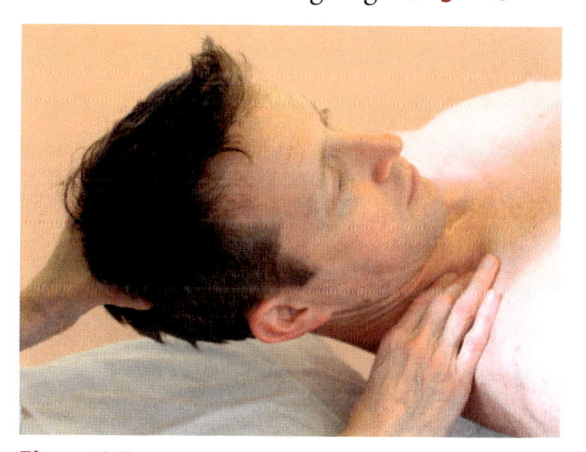

Step 4
Apply a compressive force of two to three ounces to the top of the head until you feel motion at the monitoring finger.

Step 5
Maintain the previous position. Next, rotate the patient's head from the right side towards the midline, in the direction of your monitoring finger. Make sure the rotation occurs in the horizontal plane and does not cross over the midline. Occasionally, you will need to add a minimal amount of sidebending. When the rotation reaches the monitoring finger, you should feel an immediate relaxation of the muscle being treated.

Figure 2.7
Final position for Anterior Cervical Muscle treatment.

Technique 5

Treatment of a Hypertonic Sternocleidomastoid Muscle

Example

Hypertonic sternocleidomastoid muscle on the right side.

Patient position Ask the patient to lie in the supine position.

Practitioner position
Sit by the patient's head.

Procedure

Step 1

Place a finger of the right hand (monitoring finger) on the medial, sternal attachment of the muscle. Position a second monitoring finger at the midpoint of the clavicle, where the lateral portion of the muscle attaches.

Step 2

Grasp the top of the patient's head with your left hand.

Step 3

Use your left hand to aim the patient's chin towards the lateral portion of the muscle, and forward bend his head until you feel the motion at the monitoring finger.

Step 4

Add a compressive force in the direction of your lateral monitoring finger. If the patient's head is too heavy, place it against your chest wall and create the compressive force by leaning into it.

Step 5

Once you feel the lateral portion of the muscle normalize, maintain the forward bent position and compression, and slowly rotate the patient's head medially towards the monitoring finger at the sternal attachment. You will feel an immediate release of the muscle.

Technique 6

A "Shotgun Technique" to Treat All the Superficial Muscles of the Posterior Cervical Region at Once

This is a quick method to create relaxation and return normal tone to all of the superficial muscles of the posterior cervical region. When you become proficient in this maneuver, you will find that you will be able to normalize the superficial muscles, as well as some of the deep cervical muscles. In fact, when you examine the deeper bony articulations, you may find that there are no Type II Somatic Dysfunctions left, even if they were present before you performed this technique.

Example

Treatment of the cervical muscles on the right side.

Patient position Ask the patient to lie in the supine position.

Practitioner position Sit by the patient's head and place a pillow on your lap.

Procedure

Step 1

Ask the patient to slide back until his cervical spine and the middle portion of his trapezius muscle are off the table and resting comfortably on the pillow on your lap.

Step 2

Place your left hand under the patient's neck and spread your fingers so that your pinky is below the right occiput, your middle fingers are lateral to the right cervical muscles, and your index finger is posterior and lateral to the seventh cervical vertebra. If the index finger does not reach that far down, then place the finger as far as it can reach while still remaining lateral to the cervical muscles.

Step 3

Aim your left elbow away from your side and perpendicular to the patient's neck.

Step 4

Grasp the top of the patient's head with your right hand and forward bend the patient's neck up to the level of your left index finger, or as far up as the patient can go comfortably and without pain. [Fig. 2.8]

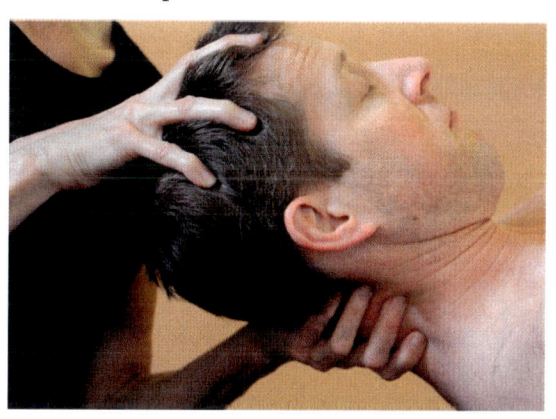

Figure 2.8
Hand position for Shotgun Technique.

Step 5

With your right hand, create a slight compressive force until you feel the motion at your left index finger.

Step 6

Maintaining the compression, slowly bend the patient's neck backwards, over each finger of your left hand, from the suboccipital area until T1. As you reach each finger, use it to pull the cervical muscle towards the left. This motion will create a right-to-left translatory force on the cervical muscles and on each of the vertebral bodies.

Step 7

The neck will automatically rotate to the right as it is extended and translated. Continue this motion until the patient's head and neck are off the table and in a backwards bent and rotated position.
[Fig. 2.9]

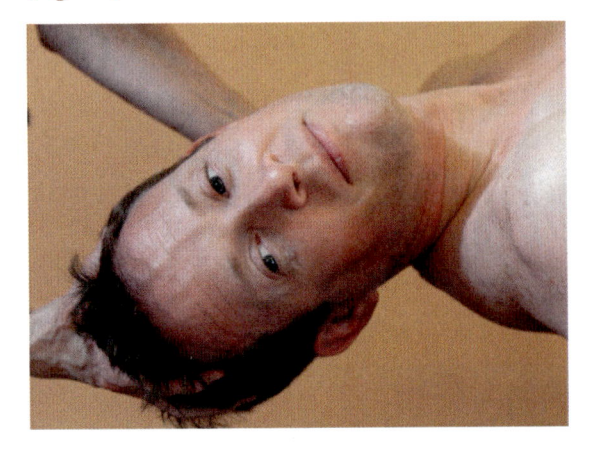

Figure 2.9
Final Head position for Shotgun Technique.

Note: Do not allow the patient to "assist" you when doing this maneuver. Stop if the patient complains of any pain.

Step 8

Reverse your hand position and repeat this process on the left side of the neck.

At the end of the treatment you will find that all of the superficial posterior cervical muscles are relaxed and normotonic. Many of the cervical Type II Somatic Dysfunctions will also be gone.

Technique 7
Combination Technique for the Diagnosis and Treatment of a Type II Somatic Dysfunction

This method is designed to increase the efficacy and efficiency of diagnosing and treating a Type II Somatic Dysfunction in the cervical region.

Patient position Ask the patient to lie in the supine position.

Practitioner position Sit by the patient's head and place a pillow on your lap.

Procedure

Step 1

Ask the patient to slide back until his cervical spine and the middle portion of his trapezius muscle are off the table and resting comfortably on the pillow on your lap.

Step 2

Slide your hands under the patient's head and neck. Starting at the occiput, place one or two fingers of each hand lateral to the patient's cervical spinous processes and beneath the articular facets.

Note: *If your patient has a small or thin neck, slide your dominant hand under it and place your thumb (monitoring finger) on the articular facet on one side. Position your index or middle finger (monitoring fingers) on the other side's articular facet. Use your free hand to introduce all other motions.* **[Fig. 2.10]**

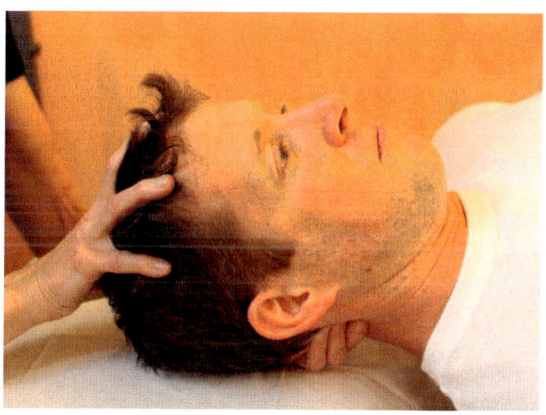

Figure 2.10
Hand Position for working on an Individual with a Small Neck.

Step 3

Use the heels of your hands to flex the patient's neck. When you feel the motion at your monitoring fingers (this is the neutral position for this vertebra), add compression.

> *Note: If the patient has a wide or heavy neck, support his head with your chest wall or abdomen. Use your chest or abdomen to exert a mild compressive force down the cervical spine.* [Fig. 2.11]

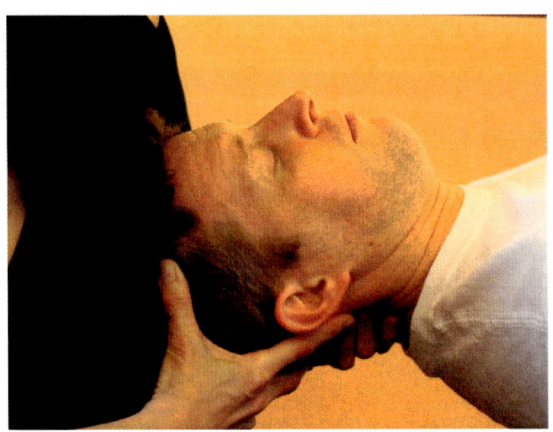

Figure 2.11
Support for head and neck.

Step 4

As you slide your fingers down the spine, continue to adjust the flexion and compression so that you can feel the motion at the level of your monitoring fingers. Maintain this flexion and compression at that level and feel for any posteriorly rotated articular facets; if you find any, pause at that spot.

Step 5

Using very small motions, pivot the posteriorly rotated vertebra over your palpating fingers into extension and flexion. If the posteriorly rotated articular process is exaggerated when either flexion or extension is introduced, then there is a Type II Somatic Dysfunction at that level.

> *Note: If the patient has a wide or heavy neck, sit up taller to introduce flexion, and slouch to create extension.*

Step 6

Return the cervical spine to its neutral position and make sure that the vertebra remains compressed up to your monitoring finger. Reintroduce either flexion or extension, depending on which position diminished the prominence of the posterior articular facet in the previous step.

Step 7

Translate the affected vertebra into its freedom of motion by pushing gently against its lateral side; depending on the diagnosis, the translatory push will be either from the right to the left side or from the left to the right side. This step will cause the vertebra to sidebend and rotate into its ease of motion.

Step 8

When you have finished treating the affected vertebra, return the patient's neck to its neutral position and compression at that level.

Proceed down the neck, increasing the compression and neutral position at each new level of your fingers and feel for any Somatic Dysfunctions.

> *Note:* *Remember to keep adjusting the neutral and compressive forces to align with the level of your monitoring finger. Repeat the above steps and treat any other Somatic Dysfunctions you find.*

Example

While palpating down the cervical spine, you find a posteriorly rotated transverse process on the right side at the level of C4, which accentuates on flexion. The name of the lesion is C4 E SR RR (C4 Extension, Sidebent right, Rotated right). Place the cervical area in its neutral position, add the necessary compression, then pivot C4 into extension over the palpating fingers and move your right palpating finger medially against the body of C4, translating C4 to its left. This will create right sidebending and rotation and eliminate the dysfunction. Return the cervical area to its neutral position and compression. Continue palpating down the rest of the cervical spine, testing for the presence of any other Somatic Dysfunctions.

Technique 8
Treatment of Chronic Restriction of Regional Motion of the Neck

The average person, by his fiftieth birthday, will experience some form of injury that leads to degenerative changes and restriction of motion of the cervical spine. The patient may not recognize his limitations, due to years of having adapted to this lack of motion. Upon examination, you will notice that, when the patient is asked to view something, he moves his head, neck, and body as one unit, rather than moving just his cervical region. Below is a technique that will dramatically increase your patient's regional motion.

Before beginning the treatment, ask the patient to be seated. Measure and record the patient's initial cervical regional motion.

⚠ CAUTION
Contraindications to "Treatment of Chronic Restriction of Regional Motions of the Neck" include any metastatic disease to the bones and severe osteoporosis with demonstrable bony collapse.

Procedure for Part One: Bilateral mobilization of T1

Patient position
Ask the patient to lie in the supine position.

Practitioner position
Sit by the patient's head and place a pillow on your lap.

Step 1
Ask the patient to slide back until his cervical spine and the middle portion of his trapezius muscle are off the table and resting comfortably on the pillow on your lap.

Step 2
Place the palm of your right hand on top of the anterior portion of the patient's right shoulder. Position your thumb underneath the patient's back and onto the posterior, lateral aspect of the right transverse process of T1. Keep your hand as close to the patient's neck as possible. Hold this position. [Fig. 2.12]

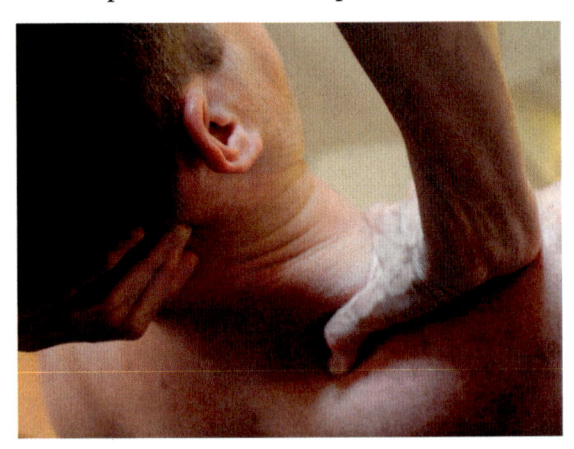

Figure 2.12
Hand Position for Mobilization of T1.

Step 3
Place your left hand under the patient's occiput and grasp it tightly in your hand.

Step 4
Lock your left elbow against the side of your body.

Step 5
Lean back so that the weight of your body creates traction on the patient's head and neck. Maintain this traction.

Step 6

Using your right thumb as a pivot, swing your body along with the patient's head to the right side. This motion will move the neck to the right and create right sidebending of the neck. At the same time, maintain an upward pressure on the T1 transverse process with your right thumb. Hold this position for three to four seconds. [Fig. 2.13]

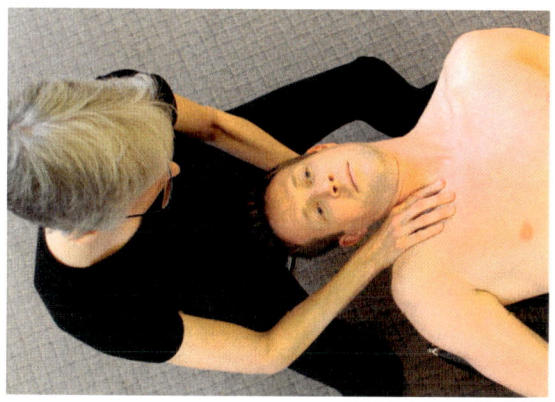

Figure 2.13
Use your right thumb as a pivot and swing your body towards the right.

Step 7

Maintain the traction and swing your body to the left, creating left sidebending of the patient's neck away from your right thumb. [Fig. 2.14]

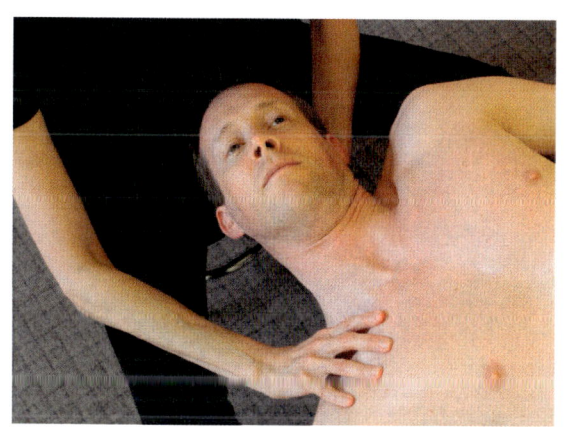

Figure 2.14
Left Sidebending of the Neck.

> **Note: Remember to use your body weight, not your arm muscles, to attain the desired traction.*

Step 8

Repeat Steps 6 and 7 several times.

Step 9

Reverse hands and repeat the same treatment on the left side's transverse process of T1.

You should now feel bilateral mobilization of T1.

Procedure for Part Two: Treatment of the Cervical Region

Patient position

Ask the patient to lie in the supine position.

Practitioner position

Stand by the patient's head.

Step 1

Forward bend the patient's neck into flexion. Stop when the slack in the fascia is gone and the area feels tight, or if the patient complains of any discomfort or pain.

Step 2

Rest your abdomen or chest wall against the top of the patient's head. This will support the forward flexion position. You may want to place a small pillow or towel between your abdomen and the patient's head.

Step 3

Gently lean your chest wall or abdomen against the patient's head. This will introduce a slight compressive force. Stop when you feel the compression at C7. Maintain the forward bent and compression position throughout this procedure.

Step 4

Point your fingers towards the floor, with your palms facing your body. With your hands in this position, place the medial side of the index finger of each hand on the sides of the patient's seventh cervical vertebra. [Fig. 2.15]

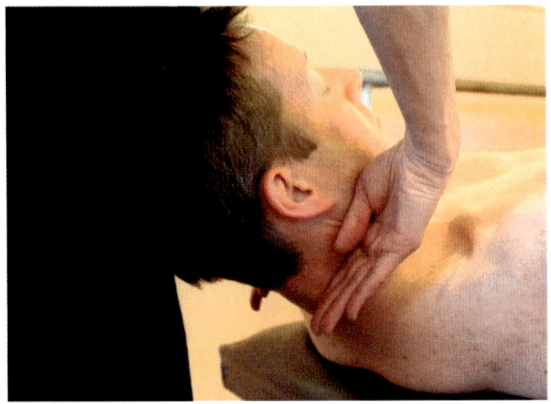

Figure 2.15
Hand Position.

Alternatively, you can place the middle and index fingers of each of your hands lateral to the sides of the body of the seventh cervical vertebra.

Step 5

Use your index fingers to translate the body, not the intervertebral disc, of the seventh cervical vertebra from right to left and then from left to right. Do not sidebend or rotate. Do this two to three times. Then, move your fingers up to the body of the sixth cervical vertebra and repeat.

Step 6

Continue translating each vertebra from side to side until you reach the suboccipital region.

Step 7

Return to the level of the seventh vertebra and repeat the process until the translatory motions have increased.

Step 8

Next, lock your arms against your body and place your fingers against the sides of the seventh cervical vertebral body. Move your body, not your hands, in a circular motion in one direction, then repeat the motion in the other direction. Note that it is your body that creates the rotary motion of the vertebral body, not your arms.

Step 9

After you introduce rotation to all levels of the cervical area, move each vertebra in a figure-eight pattern. To introduce the figure-eight motion, translate the patient's vertebra in one direction, then rotate it in the same direction. Next, move the vertebra into extension, and then rotate and translate it to the opposite direction. These motions should be fluid, with one motion leading into the next.

> *Note: When performing this maneuver, make sure that your arms are locked against your body. Your fingers should also be locked against the sides of the vertebral body so that your body, not your hands, introduces all movements.

Step 10

Repeat these steps several times. Release the compression and reevaluate the range of motion of the patient's neck.

The results are always dramatic. You may not be able to return full motion in all directions. However, even after the first treatment you will find that you have created a twenty-five to thirty percent increase in motion. Repeat the treatment weekly until you can no longer achieve any further improvement. I have performed this treatment on patients of all ages, including patients with old fractures and/or with fusion of some of their cervical vertebrae, with remarkable results.

Technique 9
Use of Spinal Vector Forces in the Treatment of Restriction of Motion in the Cervical Spine

This technique involves generating a gentle but directed vector force down a defined area of the spine by applying continuous spinal compression. This constant force creates a closed pack rod of the specified region and enables the practitioner to use very small motions to treat the somatic dysfunctions of the involved vertebra. If done properly, this technique enables the practitioner to use a fraction of the force needed for most procedures. Therefore, this technique is well-suited for use on elderly and mildly osteoporotic individuals.

Patient position Ask the patient to lie in the supine position.

Practitioner position Sit by the patient's head and place a pillow on your lap.

Procedure

Step 1
Ask the patient to slide back until his cervical spine and the middle portion of his trapezius muscle are off the table and resting comfortably on the pillow on your lap.

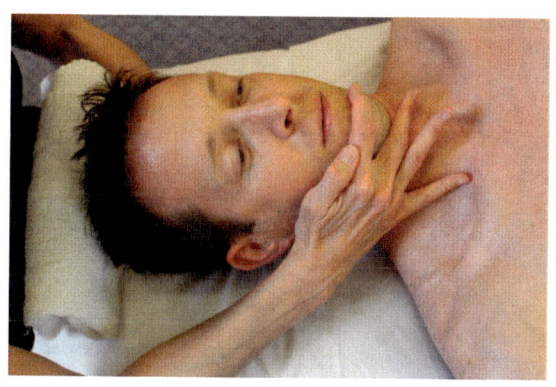

Figure 2.16
Neutral Positioning of O-A-A Articulation.

Step 2
Place your left hand under the patient's occiput and support his head.

Step 3
Place your right index finger on the anterior aspect of the patient's mandible. With the right index finger, pivot the mandible down towards the patient's chest. This motion will align the patient's occiput, atlas, and axis– the neutral position– while simultaneously creating a rod.
[Fig. 2.16]

Step 4
Keeping your right index finger on the patient's mandible, slowly pivot your left hand and the patient's head up and over your right index finger. Stop when the remaining portion of the cervical spine is in its neutral position and has formed a straight rod.

Step 5

Place your chest over the front portion of the patient's hairline and forehead. Next, direct a mild compressive force down the straight line of the rod which was formed in the cervical spine during steps three and four. Maintain this locking of the upper three articulations, C1, C2 and C3, and the closed pack rod position of C3 to C7 throughout the rest of the treatment. [Fig. 2.17]

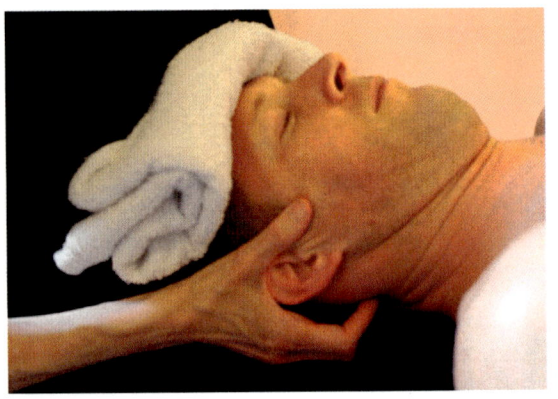

Figure 2.17
Positioning to support the Neutral Position and Rod Formation of the Cervical Spine

*Note: Holding up the patient's head and neck with your chest frees both of your hands.

Step 6

Place one or two fingers of each hand lateral to the cervical vertebral body of C7, and gently push the articular facets of C7 from side to side. This motion should be so gentle and small that you are only indenting the skin over the vertebral body.

Step 7

Move your fingers to the posterior aspect of the articulations and rotate the vertebra from side to side.

Step 8

Next, gently move your fingers against the articular facets in a figure-eight pattern. These motions should be very small and require no more than one to two ounces of force. Repeat this motion until both sides feel free.

Step 9

Repeat Steps 6 through 8 at each individual cervical vertebra. Remember that all the motions are very small and require hardly any force.

Technique 10
Use of Spinal Vector Forces to Diagnose and Treat Dysfunctions of C3 through C7

Patient position Ask the patient to lie in the supine position.

Practitioner position Sit by the patient's head and place a pillow on your lap.

Procedure One

Step 1
Ask the patient to slide back until his cervical spine and the middle portion of his trapezius muscle are off the table and resting comfortably on the pillow on your lap.

Step 2
Place your left hand under the patient's occiput and support his head.

Step 3
Place your right index finger on the anterior aspect of the patient's mandible. With the right index finger, pivot the mandible down towards the patient's chest. This motion will align the patient's occiput, atlas, and axis—the neutral position—while simultaneously creating a rod.

Step 4
Keeping your right index finger on the patient's mandible, slowly pivot your left hand and the patient's head up and over your right index finger. Stop when the remaining portion of the patient's cervical spine is in its neutral position and has formed a straight rod.

Step 5
Place your chest over the front portion of the patient's hairline and forehead. Next, direct a mild compressive force down the straight line of the rod which was formed in the cervical spine during steps three and four. Maintain this locking of the upper three articulations, C1, C2, and C3, and the closed pack rod position of C3 to C7 throughout the rest of the treatment.

Step 6
Now that your chest is holding up the patient's head and neck, place the index fingers of your hands on the sides of the body of the C7 vertebra.

Step 7
Translate C7 in both directions by pushing the right index finger to the left and then the left index finger to the right. Again, you should only be indenting the skin over the vertebra. Use approximately one to two ounces of force. Repeat this motion until both sides feel free.

Step 8
Move your index fingers to the posterior aspect of the articulations and rotate the vertebra by first pushing up the right index finger and then by pushing up on the left index finger. Again, use only one to two ounces of force.

Step 9
Repeat the translation and rotation steps on each vertebra until you reach C3.

Step 10
If at any level you feel that either the translation or rotation motion is locked, stop and treat it immediately.

Procedure Two:
Treatment to increase motion

Example

C5 cannot be freely translated from right to left.

Step 11

Keep your index fingers on the lateral aspects of the body of C5. Gently press your fingers so that they just indent the patient's skin.

Step 12

Pull the skin up towards the top of the patient's head, with a force of about one ounce. This action will create a very small amount of traction on the skin.

Step 13

Using the left index finger as a pivot, move your body to cause a left lateral flexion of the spine. At the same time, push your left index finger to the right to translate the vertebra from the left to the right side. You can add small jiggling motions of your index finger to exaggerate the translatory motion.

Step 14

Maintaining the pull on the skin, return your body to the midline. Next, place your right index finger posterior to the articulation and rotate C5 to its left. This will unlock the vertebra and restore full motion. Release the pull on the skin.

Technique 11
Treatment of Acute Posterior Hypertonic Neck Muscles

Causes of acute cervical muscle hypertonicity are too numerous to all be listed here. A few examples are traumatic whiplash, a sports injury, or even something as simple as a forceful sneeze. The affected patient presents with a neck that is rigid and painful to move. The involved area will be tender to the touch. Any attempt at examining the area will aggravate the patient's symptoms.

Example
Acute cervical hypertonicity on the left side.

Patient position
Ask the patient to sit on the table with his back facing you.

Practitioner position
Stand behind the patient.

⚠ CAUTION
This treatment should be used only for muscle dysfunctions. It should not be used in cases of nerve or discogenic dysfunctions, or recently fractured vertebrae.

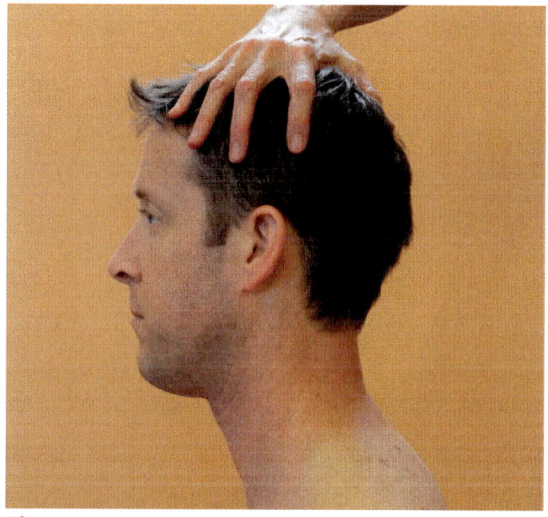

Figure 2.18
Proper Hand Position for Treatment of Acute Cervical Muscle Dysfunctions.

Procedure
Step 1
Very gently place the palm of your right hand on top of the patient's head. Extend your thumb down the posterior side of the patient's head and point your middle and ring fingers down the left side. [Fig. 2.18]

Step 2
Create a minimal compressive force by gently pressing the top of the patient's head towards the floor with your palm.

> **Note:* I must emphasize the word minimal; the effects of the created force should not be detectable to the eye. Make sure the compressive force is directed down in a straight line. It should not create any other movements of the head.

Step 3

Maintaining this compressive force, lightly press your middle and ring fingers against the left side of the skull, and your thumb against the posterior aspect of the skull. This will create extension and left sidebending. The pressure created at each fingertip should only be enough to compress the skin against the bone beneath it.

Step 4

As you feel the muscles relax, slightly increase the pressure applied by your thumb, middle, and ring fingers. If you feel that rotation is needed, turn the head in the same direction as you are sidebending it.

To treat the right side, place your left hand on top of the patient's head. If this technique is performed properly, there will be no visible motion of the head or neck during treatment, and the patient will not feel any pain. Follow-up management may include prescribing intermittent, short-term cervical support; ice; and medication to relieve inflammation, muscle spasms, and pain.

Technique 12
Treatment of a Type II Somatic Dysfunction Locked in Extension

Sometimes, a patient presents with a chronic cervical Type II Somatic Dysfunction, which is resistant to treatment. In my experience, these dysfunctions are always locked in extension; the dysfunctional vertebra will not move into flexion on the vertebra below it. In these cases, there is a locking at the vertebra's uncinate articulation. Only release of that locked articulation will restore full motion.

Example
Treatment of a locked C5 on C6.

Patient position
Ask the patient to lie in the supine position.

Practitioner position
Sit by the patient's head and place a pillow on your lap.

Procedure

Step 1

Ask the patient to slide back until his cervical spine and the middle portion of his trapezius muscle are off the table and resting comfortably on the pillow on your lap.

Step 2

Cup your hands underneath the patient's head and grasp the lateral aspects of the articulation of C5 with your index and/or middle fingers.

Step 3

Use the heels of your hands to press gently on the sides of the patient's head. Lean back to create traction on the patient's neck.

Note: Always use your body weight to create traction, not your hands.

Step 4

Maintain this traction for several seconds, until you feel a slight loosening at the vertebral articulation.

Step 5

While maintaining the traction, transfer your fingers to the posterior and inferior aspect of the C5 articulation. Pivot the patient's cervical spine over your fingers into extension. This maneuver will create a direct extension of C5 on C6.

Step 6

Maintain the traction in its new downward direction until you feel a loosening at the articulation. Your patient's head will be off the table and in extension. [Fig. 2.19]

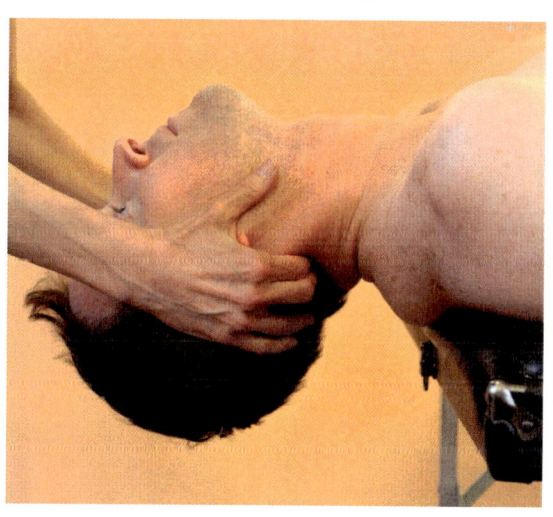

Figure 2.19
Maintain Traction in a Downward Direction.

Step 7

Continuing to maintain the traction, quickly stand up and pivot the vertebra over your fingers. This action will create a flexion motion of C5 onto C6. The articulation should now have complete freedom of motion.

OCCIPITOATLANTAL ARTICULATION (O-A)

Motion of the Occipitoatlantal Articulation

Imagine placing a hat with a straight-edged bottom atop your patient's head. I like to use the example of an old World War I German helmet. The helmet's back would be parallel to the horizontal plane, and the sides of the helmet would almost cover the patient's ears. If you tilted the right side of the helmet towards the floor until it extended below the right ear, then the back and left side of the helmet would be tilted towards the top of the head and the left ear would be exposed. This is similar to the motion that the occiput has on the atlas when it laterally flexes to the right.

Note that the articulations of C1, C2, and C3 follow coupled motion rules that differ from the rest of the cervical spine when going into flexion, extension, lateral flexion and rotation.

1 Flexion and extension of the occiput on the atlas are accompanied by a contralateral anterior and posterior slide. When you flex the occiput on the atlas, the occiput slides backwards. In a typical cervical vertebra, e.g. C3 on C4, when you flex C3 on C4, C3 slides forward.

2 Lateral flexion is accompanied by a contralateral slide and rotation. When you laterally flex the occipitoatlantal articulation to the right, the occiput translates to the left and rotates to the left. If C3 is laterally flexed to the right on C4, then C3 translates to the left and rotates to the right.

3 The motions of lateral flexion and rotation are coupled at the occipitoatlantal articulation, so there is no need to evaluate for rotation.

4 Since there is no disc between the occipitoatlantal articulation, rotation is not accompanied by disc compression.

Technique 13
Method for Diagnosing Occipitoatlantal Somatic Dysfunctions

Patient position
Ask the patient to lie in the supine position with his head resting on the table.

Practitioner position
Sit by the patient's head.

Procedure

Step 1
Slide both hands under the occiput until the tips of your middle and index fingers (monitoring fingers) are in contact with the bottom edge of the occiput. [Fig. 2.20]

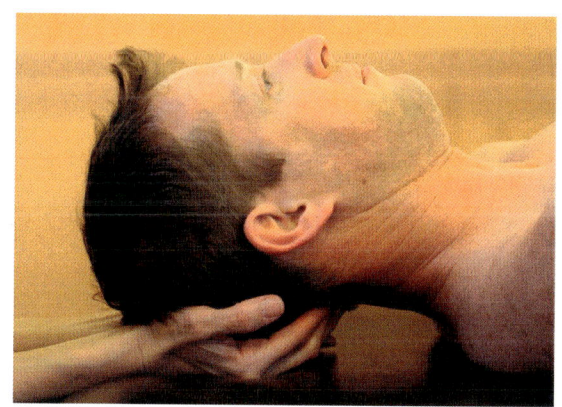

Figure 2.20
Position of hands under the Occiput.

Step 2
Maintain this position until you feel the tissue under the tips of your fingers soften. You will soon find that your fingertips are resting in the bilateral indentations created by the end of the occiput and its cervical muscle attachments.

Step 3
Feel for symmetry between the two indentations. Are the sides equal or does it feel as if one finger is in a deeper/wider indentation or a shallower/narrower groove? If the two sides do not feel even, then the occiput is laterally flexed on the atlas towards the shallower/narrower side (it helps to think about the earlier helmet example).

Step 4
To complete the diagnosis, place the occipitoatlantal articulation into its neutral position, either by flexing the occiput with the heels of your hand or by pushing the patient's mandible towards his chest wall.

Step 5
Using your monitoring fingers as a fulcrum, flex and extend the occiput over your fingers, by about one or two degrees. Use your fingertips to feel for any change in the indentations.

Step 6
If you feel a change on the shallower/narrower side, then a Type II Somatic Dysfunction is present.

If flexion changed the groove on the right narrower side, then the diagnosis is O-A E SR RL (Occipitoatlantal Extension, Sidebent right, Rotated left).

Technique 14
Treatment of an Occipitoatlantal Somatic Dysfunction

Example
Occipitoatlantal Extension, Sidebent Right, Rotated Left Somatic dysfunction (O-A E SR RL).

Patient position
Ask the patient to lie in the supine position.

Practitioner position
Sit by the patient's head.

Procedure
Step 1
Turn your left palm up, and slide your hand under the patient's occiput. Your fingers should be pointing towards the patient's right side. Place your left index finger (monitoring finger) posterior and slightly below the right mastoid process. Use the rest of your hand to support the patient's head.

Step 2
Use your right hand to grasp the top of the patient's head. Flex the occiput on the atlas, only one to two degrees, until you feel the motion at the monitoring finger. This is the neutral position. [Fig. 2.21]

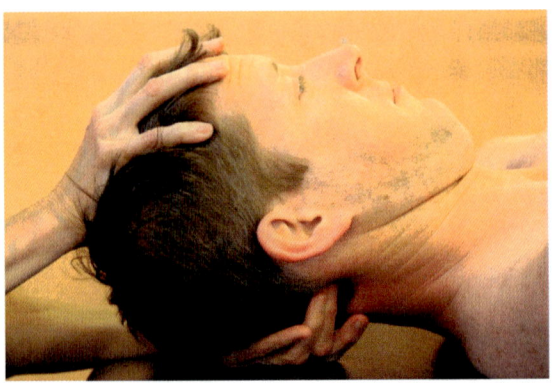

Figure 2.21
Neutral Position of the OA Articulation.

Step 3
Use your right hand to create a mild compressive force until you feel the motion at your left monitoring index finger.

Step 4
While maintaining the compression, slightly extend the occiput on the atlas.

Step 5
Introduce a translatory force from right to left by pulling your left index finger from the right side towards the left side of the vertebra. This motion will create a right lateral flexion and left rotation of the vertebra. At this point, you should feel a release of the lateral flexion restriction and normalization of the occipitoatlantal relationship.

Common Pitfalls While Treating Patients

1 A common mistake is to move the neck beyond the monitoring finger while trying to place the region in its neutral position. Always think in terms of small but exact motions.

2 The diagnosis was incorrect. If treatment in flexion does not eliminate the dysfunction, then treat the vertebra in extension. Conversely, if treatment in extension does not eliminate the dysfunction, then treat the vertebra in flexion.

3 The dysfunction is long-standing, most likely as a result of trauma. It is locked and will not release. I label this condition the "Stubborn Occipitoatlantal Somatic Dysfunction."

Technique 15
Treatment of a Stubborn Occipitoatlantal Somatic Dysfunction

Patient position

Ask the patient to lie in the supine position.

Practitioner position

Sit, preferably on a rolling stool, by the patient's head.

Procedure

Step 1

Slide your left hand under the patient's occiput. Place your left index finger (monitoring finger) posterior and slightly below the right mastoid process. Position your thumb below the patient's left mastoid process.

Step 2

Grasp the top of the patient's head with your right hand and flex the occiput on the atlas. Stop when you feel the motion at the monitoring finger. You will need to move the occiput no more than one to two degrees.

Step 3

The area is now in its neutral position. Push gently, with your right hand, to create a mild compressive force, until you feel the motion at your left monitoring index finger.

Step 4

While maintaining the compression, pull your left index finger from the right side towards the left side. This motion will create a right lateral flexion of the occiput on the atlas.

Step 5

With your right hand add a jiggling motion (small oscillations) aimed towards your left index finger and the right laterally flexed occipitoatlantal articulation.

Step 6

For this step be sure to hold the patient's occiput with your left index finger, and to place your left thumb posterior and slightly below the right mastoid process. Lock your left elbow at the side of your body. Lean your body back to create a traction force on the occiput. Do not use your hand alone to create the traction force.

Step 7

Maintain the traction, and use your left index finger as a fulcrum. Move your body, along with the patient's head, around the fulcrum, towards the patient's right side.

Step 8

Release the traction. Direct a compressive force towards your index finger. Apply a jiggling motion in the same direction as your index finger to exaggerate the right lateral flexion. At the same time, apply a right to left translatory force with your left index finger.

Step 9

Reapply the traction force. Next, swing your body and the patient's head around your left thumb, in the frontal plane, from the right to the left side.

Step 10

Release the traction. Direct a compressive force towards the thumb. Apply a jiggling motion towards your thumb, and exaggerate the left lateral flexion. At the same time, apply a left-to-right translatory force with your left thumb.

Step 11

Repeat Steps 6 through 10 until you feel a complete release of the dysfunction and can easily translate the vertebra in both directions.

Note: *If you are sitting on a rolling stool, you can swing the stool from side to side to create the motion while maintaining your hand position. Once you learn how to use your body rather than your arm muscles, you can create and maintain a force for very long periods of time, without feeling fatigued.*

Technique 16
Traction Treatment of a Stubborn O-A (Occipitoatlantal) Somatic Dysfunction

Patient position
Ask the patient to lie in the supine position.

Practitioner position
Sit, preferably on a rolling stool, by the patient's head.

Procedure

Step 1
Slide your left hand under the patient's occiput. Firmly place your left index finger and thumb immediately below the occiput. Lean back and use your body weight to create a traction force on the O-A (Occipitoatlantal) articulation.

Step 2
Place your right thumb on the patient's left parietal area, and your right index and middle fingers on the right side of the patient's head. Note that this position will allow greater control of the patient's head.

Step 3
Point your right index and/or middle finger down towards your left index finger. Pivot the patient's head over your right middle finger. This motion will create a right sidebending of the occiput on the atlas. [Fig. 2.22]

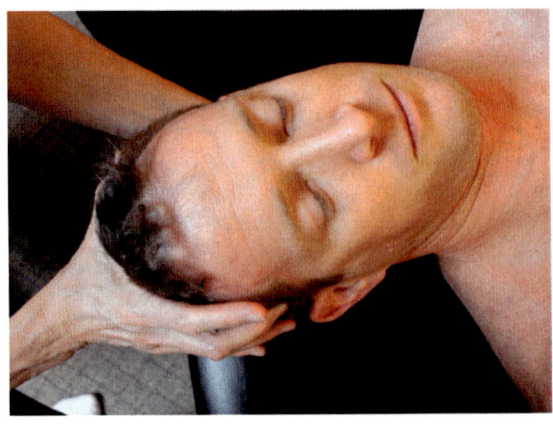

Figure 2.22
Pivot the Patient's Head over your Index or Middle Finger.

Step 4
At the same time, use your left index finger to translate the O-A from the right to the left side.

Step 5
Have your right hand direct a jiggling force (small oscillations) down towards your left index finger.

Step 6
Bring the patient's head back to the neutral position. Use your right thumb to pivot the patient's head and to create a left sidebending of the O-A (Occipitoatlantal) articulation. At the same time, use your left thumb to translate the O-A (Occipitoatlantal) articulation from the left to the right side.

Step 7
Add a jiggling motion towards your left thumb. Repeat this several times until motion at the O-A (Occipitoatlantal) articulation is restored.

Technique 17

Treatment of Cervical Pain with Radiating Nerve Pain down the Arm Secondary to Cervical Discogenic Changes or from the Narrowing of the Cervical Disc Space caused primarily by Degenerative Changes

"Doctor, how do you treat a cervical herniated disc?"

"With trepidation." However, if you feel confident in your palpatory skills and are sure that your fingers can communicate quickly and accurately what they are feeling, then there is an approach that I recommend.

First, let us define what we are treating. This is the patient with pain in the cervical region which radiates down the arm and occasionally causes cutaneous symptoms. On physical examination, you will notice restriction of motion of the cervical spine. An M.R.I. may reveal a bulging or tear of a cervical disc, or a narrowing of the disc space with mild degenerative changes. Treatment for either diagnosis is similar. The case of a bulging disc, however, is a little more difficult to treat and requires greater skill.

These patients are very uncomfortable and exhibit pain when any form of motion is applied. Usually, the most comfortable position for the patient is supine, with the head and neck flexed and rotated to the side of the radiating pain. This position will relieve some of the patient's discomfort, and allow you to treat the patient more comfortably.

Part One: Treatment of the Thoracic Component

Example
There is radiating nerve pain down the right arm, secondary to discogenic changes between the fifth and sixth cervical vertebrae.

Patient position
Cup your hand under the cervical area and support the patient's neck as the patient reclines into the supine position. To increase the patient's comfort level, try flexing, sidebending, and rotating the patient's head in the direction of the radiating pain. Then place as many pillows as necessary to maintain the patient's head in this position.

Practitioner position
Sit or stand by the patient's head.

Procedure
Step 1
Place your left hand under the patient's neck to support it.

Step 2

With your right palm facing up, slide your hand down the right side of the patient's spine and over the thoracic transverse processes. Stop when your right hand arrives at an area which feels firm and is tender to touch. This secondary thoracic component is always present when the cervical nerve root is involved and is creating radiating pain down the arm. The area involved is usually found at the level of the third or fourth thoracic transverse processes. [Fig. 2.23]

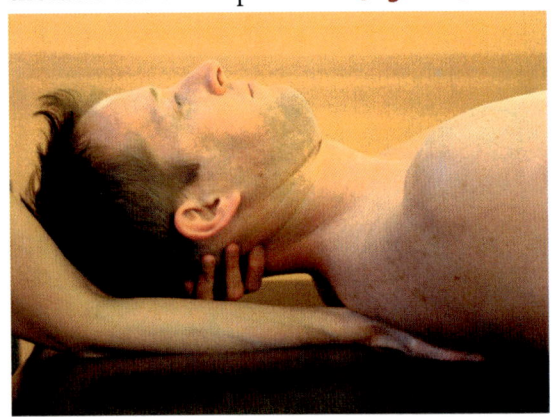

Figure 2.23
Hand Placement for Treatment of the Thoracic Component.

Step 3

Push the heel of your right hand up against the firm and tender tissue. Maintain this pressure for a slow count of five, and then relax your hand. Repeat this step until you feel the tissue soften and the pressure causes the involved transverse processes to rotate.

Part Two: Treatment of the Cervical Component

Practitioner position

Stand by the patient's head.

Procedure

Step 1

Slide your hands down the sides of the patient's neck and stop when your middle or index fingers are touching both sides of the fifth disc. The right side of the disc will be tender to touch, so do not press against it.

*Note: If symptoms are due to narrowing of the cervical disc space caused by degenerative changes, place your fingers at the side of the vertebral body instead of at the disc itself. In each subsequent step, substitute "vertebral body" for "disc."

Step 2

With the heels of both of your hands, grasp the patient's head and lean back in the direction in which you positioned the neck for relief of pain. Maintain this traction throughout the treatment.

Step 3

With the finger of your left hand, push on the left side of the disc (the side that does not have pain), and create a gentle left-to-right translatory motion. Stop if you are causing any pain to the patient.

Step 4

Hold the pressure for a count of five, then release for a count of five. Repeat this step until you create a slight translatory motion.

Step 5

Next, press your right finger against the right side of the disc. If it is tender to touch, stop and go back to translating the left side of the disc.

> ***Note:** Maintain the traction position throughout all steps of the procedure. If you become tired, relax the traction and rest for a few minutes before reapplying the traction.*

Step 6

Once both sides of the disc are no longer tender, alternate the slight translatory pressure of your fingers from right to left and then from left to right.

Step 7

If you feel good translatory motion in both directions, maintain the traction and slowly sidebend the cervical spine over your left index finger and rotate the patient's neck towards the left.

Step 8

If you feel free motion and the patient reports no increase in symptoms, increase the traction and direct the traction towards your left shoulder.

Step 9

Maintaining the traction, carefully move the patient's head in an arc in the frontal plane, from the left to the right side.

Step 10

As you pass the midline, very gently move the right side of the disc towards the left side with your right finger, and rotate the head to the right. This step will reduce the bulge or herniation of the cervical disc.

> ***Note:** Omit this last step in cases where narrowing of the cervical disc space is caused primarily by degenerative changes.*

To obtain full relief and resolution of the dysfunction, this procedure may have to be repeated over several visits.

Posterior Cervical Sympathetic Syndrome
aka Barre-Lieou Syndrome

This syndrome presents with localized symptoms which result from a disturbance of the sympathetic nervous system. Chronic dysfunctions of the upper cervical spinal region are the primary cause of Barre-Lieou Syndrome. It is a challenging diagnosis to make; the syndrome is frequently misdiagnosed, and is often left untreated.

The patient is typically between twenty-five to sixty, and may be of either sex. By the time you see the patient, he will probably have visited several practitioners and undergone multiple tests. The resulting diagnoses will range from "arthritic changes of the cervical spine" and "depressive syndrome" to "malingering."

The patient's chief complaints will affect one side of the face and are vague and poorly defined. They may include:

- A discharge, which may last from one to four hours, of clear fluid from one nostril
- Transient blurring of vision of one eye
- Unilateral tinnitus
- Intermittent hot feelings in one cheek, occasionally accompanied by itching or sensitivity
- Vertigo
- Cough
- Limitation of neck motion as a result of a whiplash injury

Upon examination, the patient will exhibit relatively normal gross motions of the cervical area. However, on palpation, the upper posterior cervical muscles will feel like a firm and rigid mass. You will find that there is a locking of the Occipitoatlantal and Atlantoaxial articulations, which causes this area to move as one unit. There will be a secondary Somatic Dysfunction present at C2 on C3.

To treat the patient, first reassure him that there is a definitive diagnosis: the vague symptoms are due to a malfunction of the sympathetic nervous system. Next, describe your treatment plan, which will include slowly softening the muscles involved and treating any Somatic Dysfunctions that are present. Eventually, normalization of the musculoskeletal functions will relieve the symptoms that have arisen from the malfunction of the sympathetic nervous system.

Use the techniques described to relieve *"Hypertonic Posterior Cervical Muscles"* and for *"Unlocking Cervical articulations."* In addition, I recommend trying the following technique.

Technique 18
Treatment for Posterior Cervical Sympathetic Syndrome

Patient position

Ask the patient to lie in the supine position.

Practitioner position

Sit by the patient's head.

Procedure

Step 1

Face your palms up, and slide them under the patient's occiput until the tips of your middle and index fingers are pressing up against the hypertonic muscles right below the occiput. Keep your hands in this position.

The weight of the patient's head will slowly cause the muscles to soften under your fingers.

Step 2

With your fingertips still pressed against the underside of the patient's occiput, lock your elbows against your sides and lean straight back. Use your fingertips to create a traction force on the occiput in a cephalic direction.

Step 3

Maintain the traction on the occiput. As you feel the muscles soften, increase the pressure of your fingers on the muscle mass. If your fingers tire, release the traction, but maintain the pressure on the patient's muscles.

Step 4

Once the muscles soften, palpate for any underlying Somatic Dysfunctions and treat accordingly.

You will typically find a severely restricted Occipitoatlantal and Atlantoaxial articulation, as well as dysfunctions at the T2 to T3 area. Treat all findings as needed.

Chapter Three

THE THORACIC REGION

TECHNIQUES ON PATIENTS IN THE PRONE POSITION

Technique 1
Treatment of Superficial Hypertonic Muscles or Tender Points in the Thoracic and Upper Lumbar Region

Example One

The patient is experiencing hypertonic upper thoracic (trapezius) superficial muscles on the left side.

Patient position

Ask the patient to lie in the prone position on the table. Place as many pillows as necessary under the patient's abdomen, so as to flatten the lumbar spine and eliminate the lumbar lordosis. This is the neutral position for the lumbar area.

Practitioner position

Stand at the patient's right side.

Procedure

Step 1

Place your right (monitoring) finger on the hypertonic muscle or tender point involved.

Step 2

Use your left hand to grasp the lateral side of the patient's left shoulder. Pull the shoulder up towards the patient's head, until his shoulder is above (higher than) your monitoring finger. [Fig. 3.1]

Step 3

Position your body and left arm so that your left forearm is directly above your monitoring finger.

Step 4

Lean away from the table so that your weight causes your left arm to pull the patient's left shoulder towards your monitoring finger. You should feel an immediate resolution of the hypertonic muscle.

> *Note:* Remember to use your body weight, not your arm, to pull on the patient's shoulder.

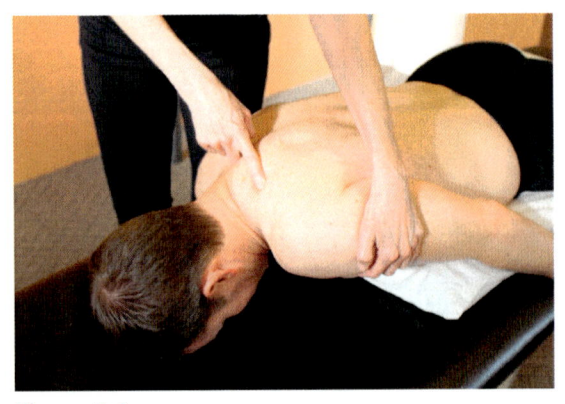

Figure 3.1
Pull the shoulder up toward the patient's head.

Example Two

The patient is experiencing hypertonic mid-thoracic to upper lumbar superficial muscles on the left side.

Patient position

Ask the patient to lie in the prone position on the table. Place as many pillows as necessary under the patient's abdomen, so as to flatten the lumbar spine and eliminate the lumbar lordosis. This is the neutral position for the lumbar area.

Practitioner position

Stand at the patient's right side.

Procedure

Step 1

Place your right index (monitoring) finger on the hypertonic muscle or tender point involved.

Step 2

Using one of the positions listed below, place your left hand on top of the patient's left shoulder and aim your hand directly towards the monitoring finger.

- If the hypertonic muscle is in the upper thoracic region, place your hand close to the patient's neck.

- If the muscle is in the mid thoracic region, place your hand halfway between the patient's neck and the lateral end of his shoulder.

- If the muscle is in the lower thoracic or upper lumbar region, place your hand on top of the patient's acromion, towards the lateral side of his shoulder.

Step 3

Grasp the patient's left shoulder and lean back, away from the table. Your body weight will create a compressive and lateral flexion force. Stop when you feel this force at your monitoring finger. [Fig. 3.2]

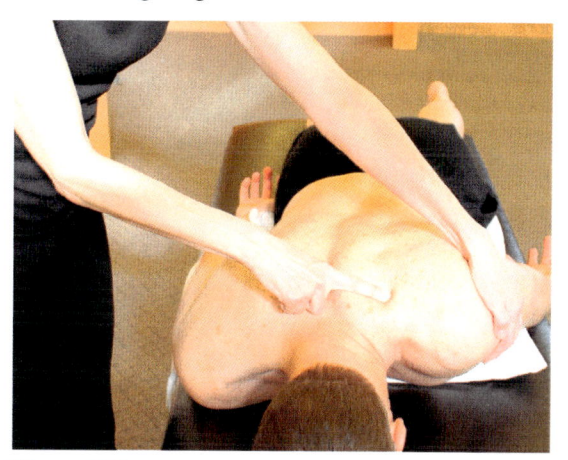

Figure 3.2
Lean away from the table.

Step 4

While maintaining the above position, turn your entire body to face the table. Then, lean away from the table. Your weight will create a rotary and an extension force, which aim towards the patient's midline. You should feel the hypertonic muscle immediately resolve.

Note: *To create a compressive and a lateral flexion force in the lumbar region, or if the patient is large, ask him to slide his left hand down towards his feet until you feel motion at your monitoring finger.* **[Fig. 3.3]**

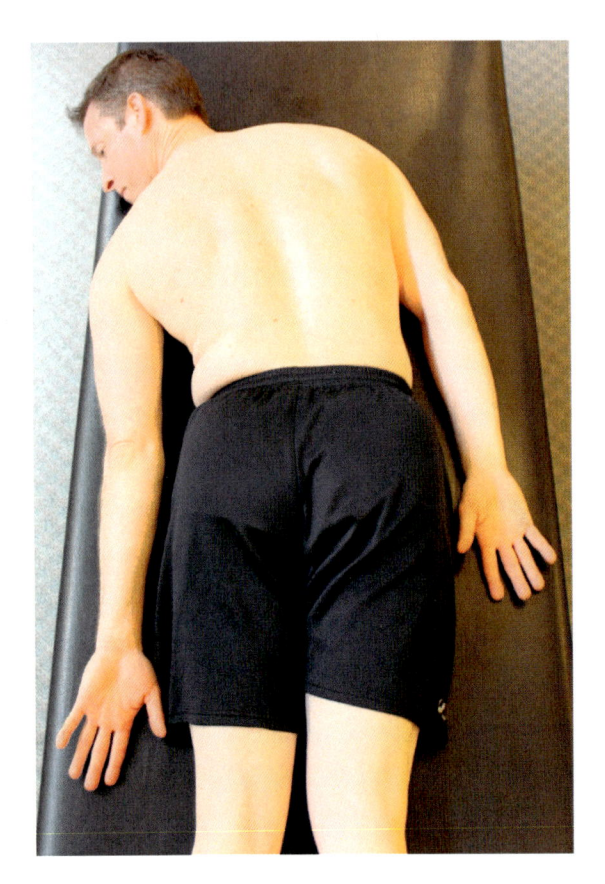

Figure 3.3
Have the patient slide his arm towards his feet.

Technique 2
A Simple Method to Diagnose a Type II Thoracic or Lumbar Somatic Dysfunction

Patient position

Ask the patient to lie in the prone position on the table. Place as many pillows as necessary under the patient's abdomen, so as to flatten the lumbar spine and eliminate the lumbar lordosis. Place a second pillow under the patient's neck and upper thoracic region. These steps will place the patient in the neutral position.

Practitioner position

You may stand on either side of the table for this technique. Pick the side at which you feel more comfortable.

Procedure

Step 1

Place your thumbs or index fingers on the posterior aspect of the transverse processes of T1. Palpate for any posterior rotations of the right or left transverse processes. Continue this process on each vertebra down to L5.

Step 2

If one transverse process is posterior as compared to the other side, you will need to distinguish if it is a Type II Somatic Dysfunction, part of a group curve, or a bony deformity.

Step 3

To test for a Somatic Dysfunction, introduce a flexion and extension motion to the affected vertebra. Introduce a flexion motion by rolling both of your thumbs simultaneously over the superior margin of the transverse processes. Push down on the superior edge of the transverse processes in a caudal direction (towards the feet). Note whether the posterior rotation of the transverse process exaggerates with this motion.

Step 4

To introduce an extension motion, roll your thumbs back onto the inferior edge of the transverse processes. Next, push the transverse processes upwards in a cephalic direction (towards the head). [Fig. 3.4]

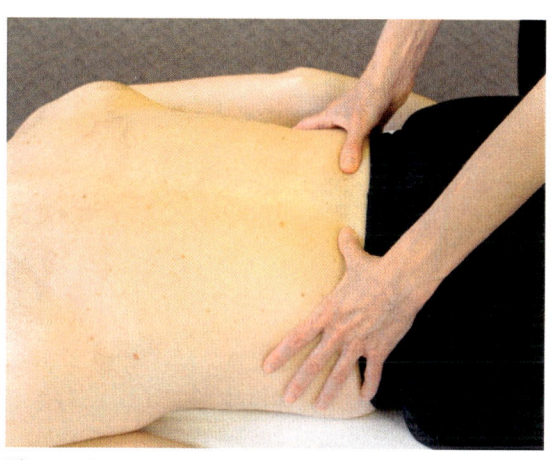

Figure 3.4
To create extension, roll your thumbs back on the inferior edge of the transverse process.

Interpreting the results

If you feel any resistance against your fingers while pushing down on the transverse processes in either flexion or extension, then there is a barrier to motion in that direction. This barrier indicates the presence of a Type II Somatic Dysfunction.

Example

If you palpate a posterior transverse process on the right side and feel increased resistance when pushing on the superior margin of the transverse process, then resistance to motion is in flexion. In this case, the ease of motion is in extension and right lateral flexion. The name of this Somatic Dysfunction is Extension, Sidebent right, Rotated right, (E SR RR)

TECHNIQUES ON PATIENTS IN THE SEATED POSITION

Technique 3
A Simple and Speedy Scanning Technique for Diagnosing Gross Deformities and Somatic Dysfunctions of the Thoracic and Lumbar Spine

Patient position Ask the patient to sit on the table with his back to you.

Practitioner position
Stand behind the patient.

Procedure

Step 1

Place your dominant hand flat against the patient's back with your fingers perpendicular to the patient's spine. [Fig. 3.5]

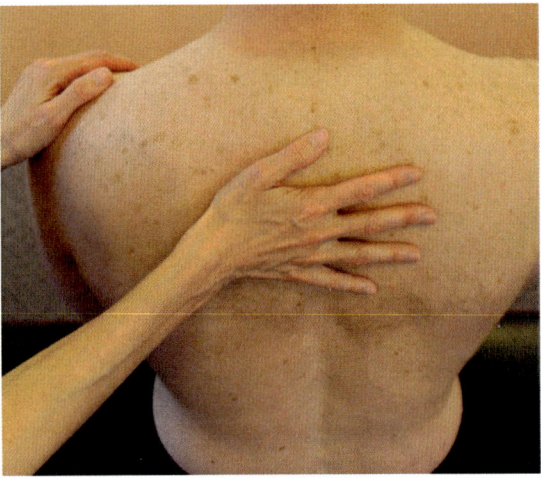

Figure 3.5
Place your hand flat against the patient's back and feel for any distortions.

Step 2

Slide your hand down the patient's back, feeling for any major gross distortions as you progress. Look for distortions such as uneven scapulas, bulging muscles, and spinal curves.

Step 3

Once you have completed Step 2, place one or two fingers of the same hand on the tip of the T1 spinous process. You can use your thumb alone, your index finger alone, or your index and middle fingers together. Run your finger(s) down the spine. Note any changes from one spinous process to the next. [Fig. 3.6]

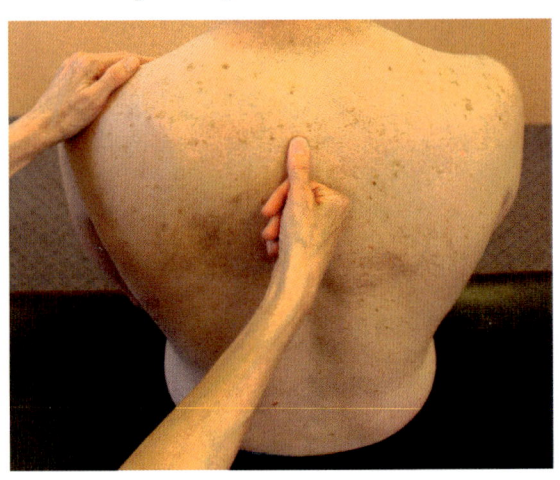

Figure 3.6
Place your thumb over the patient's spinous process.

*Note: *If you are having trouble feeling the individual spinous processes, ask the patient to flex his back slightly. You will need to increase the patient's flexion as you proceed towards T12 and the lumbar area.*

Differential Diagnosis

1 If the patient has no somatic or postural changes, then each spinous tip will be lined up directly above the one below it in all three primary planes: frontal, sagittal, and horizontal.

2 If a **kyphosis** is present, the tip of each spinous process will be slightly posterior to the one above it in the sagittal plane. If a **lordosis** is present, each spinous tip will be slightly anterior to the one above it in the sagittal plane.

- In either a kyphotic or lordotic curve, the changes in the spinous processes will continue until the peak of the kyphosis or lordosis, at which point the curve will reverse direction.

3 If a **scoliotic** curve is present, the entire spine will feel as if it is moving in the direction of the convexity.

Example

The patient has a scoliosis from T3 through T11 with its convexity to the right:

- T3 will be laterally flexed to the left and rotated to the right in relation to T4, T4 will be laterally flexed to the left and rotated to the right in relationship to T5, etc., until you reach the apex of the curve. After the apex, the relationship of the lower vertebra will reverse and gradually return to the midline.

- If you palpate the spinous tips up until the apex, you will notice a gradual shifting in the frontal plane of the tip of each spinous process to the right, as compared to the one below it. After the apex, the spinous tip will feel as if it is moving to the left, as compared to the spinous tip above it, until you reach T11.

- The individual functional units will be restricted in lateral flexion to the right and rotation to the left.

- Usually, the upper portion of the scoliotic curve will be accompanied by a kyphosis that ends at the point at which the scoliosis reverses direction. A lordotic curve may begin at this point.

- When examining a scoliotic curve, you should also look for any obvious posterior rotations of the ribs secondary to the convexity of the scoliosis. In a scoliotic pattern, patients often notice the rotation of the ribs. This deformity, especially in an advanced state, causes most of the patient's complaints.

4 If a **Type II Somatic dysfunction** is present, you will find that, while all the other spinous processes follow a fixed pattern, one spinous process has deviated from that pattern.

5 A **Type II Somatic dysfunction within a scoliotic curve** will present differently depending on whether it is a flexion or extension Somatic Dysfunction.

■ Example of a Flexion somatic dysfunction of T5, Sidebent left, Rotated left (T5 F SL RL) within a scoliotic curve with its convexity to the right:

- T5 is in flexion, so its spinous tip is slightly indented (forward slide) as compared to those of T4 and T6. In addition, the tips of T4 and T5 are closer together than expected, and the tips of T5 and T6 are further apart than expected.

- You will also notice that the spinous tip of T5 is farther to the right than expected; this is because of the coupled motion of right translatory slide and left lateral flexion motion. This may be difficult to feel. However, as your palpating finger descends to T6, you will note that T6 does not feel as if it has translated as far to the right as compared to T5.

■ Example of an Extension Somatic Dysfunction of T5, Sidebent right, Rotated right (T5 E SR RR):

- The spinous tip of T5 feels as if it is slightly posterior as compared to T4 and T6 because a dorsal translatory slide accompanies extension. In addition, the tip of T5 will be further away from T4, and closer to T6, than expected.

- The tip of the spinous process of T5 will be vertically aligned with the tip of the spinous process of T4. This is because lateral flexion is accompanied by translation in the opposite direction. In this case, T5 is laterally flexed to the right and translated to the left, while the rest of the vertebrae in the curve are translated to the right.

Technique 4
Diagnosing a Somatic Dysfunction

Patient position

Ask the patient to sit on the table with his back to you.

Practitioner position

Stand behind the patient.

Procedure

Step 1

Separate the index and middle fingers (monitoring fingers) of your dominant hand. Place one finger on each side of T1's transverse process. Alternatively, you can position one finger from each hand on each side of the transverse process.

Step 2

Ask the patient to sit up straight to eliminate the thoracic kyphosis and to place the thoracic spine in its neutral position. If necessary, ask the patient to push his chest up towards the ceiling to achieve the neutral position.

Note: If the patient has a severely locked kyphosis and is unable to straighten his back, hook your axilla over the patient's shoulder and wrap your arm around his chest. With the same hand, grab the patient's opposite shoulder and manually move him into extension, which is the neutral position. Always stop if the patient experiences any discomfort, and/or if the area is so locked that it cannot be moved. [Fig. 3.7]

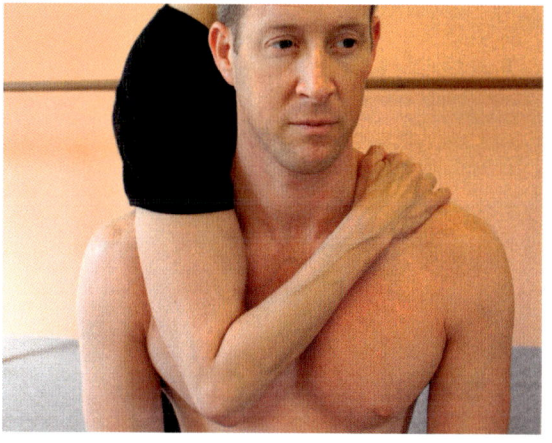

Figure 3.7
Wrap your arm around the patient's chest and grab his opposite shoulder.

Step 3

Use your monitoring fingers to determine whether one of the transverse processes is rotated in a posterior direction as compared to the other side.

Step 4

If either transverse process is posterior, then you need to confirm that this is a Type II Somatic Dysfunction. Ask the patient to inhale deeply, which will introduce extension. To introduce flexion, ask the patient to exhale fully.

Interpreting the results

If the posterior rotation becomes more pronounced with extension, then it is a Flexion Type II Somatic Dysfunction; there is an extension barrier to motion. If it becomes more pronounced with flexion, then it is an Extension Type II Somatic Dysfunction; flexion is the barrier to motion.

Example

If the right transverse process of T6 is rotated posteriorly and the posterior rotation is exaggerated when the patient inhales (extension), then the diagnosis is T6 Flexion, Sidebent right, Rotated right (T6 F SR RR). In this case extension is the barrier to motion.

Technique 5
Treatment of a Type II Somatic Dysfunction in the Thoracic and Upper Lumbar Area

Example
T6 Flexion, Sidebent right, Rotated right (T6 F SR RR).

Patient position
Ask the patient to sit on the table with his back to you.

Practitioner position
Stand behind the patient, slightly to his right side.

Procedure
Step 1
Place one or two monitoring fingers of your left hand on the patient's right sixth transverse process.

Step 2
Hook your right axilla over the patient's right shoulder, as close to the patient's neck/midline as possible. Use your right hand to grasp the patient's left shoulder.

*Note: Alternative hand positions:

1 Stand by the patient's right side. Flex your right shoulder ninety degrees. Then flex your elbow one hundred and eighty degrees (your hand should be touching your shoulder). Twist your right arm slightly, so that your forearm rests on the patient's shoulder, your elbow aims towards the patient's front, and your fingers point away from the patient's back (towards you). Make sure that your arm is as close to the patient's neck/midline as possible. [Fig. 3.8]

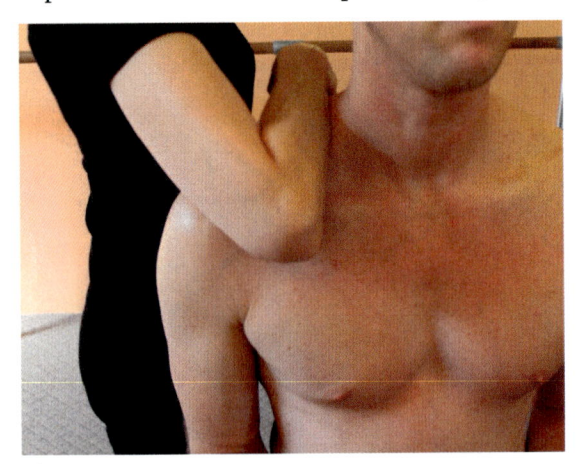

Figure 3.8
Alternative Hand Position #1.

2 Stand by the patient's right side. Flex your right elbow ninety degrees. Place your right forearm on the patient's shoulder, with your fingers pointing forwards (towards the patient's chest). Make sure your arm is as close to the patient's neck/midline as possible. [Fig. 3.9]

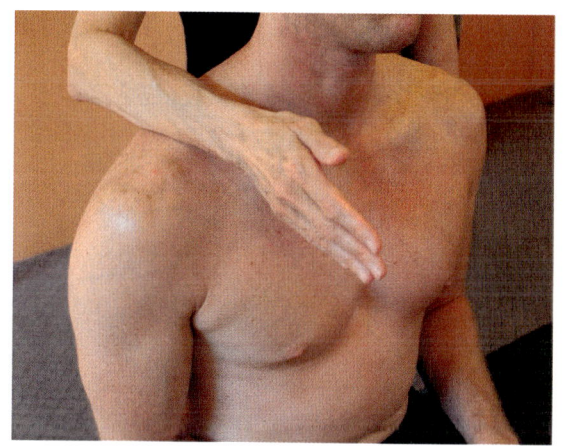

Figure 3.9
Alternative Hand Position #2.

Step 3

Sit the patient up straight until you feel motion at your monitoring finger. This is the neutral position of the thoracic spine at that level.

Step 4

Lean your body weight over your axilla or forearm until you feel motion at your monitoring finger. This motion creates compression and right sidebending of the patient's thoracic area.

***Note:** Always use your body weight, not your arm, to create the forces. Make sure your downward pressure is very close to the side of the patient's neck/midline.*

Step 5

Ask the patient to exhale so as to create flexion of the spine. While the patient exhales, rotate the patient's right shoulder posteriorly, along the horizontal plane, up to your monitoring finger. You should feel an instant release of the dysfunction.

Step 6

If you feel that the dysfunction has not resolved completely, create a jiggling motion in the direction of your monitoring finger and of the articulation, by pressing your right shoulder or forearm down towards your monitoring finger repeatedly and then releasing the pressure.

***Note:** To treat the lumbar area up to L3, ask the patient to slouch until his lumbar lordosis has flattened. The lumbar region will now be in its neutral position, and you can continue with the treatment described above.*

Technique 6

Use of Spinal Vector Forces to Treat a Severely Locked Vertebra in the Thoracic and Lumbar Area

This technique involves generating a gentle directed vector force down a defined area of the spine, by applying continuous spinal compression. This constant force creates a closed pack rod of the specified region, thereby enabling the practitioner to use very small motions to treat the Somatic Dysfunctions of the involved vertebra. If done properly, this technique enables the practitioner to use a fraction of the force usually needed to unlock a locked articular dysfunction of the vertebra.

Example
Locking of T8 on T9.

Patient position
Ask the patient to sit on the table with his back to you.

Practitioner position
Stand at the patient's midline. Turn so that your body is perpendicular to the patient, and your left side rests against the patient's back.

Procedure

Step 1
Ask the patient to sit up straight. This will flatten the thoracic spine and place the area into its neutral position.

Step 2
Use your right thumb and index finger (monitoring fingers) to grasp the spinous process of T8.

Step 3
Rest your left axilla close to the left side of the patient's neck. Wrap your left arm around the patient's front, and rest your forearm close to the right side of the patient's neck.

Step 4
Bend your knees so that your weight creates an even force down the patient's spine. Stop when you feel the force at your monitoring fingers. This compression will create a closed pack rod of the vertebrae, up to and including T8. Maintain this compression throughout the procedure. [Fig. 3.10]

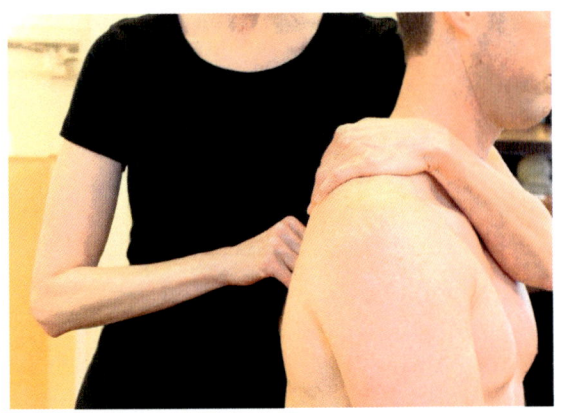

Figure 3.10
Bend your knees to create an even force down the midline.

  Note: Avoid any lateral flexion motion by making sure the force you are creating is directed down the midline of the vertebra. The degree to which you bend your knees can control the amount of force you produce.

Step 5
Create left lateral flexion of T8 on T9 by increasing the downward force of your left axilla on the patient's left shoulder. Return the patient's spine to its upright position.

Step 6
Next, create right lateral flexion of T8 on T9 by pushing down with your left forearm, which is near the right side of the patient's neck. Return the patient's spine to its upright position.

Step 7

Introduce flexion of T8 on T9 by gently pushing your left elbow down into the patient's chest. Return the patient's spine to its upright position.

Step 8

Lean backwards to create extension of the vertebra. Maintaining this position, push T8 forward with your right fingers.

Step 9

Continue to maintain the downward vector force produced by your left arm and body weight. Slowly move your body in small circles. This motion will create small circular motions of the involved vertebra.

Step 10

Repeat all of the above steps until you feel freedom of motion of the vertebra in all directions.

> ***Note 1:*** *For this technique to be effective, you MUST maintain your knees in the bent position so that the vector force on the spine remains constant.*
>
> ****Note 2:*** *If you are treating a locked lumbar vertebra, first create a closed pack rod of all the thoracic vertebrae and maintain that position. Ask the patient to slouch, one lumbar vertebra at a time, while you follow along and increase the compression at each lumbar vertebra until you have reached your monitoring finger.*

Technique 7
Chronic Localized Flattening of Two or More Segments in the Thoracic Spine

While examining the patient's thoracic spine, you may come across a localized area at which the thoracic spine feels flattened. I have noticed that many practitioners mistakenly diagnose and treat this area as two or three adjacent extension Type II Somatic Dysfunctions. The major difficulty with the area is not extension, but rather a locking of the vertebra in a ventral translatory position. To treat this area properly, you must restore and normalize the dorsal-ventral translatory slide motion.

Patient position
Ask the patient to sit as far back on the treatment table as possible.

Practitioner position
Stand behind the patient and ask him to lean his body against yours.

Procedure
Step 1
Use the thumb and bent index finger of your dominant hand to grasp the spinous process of the vertebra, which is immediately below the lowest flattened vertebra.

Step 2
Ask the patient to cross both arms across his chest. With his hands in this position, raise his arms until you feel motion at the level of the lowest dysfunctional, flattened vertebra. [Fig. 3.11]

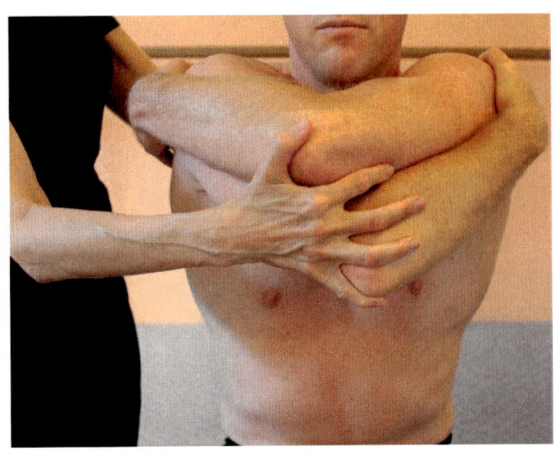

Figure 3.11
Have the patient cross his arms across his chest.

Step 3
Place your hand on the front of the patient's crossed arms and push them tightly against his chest.

Step 4
Ask the patient to push his arms straight forward, against your hand, while you maintain firm resistance against his arms to prevent any forward motion. This will create an isometric resistance.

Step 5

As the patient is pushing forward, maintain firm pressure on the vertebra's spinous process with your thumb and index finger so as to prevent any posterior motion. If you do this technique properly, you will feel the vertebra above your fingers slide in a dorsal (backwards) direction. [Fig. 3.12]

Step 6

Have the patient repeat the isometric resistance three to four times.

Step 7

Repeat all of the above steps on each successive flattened vertebra until you have treated the entire localized flattened area.

Step 8

Once the translatory motions have been normalized, you can add any other necessary manipulative procedures to normalize motion completely in that area.

> *Note:* *This is a chronic condition and will require repeated treatments to restore motion and relieve any Somatic Dysfunctions.*

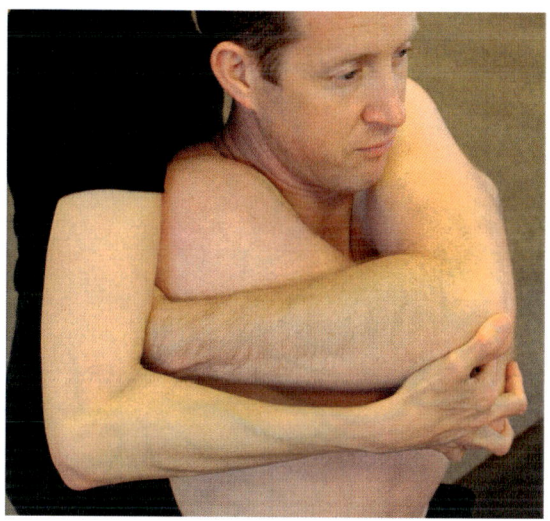

Figure 3.12
Have the patient push forward against your hand.

SCOLIOSIS

Technique 8
Treatment of an "S" Shaped Scoliosis of the Thoracic and Lumbar Spine

Treatment of an "S" shaped scoliosis consists of two parts. The first part addresses the vertebra at which the convexity of the scoliosis changes direction. This transitional point, which consists of a severely locked Type II Somatic Dysfunction, will be tender to the touch and restricted in motion. The second part of the treatment requires introducing translatory slide to each vertebra which forms part of the scoliotic pattern.

Treatment Part One

Example
The patient has an "S" Shaped scoliosis with an upper convexity to the left and a transition to the right at T9 on T10.

Patient position
Ask the patient to sit as far back on the treatment table as possible.

Practitioner position
Stand behind the patient and lean him against your body.

Procedure

Step 1
Place your right thumb and bent index finger (monitoring fingers) on the sides of the spinous process of the lowest vertebra of the upper convexity (at T9, in this case). Your hand should be on the vertebra at the transitional point of the convexity.

Step 2
Wrap your left arm around the patient's anterior chest wall and grasp his right shoulder. Make sure that you have a firm grip on the patient's thorax and chest wall.

Step 3
Ask the patient to sit up straight so as to create a flattening of the thoracic kyphosis and place the area in its neutral position.

Step 4
Use your left hand to push down on the patient's right shoulder, creating a right sidebending force on the thoracic spine. Stop when you feel the force at the monitoring fingers of your right hand.

Step 5
Bring the patient back to an upright position. Next, lean on his left shoulder to create sidebending to the left. [Fig. 3.13]

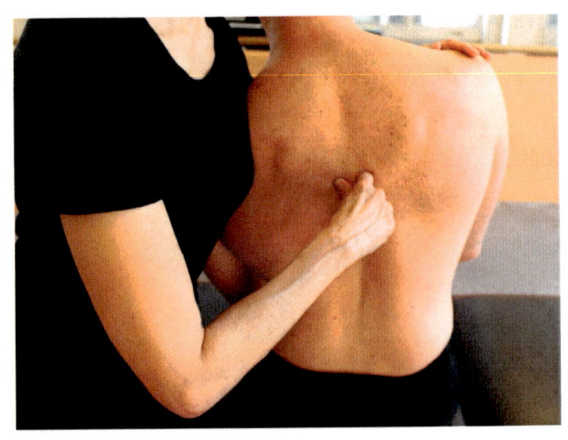

Figure 3.13
Lean on the patient's left shoulder to create sidebending to the left.

a Repeat sidebending in both directions, until you feel bilateral freedom of lateral flexion of T9 on T10.

b If you do not obtain freedom of sidebending at the articulation, then aim a jiggling force at each side of the articulation alternately.

Step 6

The next step is to introduce a circular motion of T9 on T10.

a First, ask the patient to inhale to create extension of the spine. While the patient inhales, raise the patient's entire thorax in a cephalic (up) and dorsal (back) direction over your right fingers, while you push forward on T9 with your right hand.

b Next, right sidebend the spine up to T9.

c Ask the patient to exhale. As he does so, rotate him first into flexion and then towards the front midline. Next, rotate the patient to the left. Finally, move him into a fully upright position.

Note: These movements should be performed as one fluid motion.

Step 7

Repeat this circular motion several times. Once you have finished Part One of the treatment, you will notice free motion of the locked vertebra, reduction of the kyphotic/lordotic posture of the spine, and reduction in the convexity of the spine.

Note: If you are not satisfied with the results, repeat this entire process at the next thoracic vertebra, (in this case, T10).

Treatment Part Two

This part of the treatment consists of introducing a translatory slide motion at each vertebra in the scoliotic pattern.

Patient position

Ask the patient to sit on the table with his back to you.

Practitioner position

Stand behind the patient, towards his left side (in this case, the side of the convexity).

Procedure

Step 1

Place the web of your left hand over the patient's left shoulder, and position your left thumb (monitoring finger) on the left lateral aspect of the spinous process of T1. Make sure your left hand is close to the patient's neck.

Step 2

Ask the patient to sit up straight so as to flatten the thoracic spine and to place it in its neutral position.

Step 3

Use your right hand to keep the patient's right shoulder stationary.

Step 4

Push the web of your left hand downwards to create a compressive force up to the level of T1. Next, push your left thumb medially against the lateral aspect of the T1 spinous process. This will introduce both lateral flexion and a left-to-right translatory slide of the vertebra. Repeat this motion several times and then replicate this step on T2 and T3.

Step 5

To treat T4 and beyond, change your left arm position to one of the following:

a Flex your left shoulder ninety degrees, and your left elbow one hundred and eighty degrees. Twist your left arm so that your forearm rests on the patient's shoulder, your elbow aims towards the patient's front, and your fingers point away from the patient's back (towards your body).

b Place your left axilla on top of the patient's shoulder.

c If the table is very low, flex your left elbow, point your fingers anteriorly towards the patient's front, and place your forearm on the patient's shoulder.

Step 6

Place your right thumb (monitoring finger) on the left, lateral aspect of the spinous process of T4.

Step 7

Lean your body weight down towards your monitoring finger. This will create a compressive force and a lateral flexion of T4. At the same time, push your right thumb against the left lateral aspect of the spinous process of T4. This will cause a translatory slide of the vertebra. Repeat this step several times. [Fig. 3.14]

Step 8

Lowering your monitoring finger, repeat Step 7 at each vertebra, through T9. At this point, the convexity changes to the right side. Stand to the patient's right, reverse your hand position, and repeat the above steps.

> *Note 1:* As your fingers descend down the patient's spine and you reach a lordotic area, remember to ask your patient to slouch so as to maintain the neutral position.

> **Note 2:* The above description calls for translation towards the restrictive side of each vertebra. If this does not work, reverse your hands and translate towards the freedom of motion of each vertebra involved.

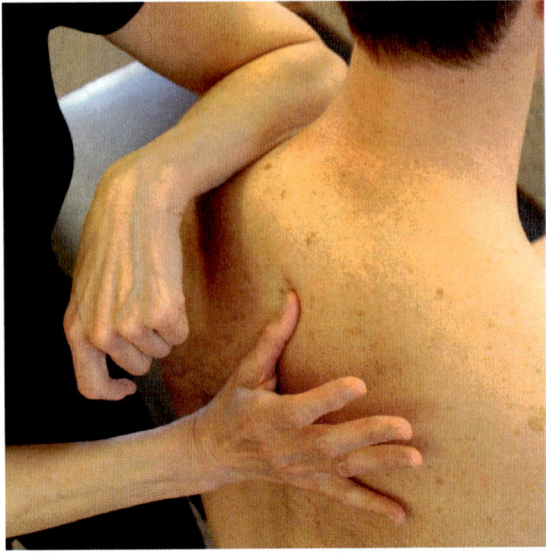

Figure 3.14
Push your thumb against the lateral aspect of the transverse process.

> ***Note 3:* Incorporate the following modifications into the above procedure to treat an "S" Shaped Scoliosis in a thin, flexible, and/or young patient.

1 Use traction rather than compression in Part 2. Wrap your arm around the patient and hold his opposite shoulder with your hand. Use your axilla and hand to lift his thorax straight up towards the ceiling.

2 Grasping the involved spinous process with your thumb and index finger, move it into flexion, extension, lateral flexion, and rotation.

> *Note:* A patient who presents with a scoliosis which is organic in nature must be told that treatment will not "cure" the condition. The treatment aims to reduce the degree of the curve's convexity, increase thoracic motion, and decrease the pain.

Technique 9

Treatment of Superficial Tender Points on the Anterior Thoracic Wall

Example

The patient requires treatment of a tender point on the anterior portion of the right fifth rib lateral to its sternal attachment.

Patient position

Ask the patient to sit on the table with his back to you.

Practitioner position

Stand behind the patient

CAUTION

This technique should not be used if a rib has been fractured or displaced or if there is any danger that further motion could perforate the lung.

Procedure

Step 1

Flex your elbows to ninety degrees. Place your left forearm on the patient's left shoulder. Your left forearm should rest by the patient's neck. Your right forearm should be over the patient's right shoulder, in line with the tender point.

Step 2

Place your left finger (monitoring finger) on the point to be treated.

Step 3

Ask the patient to sit up straight. This will place the thoracic area in its neutral position.

Step 4

Lean your body weight down from your shoulders. This will cause your forearms to push down on your patient's thoracic area. Stop when you feel motion at your monitoring finger.

*Note: The downward force will create midline compression and right sidebending due to the right arm's lever type motion.

Step 5

Treatment of an anterior point always requires flexion. To introduce this flexion motion, forward bend the patient's neck up to your monitoring finger. If greater flexion of the spine and chest wall is required in order to reach your monitoring finger, place your chest on top of the patient's upper thoracic spine, and lean your weight downward and forward until the desired flexion is produced. [Fig. 3.15]

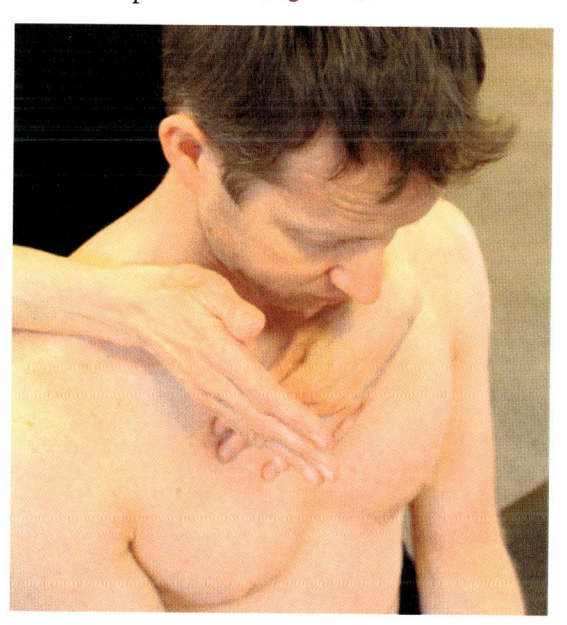

Figure 3.15

Forward bend the patient's neck to introduce flexion.

Step 6

Maintaining this position, rotate the patient's body from the right side to the left side. Keep the rotation in the horizontal plane and in the direction of the midline right up to your monitoring finger. The pain and tenderness should resolve instantly.

Technique 10

Treatment of a Tender Point on the Left Lateral Chest Wall

Patient position

Ask the patient to sit with his left side at the edge of the table.

Practitioner position

Stand behind the patient.

Procedure

Step 1

Place your right arm over the patient's left shoulder, and rest your right axilla over the shoulder.

Step 2

Ask the patient to flex his left elbow. Cup his elbow with your right hand. [Fig. 3.16]

Step 3

Ask the patient to sit up straight, so as to put the thoracic area in its neutral position.

Step 4

Place one finger of your left hand on the tender point (monitoring finger).

Step 5

Lean your body weight down on the patient's left shoulder until you feel the force at your monitoring finger. This motion should create a compressive force and a sidebending force.

  a If the tender point is in the midline, it will resolve at once.

  b If the tender point is to the right or left of the midline, maintain the above position and rotate the patient's shoulder, in the horizontal plane, up to your monitoring finger. This should immediately resolve the tender point.

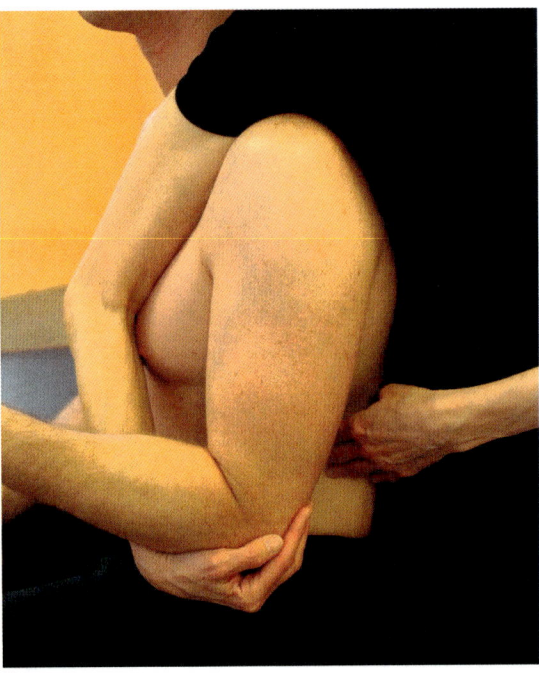

Figure 3.16
Cup the patient's elbow in your hand.

Common Pitfalls While Treating Patients

1. The spine was not in the neutral position at the start of the treatment.

2. Insufficient compression was applied. Make sure the patient's shoulders are lower than yours, so that you can lean down to create the needed compression.

3. The region to be treated was flexed beyond the monitoring finger. To correct for this, repeat the compression maneuver described above, while flexing each vertebra at a time, e.g., T1 on T2, then T2 on T3 etc. This will help you to obtain the necessary flexion without bypassing the monitoring finger.

4. You passed the midline of the body while rotating the patient.

5. You rotated the patient's left shoulder to your monitoring finger while treating a right-sided dysfunction, rather than rotating the patient's right shoulder up to the monitoring finger.

6. Remember to create the compressive force with your body weight, not your arm muscles.

TECHNIQUES ON PATIENTS IN THE SUPINE POSITION

Technique 11
Treatment of a Tender Point on the Anterior Upper Chest Wall

Example
The patient has a left anterior tender point.

Patient position
Ask the patient to lie in the supine position on the table, with a pillow under his head.

Practitioner position
Stand to the patient's right side.

Procedure

Step 1
Place your left finger (monitoring finger) on the tender point.

Step 2
Place your right thumb on the anterior aspect of the patient's left shoulder at the acromion. Place the rest of your right fingers behind his shoulder. Grasp the shoulder. [Fig. 3.17]

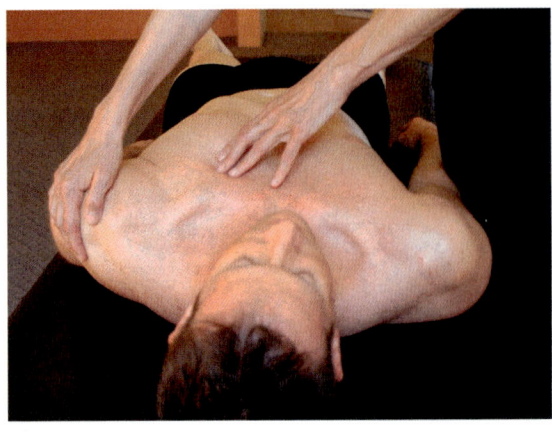

Figure 3.17
Grasp the patient's shoulder and lean back.

Step 3
Lean backwards, so that your body weight pulls the patient's shoulder down towards his feet and then up towards your monitoring finger. These motions will resolve the tender point by creating compression, flexion, rotation, and sidebending.

TECHNIQUES TO TREAT RIB AND CLAVICULAR DYSFUNCTIONS

Technique 12
Treatment of a Tender Point on a Lower Rib

Example
The patient has a tender point on the lower left sixth rib.

Patient position
Ask the patient to lie in the supine position on the table, with a pillow under his head.

Practitioner position
Stand by the patient's left shoulder.

Procedure

Step 1
Place your left finger (monitoring finger) on the tender point.

Step 2
Slide your right hand and forearm under the patient's back until your fingertips are directly aligned with the tender point, and your forearm is aligned with the superior lateral aspect of the patient's left shoulder.
[Fig. 318]

Step 3
Lift your right forearm straight up, towards the tender point. Stop when you feel motion at your monitoring finger. This motion will create both flexion and sidebending of the patient's chest wall.

Step 4
Maintaining this position, create a compressive force by leaning your body towards your monitoring finger. The tender point should resolve immediately.

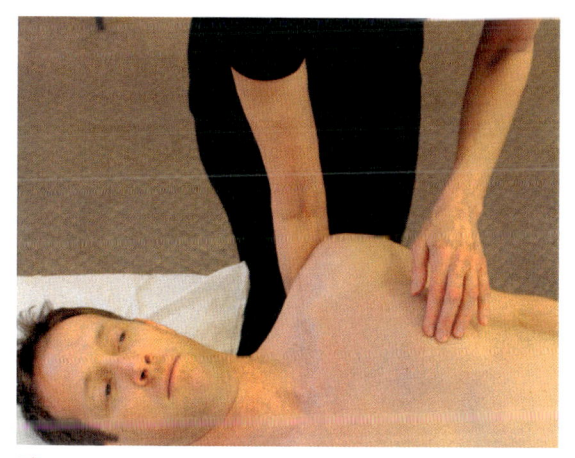

Figure 3.18
Align your forearm with the patient's tender point.

79

DYSFUNCTIONS OF THE RIBS

Many different terms have been used to describe the motion of the ribs. Often, these terms denote dysfunctions of the motion. Common terms include a "Bucket Handle," "Pump Handle," or "Inhalation/Exhalation" dysfunction. However, with FPR techniques, none of these terms apply. To diagnose a dysfunction, you only need to ask two questions:

1. Is the motion of the rib restricted?

2. Is the restriction at the ribs' posterior vertebral articulation, or is it at its anterior sternal articulation?

Note: Treatment entails restoring motion to the rib at the involved articulation.

POSTERIOR RIB DYSFUNCTIONS

Technique 13
A Simple Method for Diagnosing Posterior Rib Restrictions

Patient position
Ask the patient to sit on the table with his back to you.

Practitioner position
Stand behind the patient.

Procedure

Step 1
Place a finger of each hand lateral to the transverse process of the thoracic vertebra and at its rib attachment.

Step 2
Ask the patient to inhale and exhale deeply. Feel for bilateral rib movements.

Interpreting the results
If you detect unequal movement of a rib as the patient inhales, then the rib with less motion has a posterior rib restriction.

Technique 14
Treatment of Posterior Restriction of Motion of the First Rib

Example
The patient has posterior restriction of the right first rib.

Patient position
Ask the patient to lie in the supine position on the table.

Practitioner position
Stand to the patient's right side, facing his head.

Procedure
Step 1
Slide your left hand under the patient's back, and place your left finger (monitoring finger) at the articulation of the first rib with the transverse process.

Step 2
Ask the patient to flex his right elbow. Cup the flexed elbow with your right hand.

Step 3
Raise the patient's elbow until his shoulder is at approximately ninety degrees of flexion and ten degrees of adduction. The patient's right forearm will rest behind your right forearm and lean against the ventral side of it.

Step 4
Direct a small compressive force, of no more than one pound, down the patient's right elbow, towards your monitoring finger.

> *Note 1: If you do not feel the force localized at your monitoring finger, then you may need to add a little more adduction or flexion to the patient's arm.*
>
> **Note 2: Do not add any additional compressive forces.*

Step 5
With your right hand, rotate the patient's right elbow in a clockwise direction, using your right forearm as a fulcrum. This movement will lock the rib at its posterior articulation.

Step 6
Maintain the compressive force and the locking of the articulation. Lean down and rest your chest on your right hand; use your body, your right hand, and the patient's right elbow, humerus, and posterior rib articulation as a solid unit. [Fig. 3.19]

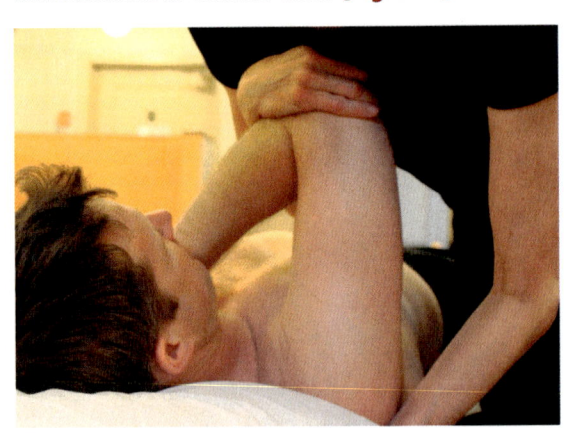

Figure 3.19
Lean down to form a solid unit composed of your hand, body, patient's elbow, humerus and posterior rib articulation.

Step 7
Move this entire unit, including and directed by your body, in a circumduction motion. This motion entails moving the unit caudally (up), medially, and finally down, until the patient's right shoulder and arm return to the patient's side.

> *Note: If the patient is flexible, this method can be used to treat posterior dysfunctions of the second and third rib.*

Technique 15
Treatment of Posterior Rib Restrictions

Example
The patient has a restriction of the posterior third rib on the right side.

Patient position
Ask the patient to lie in the supine position on the table.

Practitioner position
Stand to the patient's right side.

> ⚠️ **CAUTION**
> Do not perform this technique on a patient who has a painful physical impairment of the shoulder.

Procedure

Step 1
Slide your left hand under the patient's back and place one finger (monitoring finger) at the articulation of the patient's third rib with its transverse process.

Step 2
With your right hand grasp the patient's right arm just above the elbow joint and lock the patient's right hand under your axilla. [Fig. 3.20]

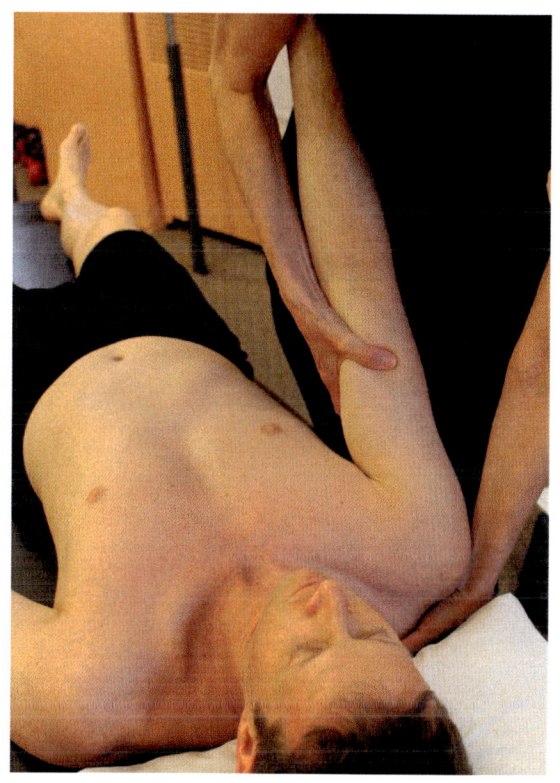

Figure 3.20
Lock the patient's hand under your axilla.

Step 3
Move your body in such a way as to place the patient's right arm at approximately one hundred and thirty five degrees of abduction, above the monitoring finger.

Step 4

Direct a mild compressive force, no more than one pound, through the patient's right glenohumeral articulation towards your monitoring finger. If you do not feel the force at your monitoring finger, add a few additional degrees of shoulder adduction and/or flexion. Do not add any additional compression.

> *Note:* At this point the right glenohumeral articulation is in a closed pack position and any force applied to the humerus will be transmitted directly to the rib at its attachment with the thoracic spine.

Step 5

While maintaining this force, rotate your body so as to create full internal rotation of the patient's arm. You will feel the rib rotate along with your body.

Step 6

When the arm has reached full internal rotation, add a jiggling motion towards your monitoring finger.

Step 7

Rotate your body in the reverse direction, creating a full external rotation of the shoulder. Add a jiggling motion towards your monitoring finger. [Fig. 3.21]

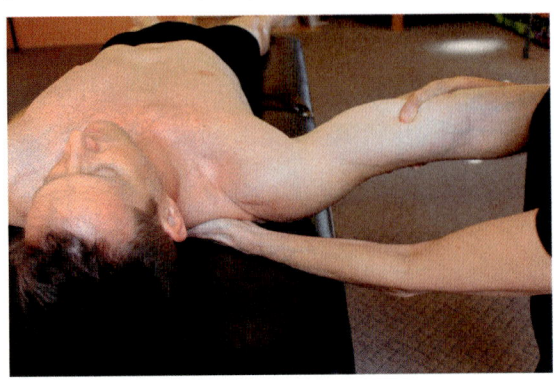

Figure 3.21
Rotate your body to create external rotation of the patient's shoulder.

Step 8

Repeat Steps 6 and 7 several times, until you feel full motion at the articulation.

> *Note:* To treat ribs at different levels, you will need to adjust your hand and body position so that you feel all forces at the monitoring finger.

ANTERIOR RIB DYSFUNCTIONS

Frequently, patients with anterior rib dysfunctions will complain of point tenderness at a specific spot. These dysfunctions are often the result of trauma or are secondary to a strain injury. An examination will reveal a slight anterior or posterior displacement of the chondral continuation of the rib at its sternal articulation. The treatment of the dysfunction consists of returning the articulation to its proper placement.

Technique 16
Treatment of an Anteriorly Displaced Rib at its Sternochondral End

Example
The patient has an anteriorly displaced right sixth rib.

Patient position
Ask the patient to sit as far back on the treatment table as possible. Ask the patient to rest both arms on his lap.

Practitioner position
Stand behind the patient, with his back against your chest wall.

Procedure

Step 1
Wrap your left arm around the front of your patient's chest and place your left finger (monitoring finger) on the right sternochondral articulation of his sixth rib.

Step 2
Ask the patient to sit up straight. Next, ask him to cross his arms and to grasp each of his elbows with the opposite hand. Instruct him to keep his arms firmly in this position. [Fig. 3.22]

Step 3
Place your right forearm between the patient's right lateral chest wall and his right arm. Make sure that your forearm is at the level of his sixth rib.

Step 4
Step to the right, shifting the patient's entire upper body to the right. This will cause a slight left lateral flexion of the ribs, which you will feel at the monitoring finger.

Step 5
Push your forearm laterally against the patient's right arm until you feel the motion at your monitoring finger. This creates a traction force at the sternochondral junction.

> **Note:* Make sure that the patient keeps gripping his elbows firmly. Ensure that his arms do not move away from his body as you push against them.

Step 6
Maintaining the traction force, move your right arm repeatedly, in first an anterior and then a posterior direction. The rib will begin to rotate internally and externally at its articulation. Repeat this step until you feel freedom of rotation.

Step 7
This step will normalize the relation of the rib to its sternal articulation. As you move your right arm forward, exaggerate the anterior motion and apply pressure to the chondral end of the rib with your monitoring finger. You will feel the rib slide posteriorly into its normal position. Maintain this chondral position while you slowly bring the patient's arm back to his side.

Technique 17
Treatment of a Depressed Rib at its Sternochondral End

Example
The patient has a depressed right sixth rib.

Patient position
Ask the patient to sit as far back on the treatment table as possible. Ask him to rest both arms on his lap.

Practitioner position
Stand behind the patient, with his back touching your chest wall.

Procedure

Step 1
Wrap your left arm around the front of your patient's chest and place your left finger (monitoring finger) on the right sternochondral end of his sixth rib.

Step 2
Ask the patient to sit up straight. Next, ask him to cross his arms and to grasp each of his elbows with the opposite hand. Instruct him to keep his arms firmly in this position.
[Fig. 3.22]

Step 3
Place your right forearm between the patient's right lateral chest wall and his right arm. Make sure that your forearm is at the level of his sixth rib.

Step 4
Step to the right, shifting the patient's entire upper body to the right. This will cause a slight left lateral flexion of the ribs, which you will feel at the monitoring finger.

Step 5
Push your forearm laterally against the patient's right arm until you feel the motion at your monitoring finger. This creates a traction force at the sternochondral junction.

> *Note: Make sure that the patient keeps gripping his elbows firmly. Ensure that his arms do not move away from his body as you push against them.

Step 6
Maintaining the traction force, move your right arm repeatedly, in first a posterior and then an anterior direction. The rib will begin to rotate internally and externally at its articulation. Repeat this step until you feel freedom of rotation.

Step 7
This step will normalize the relation of the rib to its sternal articulation. As you move your right arm back, exaggerate the posterior motion by pushing your chest wall against the patient's back at the level of the sixth rib. You will feel the rib slide anteriorly into its normal position with your monitoring finger. Maintain this chondral position while you slowly bring the patient's arm back to his side.

CLAVICLE

Technique 18
Treatment of an Anteriorly Displaced Sternoclavicular Articulation

Example
The patient has an anteriorly displaced right sternoclavicular articulation.

Patient position
Ask the patient to sit as far back on the treatment table as possible. Ask the patient to rest both arms on his lap.

Practitioner position
Stand behind the patient, with his back against your chest wall.

> **CAUTION**
> This is not a treatment for a dislocated sternoclavicular articulation.

Procedure

Step 1
Wrap your left arm around the front of the patient's chest and place your left finger (monitoring finger) on the anterior aspect of his right sternoclavicular articulation.

Step 2
Ask the patient to sit up straight. Next, ask him to cross his arms and to grasp each of his elbows with the opposite hand. Instruct him to keep his arms firmly in this position.

Step 3
Place your right forearm as high up as possible under the patient's right axillary region and point your fingers anteriorly. [Fig. 3.22]

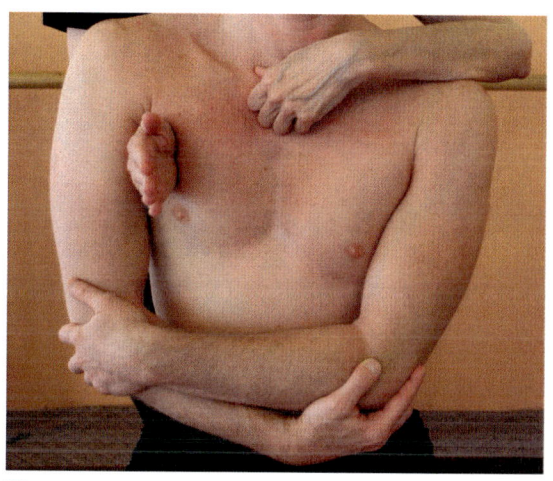

Figure 3.22
Place your hand high up under the patient's axilla.

Step 4
Step to the right while lifting your right forearm up into the axilla to raise the patient's shoulder. This action will create a left sidebending of the clavicle at the monitoring finger.

Step 5

Create a lateral traction force at the sternoclavicular articulation by pushing your right forearm laterally against the patient's right arm. Stop when you feel motion at the monitoring finger. [Fig. 3.23]

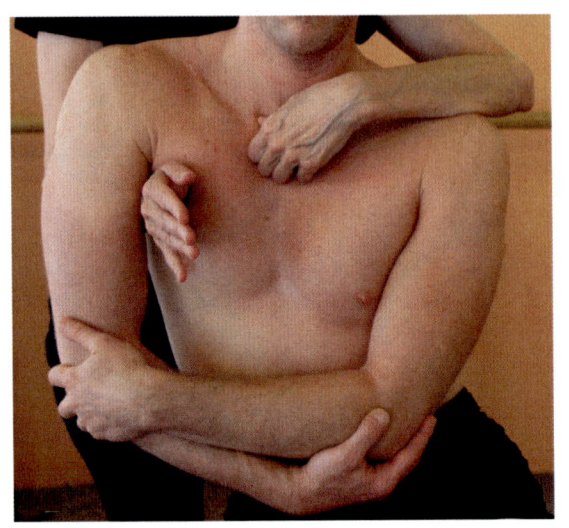

Figure 3.23
Create a traction force by pushing your forearm laterally against the patient's arm.

Note: *Make sure that the patient keeps gripping his elbows firmly. Ensure that his arms do not move away from his body as you push against them.*

Step 6

Maintaining this traction force, repeatedly move your right arm in a posterior, then an anterior, direction until you feel free motion of the clavicle at the sternoclavicular articulation.

Step 7

When you begin to feel free motion at the articulation, exaggerate your forward forearm motion. This will cause the sternal end of the clavicle to slide posteriorly into its articulation. Maintain this position with your monitoring finger as you slowly bring the patient's arm back to his side.

Technique 19
Treatment of a Posterior Sternoclavicular Displacement

Example
The patient has a posteriorly displaced right sternoclavicular articulation.

Patient position
Ask the patient to sit as far back on the treatment table as possible. Ask the patient to rest both arms on his lap.

Practitioner position
Stand behind the patient, with his back against your chest wall.

Procedure

Step 1

Wrap your left arm around the front of your patient's chest and place your left finger (monitoring finger) on the anterior aspect of his right sternoclavicular articulation.

Step 2

Ask the patient to sit up straight. Next, ask him to cross his arms and to grasp each of his elbows with the opposite hand. Instruct him to keep his arms firmly in this position.
[Fig. 3.22]

Step 3

Tuck your right forearm as high up as possible under the patient's right axillary region and point your fingers anteriorly.
[Fig. 3.23]

Step 4

Step to the right while lifting your right forearm up into the axilla to raise the patient's shoulder. This action will create a left sidebending of the clavicle at the monitoring finger.

Step 5

Create a lateral traction force at the sternoclavicular articulation by pushing your right forearm laterally against the patient's right arm. Stop when you feel motion at the monitoring finger.

Step 6

Maintaining the traction force, move your right arm repeatedly in an anterior, then a posterior, direction until you feel free motion of the clavicle at the sternoclavicular articulation. The posterior motion should be much greater than that used for anterior displacement.

> ***Note:*** *Make sure that the patient keeps gripping his elbows firmly. Ensure that his arms do not move away from his body as you push against them.*

Step 7

When you start to feel free motion at the articulation, add an additional lateral traction force by moving your arm farther to the right.

Step 8

Add an exaggerated posterior motion by pushing your chest wall anteriorly against the patient's posterior rib cage. This will cause the sternal end of the clavicle to slide anteriorly into its articulation and normalize its relationship to the sternum. Hold the clavicle in its proper position with your monitoring finger as you return the patient's arm slowly back to his side.

Technique 20
Normalizing Rotation Motion of the Clavicle on the Acromium

Example
The patient's right acromioclavicular motion must be normalized.

Patient position
Ask the patient to sit as far back on the treatment table as possible. Ask the patient to rest both arms on his lap.

Practitioner position
Stand behind the patient, with his back against your chest wall.

Procedure:

Step 1
Wrap your left arm around the front of your patient's chest and place your left finger (monitoring finger) on the anterior aspect of the right acromioclavicular articulation.

Step 2
Ask the patient to sit up straight. Next, ask him to cross his arms and to grasp each of his elbows with the opposite hand. Instruct him to keep his arms firmly in this position.
[Fig. 3.22]

Step 3
Tuck your right forearm as high up as possible under the patient's right axillary region and point your fingers anteriorly.
[Fig. 3.23]

Step 4
Step to the right while lifting your right forearm up into the axilla to raise the patient's shoulder. This action will create a left sidebending of the clavicle at the monitoring finger.

Step 5
Create a lateral traction force at the acromioclavicular articulation by pushing your right forearm laterally against the patient's right arm. Stop when you feel motion at the monitoring finger.

> *Note 1:* Make sure that the patient keeps gripping his elbows firmly. Ensure that his arms do not move away from his body as you push against them.

> **Note 2:* You will need less force to create traction at the acromioclavicular articulation than at the sternoclavicular articulation.

Step 6
Maintaining the traction force, move your right arm repeatedly, in an anterior, then a posterior, direction until you feel free rotary motion at the acromioclavicular articulation.

Chapter Four

THE LUMBAR AND SACRAL REGION

THE LUMBAR AND SACRAL REGION

A Quick Scan to Evaluate Lumbar, Iliac and Femoral Motion

Ask the patient to stand with his back to you. Place your right thumb on the patient's right posterior superior iliac spine, and your left thumb on the patient's left posterior superior iliac spine. Spread your fingers so that the pinky (5th finger) of each hand is resting on the greater trochanter of the femur. Ask the patient to bend forward slowly into flexion. While he is flexing forward, consider the following questions: [Fig. 4.1]

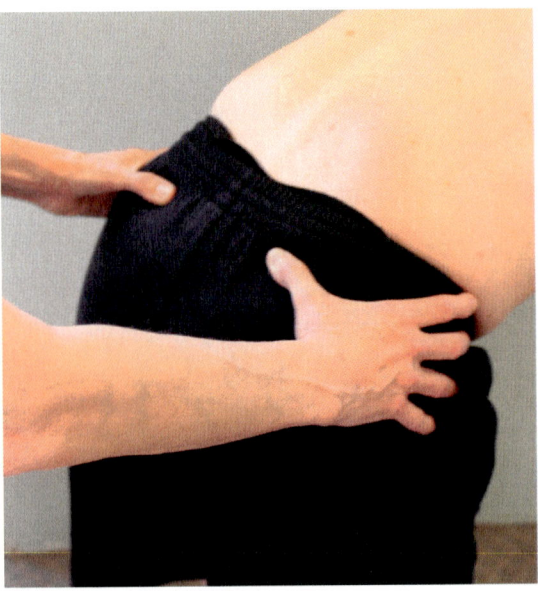

Figure 4.1
Quick scan to evaluate lumbar, iliac and femoral motion.

1. Is each vertebra freely flexing on the one below it?
2. Are the posterior superior iliac spines and the innominate bones rotating forward and downwards?
3. Are both sides moving equally? If motion is unequal, is there a sacroiliac dysfunction?
4. As the innominate bones rotate forward, are the femurs moving equally back towards you?

Note: *The answers to these questions will help to determine which areas you will need to investigate further.*

Technique 1
Treatment of Hypertonic Muscles or Tender Points in the Lower Lumbar Area

Example
The patient has hypertonic muscles, ranging from the third to the fifth lumbar vertebrae, on the left side.

Patient position
Ask the patient to lie in the prone position. Place as many pillows as necessary under the patient's abdomen to flatten his lumbar lordosis. This is the neutral position of the lumbar spine. Maintain this position for the rest of the procedure.

Practitioner position
Stand to the patient's left.

Procedure
Step 1
Spread your left (monitoring) fingers along the involved muscle.

Step 2
Use your right hand to grasp the outside of the patient's right ankle. Slide the patient's legs towards you until you feel motion at your monitoring fingers. This will create a left sidebending of the patient's trunk. [Fig. 4.2]

Step 3
Face your right palm up towards the ceiling and rotate your arm so that your fingers point towards you. Maintaining this hand position, slide your right hand around the outside of the patient's right thigh. Your hand should remain above the patient's right knee.

Step 4
Continue to slide your right hand medially and towards you. Stop when your hand is between the patient's thighs and your fingers are pointing up towards the ceiling.

Step 5
Firmly grasp the patient's lower right thigh above the knee joint. [Fig. 4.3]

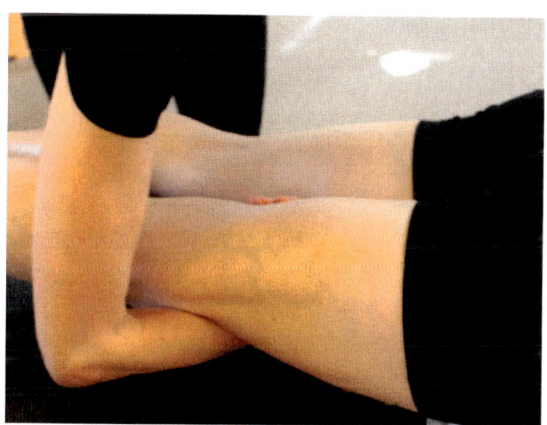

Figure 4.3
Grasp the patient's thigh above the knee joint.

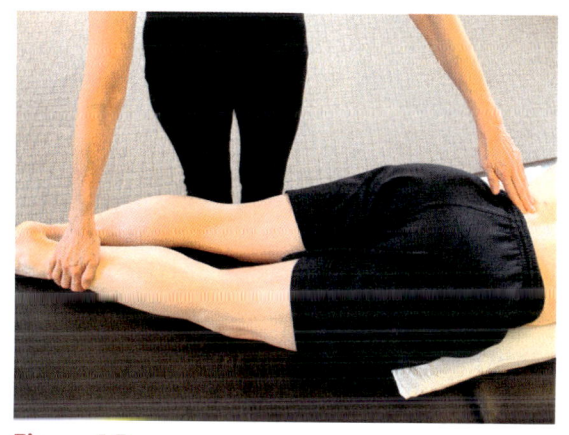

Figure 4.2
Slide the patient's legs towards you.

Step 6

Continuing to firmly grasp the patient's thigh, unwind your right wrist until you feel motion at your monitoring fingers.
You will feel an instantaneous softening of the hypertonic muscles. [Fig. 4.4]

Figure 4.4
Unwind your wrist.

Note 1: *This torsional motion places the patient's right femur into external rotation. The motion locks the femoroacetabular articulation into the sacrum, from the lower lumbar vertebra up to your monitoring finger. To understand this step better, I like to picture tightening up all the loose fascia right up to my monitoring fingers.*

Note 2: *Although the patient's femur may rise off the table during this step, you should never raise the femur intentionally.*

Note 3: *With a few adjustments, you can use this technique to relieve tender points down to the tip of the coccyx.*

1 If the tender point is located lower down on the body, you will need less sidebending in Step 2.

2 If the tender point is located closer to the midline, you will need less rotation in Step 6.

3 If the tender point is located at the tip of the coccyx, skip Step 2 (no sidebending) and only add rotation.

Technique 2
Treatment of a Lumbar Flexion Type II Somatic Dysfunction

Example

The patient is experiencing a Type II Somatic Dysfunction at L4 F SR RR (Fourth lumbar vertebra in Flexion, Sidebent right, Rotated right).

Patient position

Ask the patient to lie in the prone position on the table, with his right side close to the edge. Place as many pillows as necessary under the patient's abdomen to flatten his lumbar lordosis and to place the area in its neutral position. Maintain this neutral position throughout the procedure.

Practitioner position

Sit, preferably on a rolling stool or chair, to the patient's right, and face the patient's head. Make sure to position your legs as close to the edge of the table as possible. Your knees and legs should be parallel to the table, pointing towards your patient's head.

Procedure

Step 1

Ask the patient to drop his right leg off the table and onto your lap.

Step 2

Flex the patient's right knee and grasp it firmly between your knees. If you need help supporting the leg, wrap your left hand underneath the patient's right knee. [Fig. 4.5]

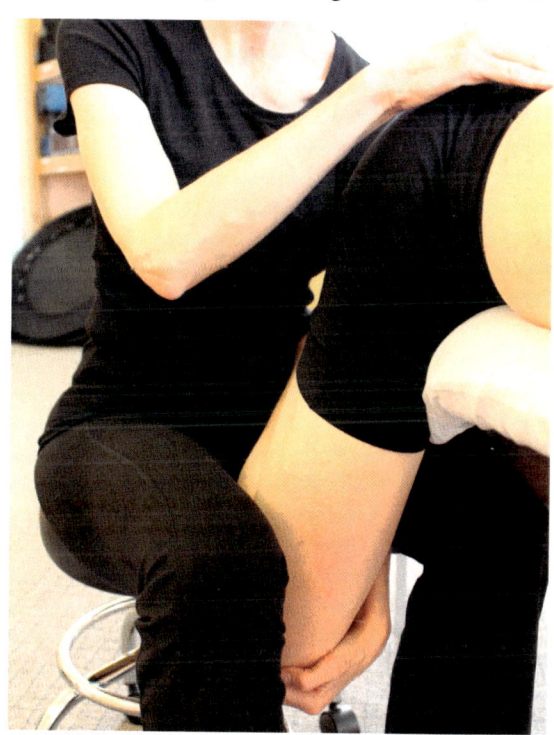

Figure 4.5
Use your free hand to support the leg.

Step 3

Place your right (monitoring) finger on the right transverse process of L4.

Step 4

Move the stool, and/or your body, towards the patient's head to increase flexion of the patient's right hip and lower lumbar vertebrae. Stop when you feel motion at your monitoring finger. [Fig. 4.6]

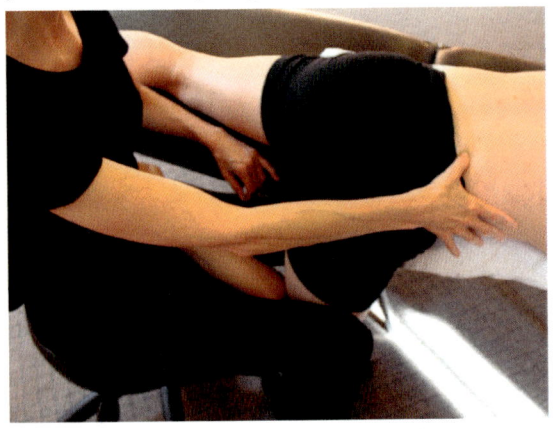

Figure 4.6
Move the stool towards the patient's head.

Step 5

Move your knees in towards the table, bringing the patient's leg as close to the edge of the table as possible. This motion will create adduction of the patient's right knee and leg.

Step 6

Move your body, and/or the stool, in a semi-circle, until the front of your body and both your knees are facing towards the side of the table. Stop moving when you feel motion at the monitoring finger. [Fig. 4.7]

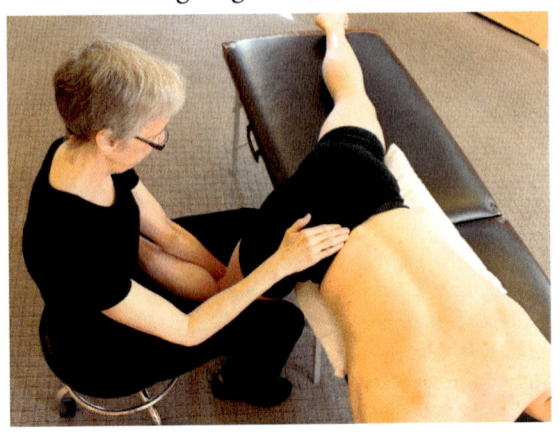

Figure 4.7
Move your body in a semi-circle, until the front of your body and both your knees are facing towards the side of the table.

*Note: *This rotary motion will create a closed pack position of the right femoroacetabular articulation, the sacrum, and the lower lumbar vertebrae, right up to your monitoring finger. In addition, the motion will place the involved vertebrae in lateral flexion.*

Step 7

Raise your heels towards the ceiling, or push your left hand, which is under the patient's right knee, up towards your monitoring finger. This motion will propel a compressive force into the involved articulation. You should feel an instant normalization of the dysfunction at your monitoring finger.

Technique 3
Treatment of a Lumbar Extension Type II Somatic Dysfunction

Example
The patient is experiencing a Type II Somatic Dysfunction at L4 E SR RR (Fourth lumbar vertebra in Extension, Sidebent right, Rotated right).

Patient position
Ask the patient to lie in the prone position on the table, with his right side close to the edge. Place as many pillows as necessary under the patient's abdomen to flatten his lumbar lordosis and to place the area in its neutral position. Maintain this neutral position throughout the procedure.

Practitioner position
Stand by the patient's right hip.

Procedure

Step 1
Place a firm wedge (either a rolled up towel or a small pillow) under the patient's right hip joint. This will allow the patient's propped up leg to function as a first-class lever and to move around a fulcrum.

Step 2
Place your right (monitoring) finger on the right transverse process of L4.

Step 3
Use your left hand to grasp the patient's right ankle. Rotate his right leg until his toes are pointing towards his left leg. Stop when you have removed all the slack in the fascia, right up to your monitoring finger. This will create internal rotation of the patient's hip and lock the femoroacetabular, sacral, and lumbar articulations into a closed pack position. [Fig. 4.8]

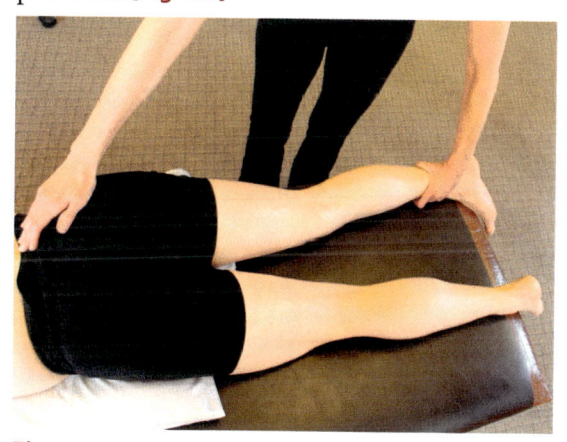

Figure 4.8
Rotate the leg until you have removed all the slack in the fascia.

Step 4
Compress the patient's leg towards your monitoring finger. The compressive force will be in a caudal direction (towards the patient's head).

Step 5

With your left hand, abduct the patient's right leg until you feel the motion at your monitoring finger. This will create lateral flexion.

Step 6

Push the patient's right ankle down towards the floor until you feel motion at your monitoring finger. You will feel an instant release of the articulation and a normalization of the somatic dysfunction. [Fig. 4.9]

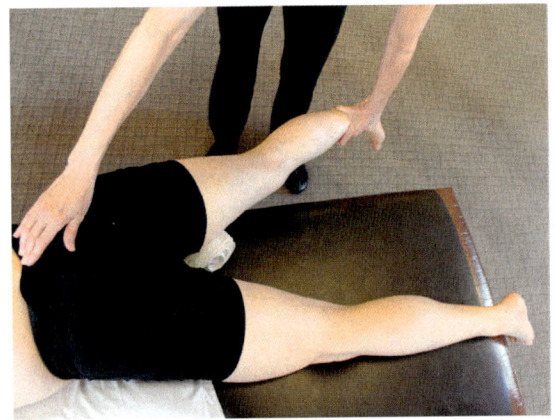

Figure 4.9
Push the patient's right ankle down towards the floor until you feel motion at your monitoring finger.

Note: *The wedge placed under the right anterior hip joint creates a first-class lever action. As the leg is pushed down, the unit (composed of the ilium, sacrum, and lower lumbar vertebrae) will lift up into extension.*

Alternative Ways to Create a First-Class Lever and Fulcrum

Substitute one of the below alternatives for the firm wedge under the patient's hip:

1 In Step 3, place your left thumb on top of the patient's leg and your index finger underneath the leg, slightly superior to your thumb. When you reach Step 6, push your thumb down towards the table and your index finger up towards the ceiling. [Fig. 4.10]

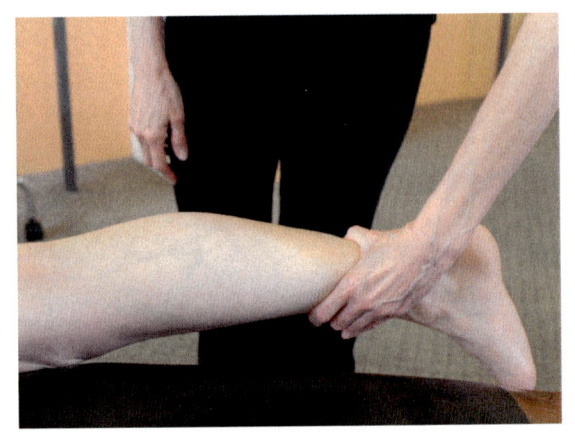

Figure 4.10
Alternative Hand Position #1.

2 If your patient is large, use your knee, rather than your hand, as the fulcrum. Ask the patient to slide to the edge of the table, so that his leg is slightly off the table. Place your knee underneath the patient's leg, right above his knee, and push the patient's leg towards the floor. [Fig. 4.11]

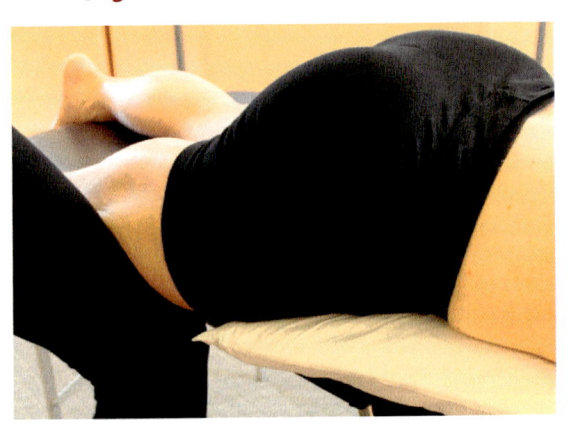

Figure 4.11
Place your knee underneath the patient's leg.

Technique 4
Treatment of a Lumbar Flexion Type II Somatic Dysfunction

Example
The patient is experiencing a Type II Somatic Dysfunction at L4 F SR RR (Fourth lumbar vertebra in Flexion, Sidebent right, Rotated right).

Patient position
Ask the patient to lie on his left side with his knees bent and his body close to the front edge of the table.

Practitioner position
Stand in front of the patient, facing him.

Procedure
Step 1
Place your right hand on the patient's abdomen. Use your left hand to push on the posterior/inferior aspect of the patient's sacrum. This motion will move the sacral tip towards you. It will also create an extension of the patient's sacrum, a straightening of the patient's lumbar lordosis, and the neutral position of the patient's lumbar region.

Step 2
Turn your left palm down towards the table. Weave your hand first under the lower part of the patient's right leg, and then over his upper right thigh. When you reach the top of the patient's thigh, grasp it. [Fig. 4.12]

*Note 1: You can also lean in and use the side of your body to hold up the patient's leg.

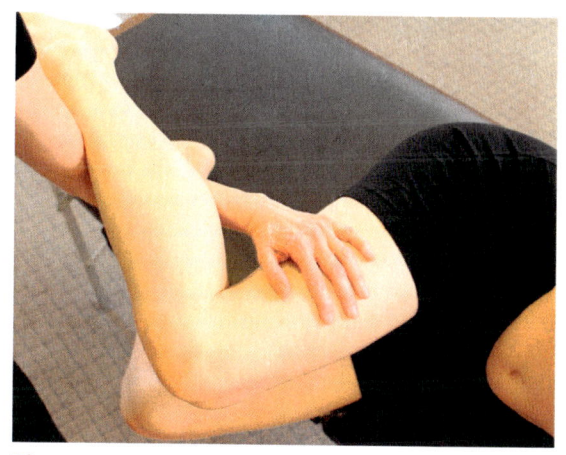

Figure 4.12
Weave your hand first under the lower part of the patient's leg, and then over his upper thigh.

*Note 2: Alternatively, you can hold the patient's leg by turning the palm of your right hand up to face the ceiling. Place your right hand under the patient's right leg and grasp his distal femur, just above the knee. The lower portion of the patient's right leg should be resting on your right forearm. [Fig. 4.13]

Figure 4.13
Alternative hand position.

Step 3

Place your right (monitoring) finger on the right transverse process of L4.

Step 4

Raise your left forearm towards the ceiling to create a pivoting motion of the patient's lower leg and an internal rotation of his hip. Stop when you feel the motion at your monitoring finger. This torsional motion creates a closed pack position of the patient's hip joint, pelvis, and lumbar area, right up to your monitoring finger.

Step 5

Use your left hand to move the patient's right knee and hip into flexion, until you feel motion at your monitoring finger. This will create flexion of the lumbar spine.

Step 6

Introduce slight adduction of the leg by letting the patient's right knee drop down towards the table.

Step 7

Introduce a compressive force by pushing the patient's knee and femur towards your monitoring finger. To create this compressive force, either use your arm (which is holding up the lower end of the femur), or press your hip or abdomen against the distal end of the patient's femur. You will feel an instant release of the articulation and a normalization of the Somatic Dysfunction.

Technique 5
Treatment of a Lumbar Extension Type II Somatic Dysfunction

Example
The patient is experiencing a Type II Somatic Dysfunction at L4 E SR RR (Fourth lumbar vertebra in Extension, Sidebent right, Rotated right).

Patient position
Ask the patient to lie on his left side with his knees bent and his back near the edge of the table.

Practitioner position
Stand behind the patient.

Procedure

Step 1

Stabilize the patient's right iliac crest by placing your left hand on it. Push on the posterior/inferior aspect of his sacrum with your right hand and move its tip away from you. This will create extension of the sacrum and a straightening of the patient's lumbar lordosis, and will place the lumbar region into its neutral position.

Step 2

Turn your right palm down towards the table. Weave your hand first under the lower part of the patient's right leg, and then over his upper right thigh. When you reach the top of the patient's thigh, grasp it. This position will help you maintain control over your patient's leg.

Step 3

Place your left (monitoring) finger on the patient's right L4 transverse process.

Step 4

Place the patient's leg in abduction by lifting your right arm up towards the ceiling.

Step 5

Pivot your distal forearm up, allowing the patient's knee to drop towards the table.

Step 6

Continue to pivot until you feel a locking of the femoroacetabular and the lumbosacral articulation, up to your monitoring finger. This area is now in a closed pack position.

Step 7

Extend the patient's hip, pelvis, and lower lumbar articulations by slowly walking away from him.

Step 8

Next, create a compressive force by pushing the patient's leg directly into your monitoring finger. You will feel the Somatic Dysfunction resolve instantly.

Technique 6
Treatment of Lumbar Nerve Root Pain

This technique uses traction to widen the involved space and to reduce symptoms caused by nerve root impingement at the intervertebral foramen. Note that I avoid using any language which implies that you are reducing a herniated disc or decreasing a partial disc protrusion.

Example
The patient is experiencing pain radiating down his right leg.

Patient position
Ask the patient to lie in the prone position on the table, with his right side close to the edge. Place as many pillows as necessary under the patient's abdomen to flatten his lumbar lordosis and to place the area in its neutral position. Maintain this neutral position throughout the procedure.

Practitioner position
Sit, preferably on a rolling stool or chair, by the patient's right side, facing his head. Make sure that your legs and knees are parallel to the table, and that they are pointing towards the patient's head.

Procedure
Step 1
Place your left (monitoring) finger at the area of the involved disc or intervertebral space.

Step 2
Ask the patient to lower his right leg off the table and onto your lap. Position the leg so that the right femur is resting on top of your knees, with the patient's knee joint lateral to your outside leg. To make the patient a little more comfortable, you may want to put a pillow or towel over your knees. [Fig. 4.14]

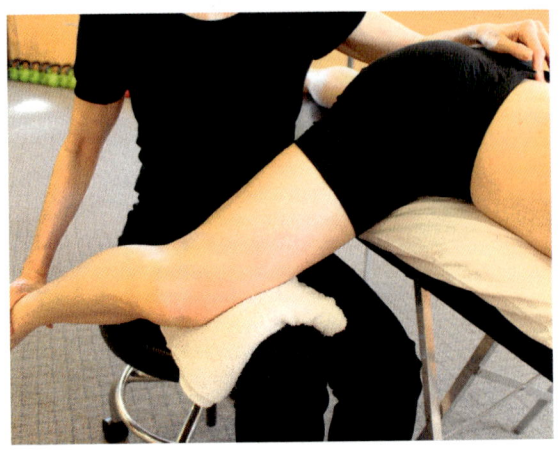

Figure 4.14
Rest the patient's leg on top of your knees, so that the patient's knee joint is lateral to your outside leg.

Step 3
Roll the stool, or move your body, forward. This will cause the patient's right hip and knee joints to flex. Stop when you feel the motion at your monitoring finger.

Step 4
Grasp the patient's right ankle with your right hand.

Step 5
Push the outside of your right knee against the medial (inside) aspect of the patient's right knee joint to move his knee laterally away from his body. This action will remove all ligamentous and muscle slack from the involved joints.

Step 6
Raise your outside leg off the floor until you feel motion at your monitoring finger. This creates abduction of the patient's leg.

Step 7

With your right hand, push the patient's ankle down towards the floor. This will create a rotary motion of the patient's right leg; this motion will automatically be transmitted through the knee, to the hip, and then to the involved vertebrae. This will create a gapping of the joint space.

Note: *Do not use more than one to three ounces of pressure to create the gapping of the joint space.*

Step 8

Hold this position for a slow count of four, then release for a count of four.

Step 9

Repeat Steps 7 and 8 several times.

To resolve this condition, you may have to repeat the process on the opposite side and treat more than one intervertebral area.

Technique 7
Diagnosis and Treatment of an Increased Lumbosacral Angle

Patients typically present with pain that radiates across the lower back and down both legs while the patient is standing. The pain is relieved when the patient assumes a non-weight-bearing position. Examination of the patient's upright back will reveal a severe lordosis with depression of the fifth lumbar spinous process. As the patient bends forward, you will note that the uppermost lumbar vertebra of the lordosis maintains a fixed lordotic position. This is due to a severe locking of the involved articulation.

First, you must treat the severely restricted juncture at which the kyphosis meets the lordosis. This is done by using Technique 6 from Chapter 3, *"Use of Spinal Vector Forces to Treat a Severely Locked Vertebra in the Thoracic and Lumbar Area."*

Example
The patient has a locked L3.

Patient position
Have the patient sit on the table, with his back to you.

Practitioner position
Stand at the patient's midline. Turn so that your body is perpendicular to the patient, and your right side is against his back.

Procedure 1

Step 1
Ask the patient to sit up straight so as to flatten the thoracic spine and place the area in its neutral position.

Step 2
Wrap your right arm around the front of the patient and rest your axilla close to the right side of his neck. Extend your right forearm over the patient's left shoulder, close to the left side of the patient's neck.

Step 3
Grasp the spinous process of L3 with your left thumb and index finger.

Step 4
Bend both of your knees so that your weight exerts a downward, even force on the patient's spine. This will create a closed pack rod of the thoracic vertebrae. Now ask the patient to slouch, one vertebra at a time, while you follow along and increase the compression at each vertebra until you have reached your monitoring finger at L3. Maintain this compression throughout the procedure.

Note: *Avoid any lateral flexion motion by making sure the force you are creating is directed towards the midline of the vertebra. The amount of force you produce down the spine is controlled by how far you bend your knees.*

Step 5
Create right lateral flexion of L3 on L4 by increasing the downward force of your right axilla on the patient's right shoulder. Return the patient's spine to its upright position.

Step 6
Next, create left lateral flexion of L3 on L4 by pushing down with your right forearm, which is near the left side of the patient's neck. Return the patient's spine to its upright position.

Step 7
Introduce flexion of L3 on L4 by pushing your right elbow down gently into the patient's chest. Return the patient's spine to its upright position.

Step 8

Lean backwards to create extension of the patient's vertebra. While you are leaning back, push L3 forward with the fingers of your left hand.

Step 9

Maintain the downward vector force supplied by your right arm and body weight as you slowly move your body in small circles. This will create small circular motions of the involved vertebra.

Step 10

Repeat Steps 5-9 until you feel freedom of motion of the vertebra in all directions.

Note: For this technique to be effective, you MUST maintain your knees in the bent position so that the vector force on the patient's spine remains constant.

Procedure 2

Next, you must increase motion of the vertebrae which make up the lordosis.

Step 1

Ask the patient to lie in the prone position on the table. Place as many pillows as necessary under the patient's abdomen, to reverse the lordotic lumbar region and to produce a slight convexity in the lumbar region.

Step 2

Stand to the patient's right. Place your left thumb on the left lateral aspect of the spinous process of the uppermost involved vertebra. Position your right thumb on the right lateral aspect of the spinous process of the vertebra right below it.

Step 3

Push the top vertebra towards you with your left thumb. At the same time, push your right thumb away from you. This will create a forced rotation of one vertebra on the other. [Fig. 4.15]

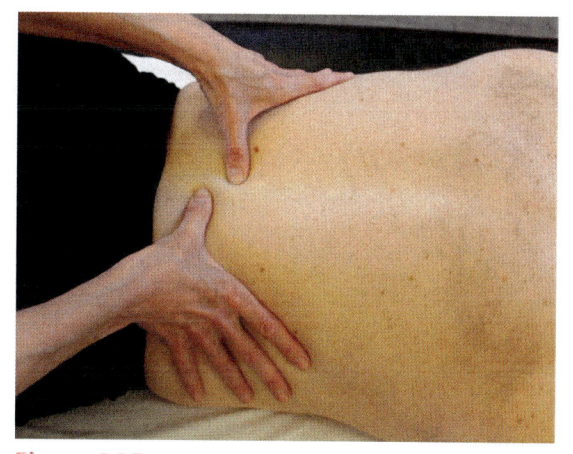

Figure 4.15
Push the top vertebra towards you with your left thumb. At the same time, push your right thumb away from you.

Step 4

Repeat Step 3 several times. Then move down one level to the next vertebra and repeat the process.

Step 5

After treating all the vertebrae, move to the other side of the table, reverse your finger placement, and repeat Steps 3-4.

Procedure 3

Normalize the motions of the lower lumbar vertebra.

Step 1
Stand to the patient's left.

Step 2
Place your left (monitoring) fingers on the spinous processes of L4 and L5 and the heel of your left hand on the posterior rim of the left ileum.

Step 3
Use your right hand to grasp the outside of the patient's right ankle. Slide the patient's legs toward you until you feel motion at your monitoring fingers. This movement will create a left sidebending of the patient's trunk. **[Fig. 4.16]**

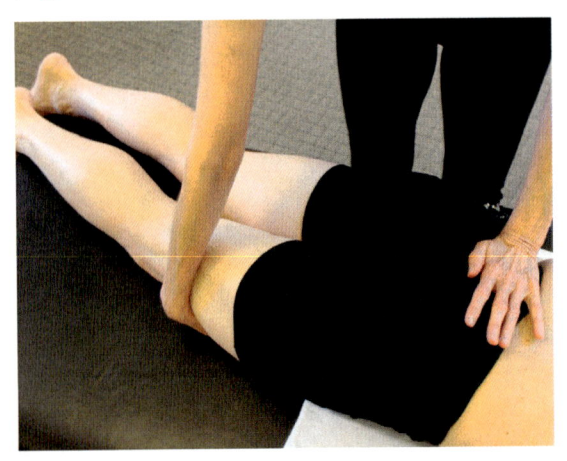

Figure 4.16
Slide the patient's legs toward you.

Step 4
Face your right palm up towards the ceiling and rotate your arm so that your fingers point towards you. Maintaining this hand position, slide your right hand around the outside of the patient's right thigh. Your hand should remain above the patient's right knee.

Step 5
Continue to slide your right hand medially and towards you. Stop when your hand is between the patient's thighs and your fingers are pointing up towards the ceiling.

Step 6
Firmly grasp the patient's lower right thigh above the knee joint. **[Fig. 4.3]**

Step 7
Continuing to firmly grasp the patient's thigh, unwind your right wrist so that the patient's right femur moves into external rotation.

Step 8
Slightly exaggerate the right thigh's rotation motion while you use the heel of your left hand to push the patient's left ileum downwards and medially. You should feel an immediate relaxation of the left side of the lower lumbar region, as well as a marked increase of motion.

Step 9
Move to the right side of table and reverse your hand positions. Repeat Steps 2-8.

Procedure 4

Increase posterior translatory slide of L5. Once you have created relaxation in the involved area, the next phase of treatment entails creating a dorsal (posterior) slide of L5 with the use of isometric muscle contractions.

Step 1

Sit, preferably on a rolling stool or chair, to the patient's left, facing his head. Make sure your legs are as close as possible to the edge of the table, and that your knees/legs are parallel to the table and are pointing towards the patient's head.

Step 2

Ask the patient to lower his left leg off the table and onto your lap.

Step 3

Flex the patient's left knee and grasp it firmly between your knees.

Step 4

Place your left hand under the patient's knee. Position your right (monitoring) finger at the spinous process of L5. [Fig. 4.5]

Step 5

Move your body (and the stool, if you are using one) towards the patient's head to create an increased flexion of the patient's left hip. Stop when you feel motion at your monitoring finger.

Step 6

Move your body (and the stool, if you are using one) in a semi-circle until the front of your body and both of your knees are facing the side of the table. Stop moving when you feel motion at your monitoring finger.

Note: This rotary motion will create lateral flexion of the involved vertebrae and a closed pack position of the right femoroacetabular articulation, sacrum, and lower lumbar vertebrae, right up to your monitoring finger. [Fig. 4.7]

Step 7

Use your left hand to lift the patient's flexed knee up a few inches towards the ceiling.

Step 8

Grasp the patient's raised knee tightly between your knees. Ask the patient to push his flexed left knee straight down towards the floor and against your left hand (isometric resistance). Resist any downwards motion of the patient's left leg with your knees and left hand. Your monitoring finger will feel a sliding of L5 in an upwards direction.

Step 9

Ask the patient to hold the contraction for a count of four and then to relax. The patient should repeat this process several times.

Step 10

Move to the right side of the table, reverse your hand positions and repeat Steps 2-9 on the patient's right leg. The patient should have immediate relief of symptoms.

Note: To maintain symptom relief, you will need to address any factors that may be contributing to this problem. Factors may include the patient being overweight, wearing high heels or worn-out shoes, and having calcaneal valgus and/or weak abdominal muscles.

An Exercise to Relieve Lordosis and Accompanying Pain in the Lumbar Region

Step 1

Ask the patient to stand with his feet six to ten inches apart.

Step 2

Instruct the patient to imagine squeezing a pencil between his buttocks.

Step 3

Next, ask the patient to contract his abdominal muscles.

Step 4

Ask the patient to maintain this position, and to rotate his upper thighs towards each other without moving his feet. Patients usually experience difficulty performing this motion. If the exercise is performed correctly, you will note that the lumbar lordosis is reduced along with the pain.

Step 5

Ask the patient to hold this position for ten to fifteen seconds, to relax, and then to repeat. Instruct the patient to repeat this exercise several times per day.

Sacroiliac and Iliosacral Dysfunctions

The sacroiliac articulation is located at the juncture of the lateral sides of the sacrum and the right and left ilium. Ligaments hold together the sacroiliac articulations. Each side of the articulation is thought to have three main sections: a flat superior segment, a middle convex-concave segment, and an inferior wedge-shaped section. Anatomists have found vast differences between the right and left sacroiliac articulations. One individual's sacrum may vary markedly from the next. Since there are so many sacroiliac variations, it is difficult to say whether a patient who has been diagnosed with a "low back syndrome" has a "typical" or "specific" type of sacroiliac articulation.

The descriptions of motion at the sacroiliac articulation further complicate matters. These motions are said to occur along several theoretical axes, including horizontal, sagittal, and frontal axes, as well as along a right and left torsional axis. Taking into account the shape of the sacroiliac articulation and the number of axes along which it can move, there are numerous possible combinations of motions along these axes. If you consider the many ways in which the ilium can move on the sacrum and that motion may be restricted in any of these movements, you can see how confusing diagnosis and treatment can be. In my opinion, this is all needlessly complicated.

My philosophy is very simple. There are only two diagnoses applicable to the sacroiliac articulation: dysfunction caused by trauma from above, and dysfunction caused by trauma from below. The former, a sacroiliac dysfunction, results from a force which has been transmitted through the fifth lumbar vertebra into the sacroiliac articulation. The latter, an iliosacral dysfunction, derives from a force which has been transmitted through the leg into the acetabular articulation and through the ilium into the sacrum.

Both etiologies will create motion disparities. However, in an iliosacral dysfunction, the restriction of motion will be accompanied by a rotation of the involved innominate bone and a functional shortening or lengthening of the leg on the involved side. In either case, the goal is the same: to normalize any limitation of motion that is present.

In many cases, the history of the patient will lead you to the correct differential diagnosis. Nonetheless, I would suggest not getting so caught up in a specific diagnosis, because moving the sacrum causes the ilium to move in the same direction. This principle also holds true when the primary source of dysfunction is the ilium; the sacrum will move in the same direction as the ilium, just a little less and a little more slowly.

Technique 8

Diagnosis of Restriction of Motion at the Sacroiliac Articulation

Patient position
Ask the patient to lie in the prone position on the table. Place as many pillows as necessary under the patient's abdomen to flatten his lumbar lordosis and to place his lumbar area in its neutral position. Maintain this position throughout the procedure.

Practitioner position
Stand to the patient's right, facing his head.

Procedure

Step 1
Place the heel of your right hand below the right inferior lateral angle ((ILA) of the patient's sacrum. Your fingers should be pointing up towards the patient's head, and should be parallel to his spine.

Step 2
With the heel of your right hand, push against the right ILA in a straight cephalic (up) and horizontal direction to feel for motion.

Note 1: When you push with the heel of your hand, make sure to keep directing the force in as close to a straight line, and as parallel to the table, as possible. There is a tendency to apply a downwards force or a medial force. This must be avoided.

Step 3
Move to the patient's left, and repeat Step 2 against the left inferior lateral angle. [Fig. 4.17]

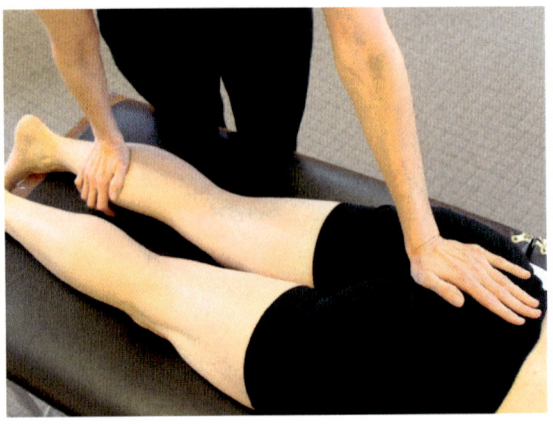

Figure 4.17
With the heel of your hand, push against the ILA in a straight cephalic direction.

Interpreting the results
If the motion of the sacrum feels equal on both sides, then there is no dysfunction. If one side's freedom of motion is less than the other side's, then that articulation is restricted.

Note 2: Once you have become more adept at this maneuver, you can stay on one side of the table to test for restriction of motion. Place both hands on the patient's ILAs and alternate creating an upward force. [Fig. 4.18]

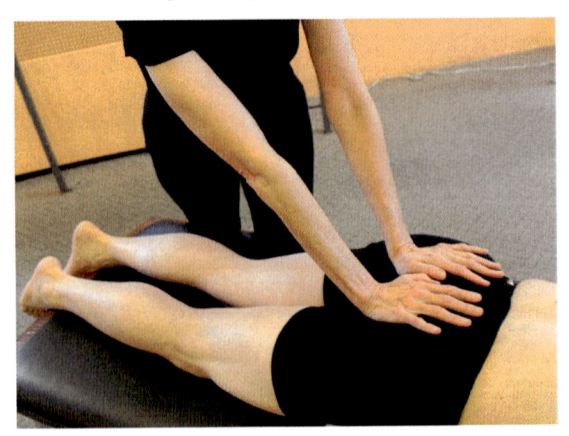

Figure 4.18
Alternate hands to create an upward force.

Technique 9
Treatment of Restriction of Motion at the Sacroiliac Articulation

A primary goal of FPR is to increase motion. Although no muscles directly attach the sacrum to the ilium at the sacroiliac articulation, "FPR and Beyond" treatments still apply. The techniques listed below use basic FPR philosophy, with the aim of increasing motion at these articulations.

Example
The patient is experiencing sacroiliac restriction on his right side.

Patient position
Ask the patient to lie in the prone position on the table. Place as many pillows as necessary under the patient's abdomen to flatten his lumbar lordosis and to place the area in its neutral position. Maintain this neutral position throughout the treatment.

Practitioner position
Stand to the patient's right, facing his head.

Procedure

Step 1
Place a small rolled-up towel, a firm pillow, or your hand under the patient's upper right thigh to create a fulcrum. Refer to *"Technique 3's "Alternative Ways to Create a First-Class Lever and Fulcrum."*

Step 2
Place the heel of your right hand below the right inferior lateral angle of the patient's sacrum, and your monitoring finger on his sacroiliac articulation.

Step 3
With your left hand, internally rotate the patient's right leg so that the patient's right toes are pointing towards his left foot. Stop when you feel that there is no slack left. This step will put the femoroacetabular articulation into a closed pack position.

Step 4
Push the patient's right leg straight up towards his head, so as to introduce compression and maximize the closed pack position.

Step 5
With your left hand, abduct the patient's right leg until you feel the motion at your monitoring finger. This step will open up the sacroiliac articulation.

Step 6
While maintaining the internal rotation, push the patient's leg straight down towards the floor. You will feel his sacrum rise in a dorsal direction, primarily at the lower end of the sacroiliac articulation (a first-class lever action). [Fig. 4.19]

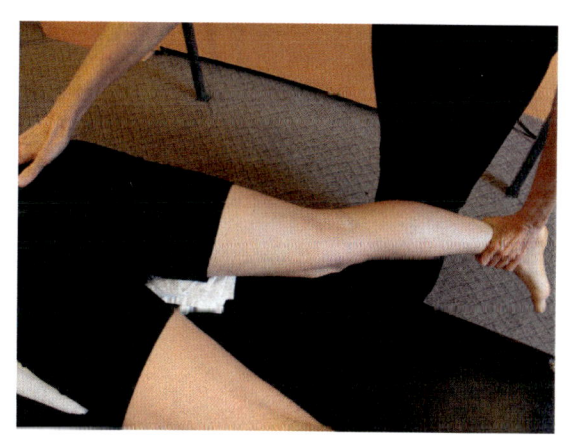

Figure 4.19
Maintain the internal rotation while you push the patient's leg straight down towards the floor.

Step 7

Reposition the heel of your right hand so that it sits lower on the inferior lateral angle of the patient's sacrum. Maintain firm contact at this new position.

Step 8

Ask the patient to take a deep breath in. As he exhales, push the heel of your right hand against the right inferior lateral angle in a cephalic, horizontal direction. This will create motion of the sacrum in the same direction.

Step 9

Release, and recheck the sacroiliac articulation's motion.

Note: *I recommend that, regardless of the diagnosis, you perform the same maneuver on the other side of the sacrum. This will equalize motion on both sides.*

Technique 10
Treatment to Increase Motion of a Severely Restricted Sacroiliac Articulation

Example
The patient is experiencing severe sacroiliac restriction on the left side.

Patient position
Ask the patient to lie in the prone position on the table. Place as many pillows as necessary under the patient's abdomen to flatten his lumbar lordosis. Maintain this neutral position throughout the treatment.

Practitioner position
Stand to the patient's left, facing his head.

Procedure
Step 1

Place the heel of your left hand below the left inferior lateral angle of the patient's sacrum. Place your left (monitoring) finger diagonally across the sacrum, at the upper-right sacroiliac articulation.

Step 2

Use your right hand to grasp the patient's right ankle, and pull his legs towards you until you feel motion at your monitoring finger. This move will create left sidebending of the hips and pelvis.

Step 3

Face your right palm up towards the ceiling and rotate your arm so that your fingers point towards you. Maintaining this hand position, slide your right hand around the outside of the patient's right thigh. Your hand should remain above the patient's right knee.

Step 4

Continue to slide your right hand medially and towards you. Stop when your hand is between the patient's thighs and your fingers are pointing up towards the ceiling.

Step 5

Firmly grasp the patient's lower right thigh above the knee joint. [Fig. 4.3]

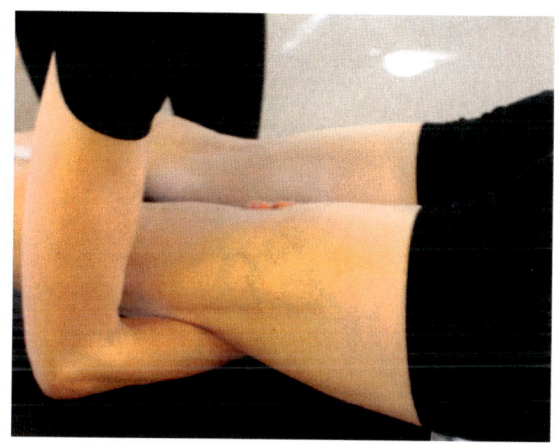

Figure 4.3
Grasp the patient's thigh above the knee joint.

Step 6

Continuing to firmly grasp the patient's thigh, unwind your right wrist so that the patient's right femur moves into external rotation.

Step 7

Exaggerate this external rotation. At the same time push, with the heel of your left hand, on the lateral edge of the sacrum's left inferior lateral angle towards the upper right sacroiliac articulation. The force of your left hand is directed up towards the patient's head, and is aimed diagonally towards the right sacroiliac articulation at which your monitoring finger is positioned. [Fig. 4.20]

Step 8

Repeat Step 7 several times. It should feel as if you are springing the articulation.

Step 9

These restrictions are usually bilateral, so I recommend treating both sides to increase motion. When you have treated both sides, release your hands and retest sacral motion.

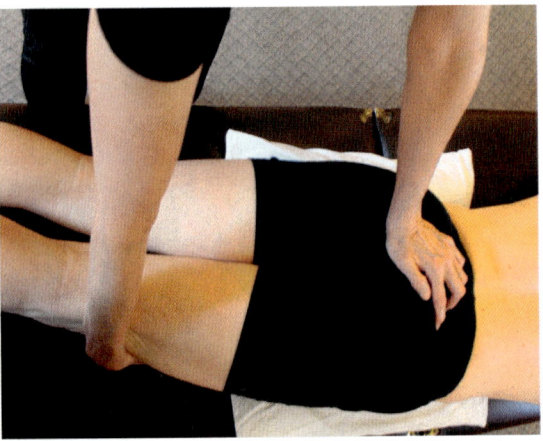

Figure 4.20
The force of your left hand is directed towards the patient's head, and aimed diagonally towards the right sacroiliac articulation.

*Note: Try to visualize your left hand creating a motion similar to the letter "J." The hand is pushing the articulation down slightly and then up towards the top of the right sacroiliac articulation.

Technique 11

Diagnosis and Treatment of a Severely Locked Sacrum Creating a Chronic "Low Back Syndrome"

Most patients with this syndrome will present with a history of chronic low back pain, which is concentrated on one side of the back. They may also experience pain radiating down the corresponding leg. The etiology is almost always from some form of trauma.

Procedure 1

Diagnosis of a Locked Sacrum.

Patient position

Ask the patient to lie in the prone position on the table. Place as many pillows as necessary under the patient's abdomen to flatten his lumbar lordosis and to place the area in its neutral position. Maintain this neutral position throughout the treatment.

Practitioner position

Stand next to the patient, on the symptomatic side of the sacrum.

Step 1

Place your hand on the patient's sacrum, with your fingers at its base. You will note that the base of the sacrum is rotated backwards and is posterior to the ilium.

Step 2

Move your fingers up until they are over the transverse process of the fifth lumbar vertebra. You will note that the transverse process is rotated to the same side as that of the locked sacrum.

Step 3

To confirm that the sacrum is locked, place the heel of your hand on the involved ilium and point your fingers medially towards the sacroiliac articulation. Press down on the ilium with the heel of your hand. If the sacrum is locked, then the entire area will move as one fused articulation.

Procedure 2

Unlock a restricted sacroiliac articulation.

First, you will need to normalize the muscles of the lumbar region and to restore motion to the fifth lumbar vertebra. To normalize the motions of the lower lumbar vertebra, use *Technique 7: Procedure 3 "Diagnosis and Treatment of an Increased Lumbosacral Angle."*

Step 1

Stand to the patient's left.

Step 2

Place your left (monitoring) fingers on the spinous processes of L4 and L5. Position the heel of your left hand on the posterior rim of the patient's left ileum.

Step 3

With your right hand, grasp the patient's right, outer ankle and slide both legs towards you. Stop when you feel motion at your monitoring fingers. This movement will create a left sidebending of the patient's trunk.

Step 4

Face your right palm up towards the ceiling and rotate your arm so that your fingers point towards you. Maintaining this hand position, slide your right hand around the outside of the patient's right thigh. Your hand should remain above the patient's right knee.

Step 5

Continue to slide your right hand medially and towards you. Stop when your hand is between the patient's thighs and your fingers are pointing up towards the ceiling.

Step 6

Firmly grasp the patient's lower right thigh above the knee joint. [Fig. 4.3]

Step 7

Continuing to firmly grasp the patient's thigh, unwind your right wrist so that the patient's right femur moves into external rotation.

Step 8

Slightly exaggerate the right thigh's rotation motion while you use the heel of your left hand to push the left ileum downwards and medially. You should feel an immediate relaxation of the left side of the lower lumbar region, with a marked increase of motion.

Step 9

Move to the right side of the table and reverse your hand positions. Repeat Steps 2-8.

Procedure 3

Treatment of a Locked Sacrum on the Right Side.

Step 1

Ask the patient to lie in the supine position on the table. Stand at his right side.

Step 2

Face your left palm up towards the ceiling. Maintaining this position, slide your hand under the patient's back. Place your fingers under the patient's sacrum, with the crease of your hand under the sacroiliac articulation and the heel of your hand under the ilium.

Step 3

With your right hand, flex the patient's right hip and knee and place his leg under your right axilla. Grasp the patient's anterior thigh with your right hand to control the movement of the patient's right hip and knee.

Step 4

Lean on the patient's flexed knee and add a slight compressive force of two to three pounds. Maintain this force throughout the remainder of this procedure. [Fig. 4.21]

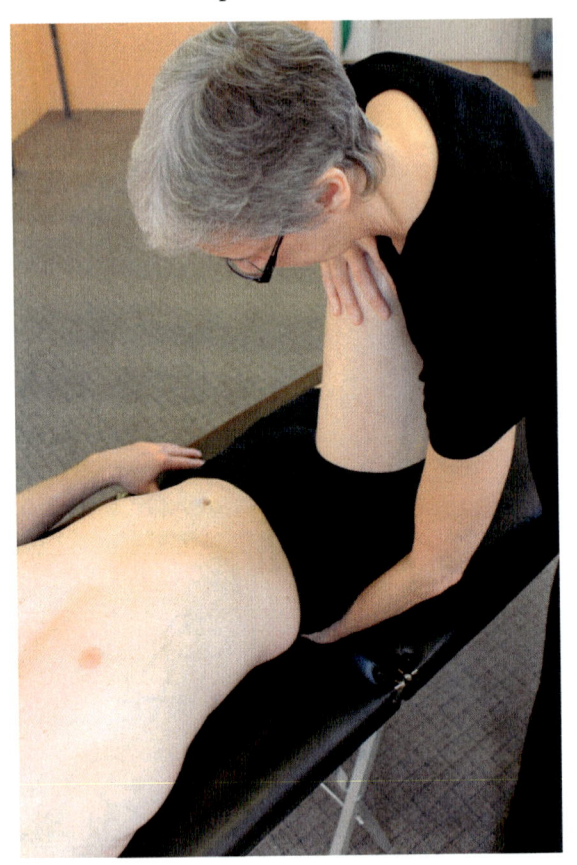

Figure 4.21
Lean on the patient's flexed knee to add a slight compressive force.

*Note: *If the patient has any knee dysfunctions or pain, add the compressive force by pushing your hand against the patient's thigh area.*

Step 5

Flex the patient's hip until you feel the maximum force directly in the crease of your left hand. If you do not feel the force, then adjust the patient's hip by moving it either medially or laterally, or by increasing its flexion or extension.

*Note: *The crease of your hand should be directly under the dysfunctional area of the sacroiliac articulation.*

Step 6

Turn the patient's hip into internal and external rotation and feel for freedom of motion. Maintain the hip in the position with the greater freedom of motion for the rest of this procedure.

Step 7

Push the heel of your left hand up against the patient's ilium. Hold for a count of four and then rest. Repeat this step four or five times. As you perform this maneuver, you should start to feel motion of the ilium on the sacrum.

Step 8

Once you have established iliac motion, use your left fingers, which are firmly in contact with the sacrum, to grasp the sacrum. Rotate the sacrum by moving your wrist from side to side. Then, move your wrist first in a clockwise, then in a counter-clockwise, direction. You will find that one direction has greater freedom of motion than the other. Exaggerate the motion on the side with the greater freedom of motion, and move the sacrum as far as it will go. Maintain this position for a count of four. Then, try to move the sacrum in the opposite direction. Keep repeating these clockwise and counter-clockwise rotations until you feel full motion at the articulation and you have restored the proper relationship of the sacrum to the ilium.

Step 9

Release the force and lower the patient's right leg to the table.

Step 10

Re-examine the sacroiliac articulation's motion.

Tests for Iliosacral Dysfunctions and Functional Leg Length Differences

Test 1
Standing Flexion Test

Patient position
Ask the patient to stand with his feet six to eight inches apart and his toes pointing forward.

Practitioner position
Stand behind the patient.

Procedure
Step 1
Place your right thumb on the inferior side of the right posterior superior iliac spine (PSIS) and position your left thumb under the left PSIS.

Step 2
Ask the patient to bend slowly forward, as far as he can comfortably flex.

Step 3
Ask the patient to straighten up about thirty degrees. Reset your thumbs directly under each PSIS so that the palmer surfaces of your thumbs are both under and in direct contact with the PSIS.

Step 4
Ask the patient to bend as far forward as possible. Monitor how far your thumbs roll forward during this movement.

Step 5
Measure the distance each thumb has moved.

Interpreting the results
If the motion of one side's PSIS to the other is greater than a half inch or more, then the test is positive. The PSIS with greater movement is the side which has the restricted iliosacral motion.

Test 2
Measuring Leg Length Differences

Step 1
Ask the patient to lie in the supine position on the table, with his hips and knees flexed and his feet resting flat on the table. Make sure his feet are aligned with each other.

Step 2
Place your thumbs on the inferior and medial end of each tibia and, with the rest of each hand, grasp each of the patient's ankles.

Step 3
Ask the patient to lift his buttocks completely off the table, and then to return his buttocks to the table.

Step 4
Keeping your thumbs on the inferior end of each tibia, straighten out the patient's legs.

Step 5
Lean your body over the patient's ankles so that your head is positioned directly over your thumbs. Measure any differences in the alignment of your thumbs. [Fig. 4.22]

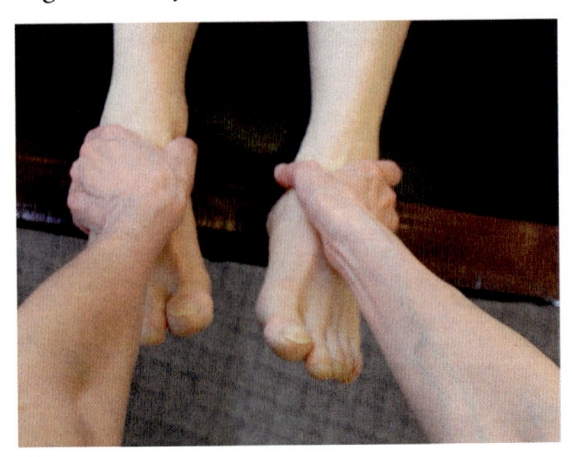

Figure 4.22
Measuring Leg Length Differences, Test 2.

Step 6

Repeat Steps 1-5 to confirm your findings.

Interpreting the results

If there appears to be half an inch or more between the position of your thumbs, then the patient may have a functional short or long leg.

*Note: Combining the results of the Standing Flexion test with the Leg Length Difference measurement will help you diagnose which side has the restricted articular motion and needs to be treated.

Test 3

A Scanning Technique to Determine Anatomical versus Functional Leg Length Differences

Step 1

Ask the patient to bend his knees and to place the soles of his feet flat on the table. Align the patient's feet with each other.

Step 2

Ask the patient to bring his knees together, so that they touch each other.

Step 3

Place a flat object, such as a straight-edged ruler, on top of one of the patient's knees. Rest the other end of the ruler on the patient's other knee. The ruler should be level. If there is a marked tilt of the ruler, it may signify that one tibia is longer than the other. [Fig. 4.23]

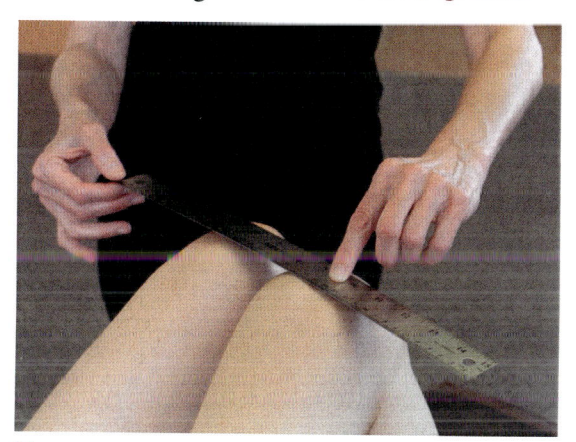

Figure 4.23
Measuring Leg Length Differences, Test 3.

Step 4

Next, place one end of the ruler in front of one of the patient's knees, directly below the patella. Place the other side of the ruler in front of the other knee, just below the patella. If there is a marked tilt of the ruler, it may signify that one femur is longer than the other. [Fig. 4.24]

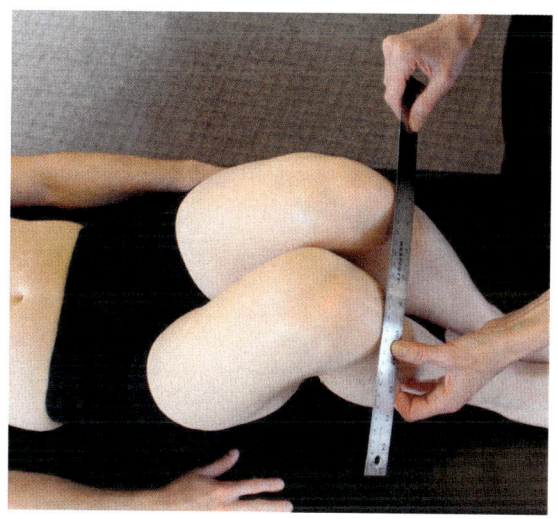

Figure 4.24
Measuring Leg Length Differences, Test 3.

*Note: This is only a scanning technique. If the clinical examination deems it necessary, the patient should be sent for a structural x-ray to obtain a definitive diagnosis.

Technique 12
Treatment of a Functional Short Leg due to an Iliosacral Dysfunction

Example
The patient has a posteriorly rotated ilium on the right side, causing his right leg to be shorter.

Patient position
Ask the patient to lie in the supine position, with both legs extended, on the table.

Practitioner position
Stand next to the patient, on the side of the functional short leg (in this case, the right side), and face his feet.

Procedure

Step 1
Ask the patient to flex his right hip and knee joints. Ask him to place the plantar surface of his right foot flat on the table, alongside and touching his left knee joint.

Step 2
Place your right hand on the patient's flexed knee, and adduct the knee over the midline, so that the patient's right buttock rises off the table.

Step 3
Turn your left palm up to face the ceiling. Point your fingers down towards the patient's feet. Keeping your hand in this position, place it under the patient's raised buttock.

Step 4
Bring the patient's right leg back into its resting position and alongside his left knee, so that his buttock is lying in your left palm.

Step 5
Flex your left fingers so that they are in firm contact with the inferior aspect of the patient's right ischial tuberosity.

Step 6
With your right hand, which is on the patient's flexed knee, pivot the knee laterally into abduction and down towards the table. Use the patient's planted right foot as a pivot point around which his right leg can rotate. Move the leg only as far as it can move comfortably. [Fig. 4.25]

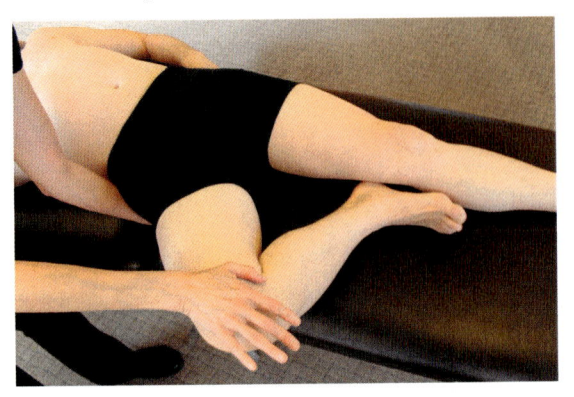

Figure 4.25
Pivot the knee laterally into abduction.

Step 7
Maintaining mild pressure on the patient's abducted right knee, ask the patient to slowly slide his right foot down the side of his left leg until his right leg is fully extended. Make sure you maintain sufficient pressure on the abducted knee so that your patient has to exert some force to move his leg.

Step 8
While the patient slides his right foot down, use your left hand to pull on his ischium in a cephalic (upwards) direction. This will cause the right ilium to rotate anteriorly. As the leg slides down, you will note that the right leg will suddenly internally rotate. The abduction motion of the right knee, accompanied by the resistant force, creates a gapping of the sacroiliac articulation, which allows your left hand to rotate the ilium anteriorly.

Step 9
Repeat the test for a leg length discrepancy. The short leg should now be close to or level with the other side.

Technique 13
Treatment of a Functional Long Leg due to an Iliosacral Dysfunction

Example
The patient has an anteriorly rotated ilium on the right side, which causes a longer leg on the right.

Patient position
Ask the patient to lie in the supine position on the table.

Practitioner position
Stand next to the patient, on the side with the functional long leg (in this case, the right side).

Procedure
Step 1
Ask the patient to flex his right hip and knee joint. Ask him to place the plantar surface of his right foot flat on the table alongside and touching his left knee joint.

Step 2
Place the palm of your right hand on the patient's right anterior superior iliac spine, and gently press down until you feel the bone. If the patient is very sensitive over his anterior iliac spine, place a small pillow or towel on this area.

Step 3
Place your left hand on the patient's flexed knee, and pivot the knee laterally into abduction and down towards the table. Use the patient's planted right foot as a pivot point around which his right leg can rotate. Move the leg only as far as it can move comfortably.

Step 4
Maintaining a mild pressure on the patient's abducted right knee, ask the patient to slowly slide his right foot down the side of his left leg until his right leg is fully extended. Make sure you maintain sufficient pressure on the abducted knee so that your patient has to exert some force to move his leg down.

Step 5
While the patient slides his right leg down, push your right hand in a cephalic (upwards) direction against the anterior superior iliac spine and create a posterior rotation of the ilium. As the leg slides down along the other leg, you will note that the right leg will suddenly internally rotate. [Fig. 4.26]

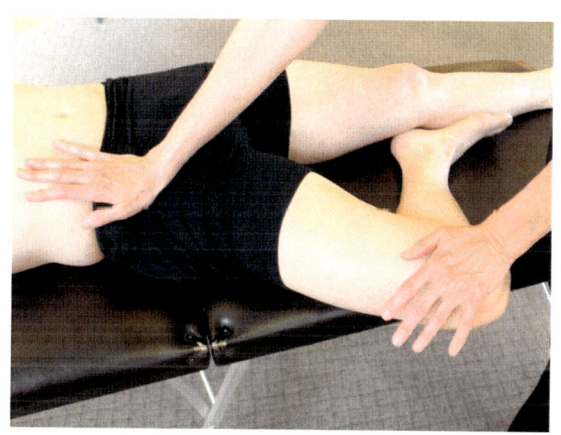

Figure 4.26
Push your right hand in a cephalic direction as the patient slides his right leg down.

Step 6
Repeat the test for a leg length discrepancy. If the leg lengths are equalized, then the patient had a functional leg length discrepancy caused by an iliosacral dysfunction.

Pelvic Tender Points

Technique 14
Diagnosis and Treatment of a Piriformis Hypertonic Muscle or Tender Point

The location of the piriformis muscle may be difficult to pinpoint at times. Here is an easy way to locate it. While the patient is in the prone position, visualize an imaginary line which starts at the superior tip of the greater trochanter and ends at the sacral sulcus. The piriformis muscle will lie along the distal third of the line, which begins at the greater trochanter. Feel for any hypertonic muscles or tender points.

Example
The patient has a piriformis muscle tender point on the right side.

Patient position
Ask the patient to lie in the prone position on the table, with a pillow under his lumbar spine.

Practitioner position
Sit, preferably on a rolling stool or chair, to the patient's right, and face his head.

Step 1
Place your left (monitoring) finger on the hypertonic or tender point of the patient's muscle.

Step 2
Ask the patient to lower his right leg off the table and onto your lap.

Step 3
Flex the patient's hip and knee. Grasp his knee firmly between your knees.

*Note: If you cannot hold on to the patient's knee comfortably, then place your right hand underneath the patient's right knee to help support it.

Step 4
Introduce flexion at the right hip and knee joint by moving the rolling stool forward. Stop when you feel motion at your monitoring finger. In most cases, you will need only a small amount of flexion.

Step 5
Move the patient's right knee into slight adduction (towards the table), then turn your body to face the table. Stop when you feel motion at your monitoring finger. This step will internally rotate the patient's hip. **[Fig. 4.7]**

Step 6
Direct a compressive force through the patient's knee, towards your monitoring finger. You will feel an immediate normalization of the muscle.

Technique 15
Diagnosis and Treatment of a Gluteus Maximus Hypertonic Muscle or Tender Point

Procedure 1

Diagnosis of a gluteus maximus tender point.

Patient position
Ask the patient to lie in the prone position on the table.

Practitioner position
Stand to the patient's right, facing his head.

Step 1
Place the tip of your fingers on top of both ilia. Slide your fingers down and palpate for any hypertonic or tender points along the patient's gluteus maximus muscle mass.

Procedure 2

Treatment of a gluteus maximus tender point on the right side.

Step 1
Sit, preferably on a rolling stool or chair, to the patient's right, and face the patient's head.

Step 2
Place your left (monitoring) finger on the hypertonic muscle or tender point.

Step 3
Ask the patient to lower his leg off the table and onto your lap.

Step 4
Move the patient's leg into full abduction, and place the front of his right knee on top of your right knee. At this point, the patient's lower leg should be bent at the knee, with the plantar aspect of his foot facing the ceiling.
[Fig. 4.27]

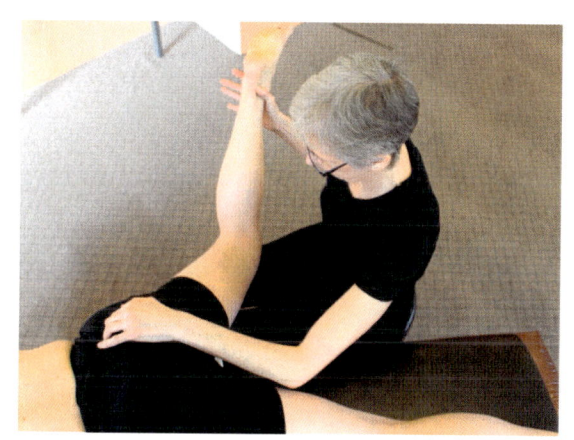

Figure 4.27
Place the patient's knee on top of your knee.

Step 5
Raise your right heel off the floor until you feel motion at your monitoring finger. This step will create extension of the patient's right hip.

Step 6
Next, introduce internal rotation of the hip by pivoting the patient's lower leg away from you, towards his head. As the rotation is completed, you will feel a normalization of the muscle.

Technique 16

Diagnosis and Treatment of a Tensor Fascia Lata Hypertonic Muscle or Tender Point

Procedure 1

Diagnosis of a tensor fascia lata tender point.

Begin by palpating from the patient's anterior superior iliac spine down along the lateral aspect of the leg, towards the patient's knee. The muscle will normally feel like thin bands of fibers, similar to a tendon, and will be non-tender. If there are any areas of hypertonicity or tender points, however, the area will feel thick and will be very tender to the touch.

Procedure 2

Treatment of a tensor fascia lata tender point on the right side.

Patient position

Ask the patient to lie in the prone position on the table, with a pillow under his lumbar spine.

Practitioner position

Sit, preferably on a rolling stool or chair, to the patient's right, and face his head.

Step 1

Ask the patient to lower his right leg off the table and onto your lap.

Step 2

Flex the patient's hip and knee. Grasp his knee firmly between your knees.

Step 3

Place your right (monitoring) finger on the tender area.

Step 4

Increase flexion of the patient's hip by moving your knees forward towards the head of the table. Stop when you feel motion at the monitoring finger.

Step 5

Push the patient's knee as far as possible under the table into adduction. [Fig. 4.6]

Step 6

Turn your entire body in a semi-circle towards the table. This will create internal rotation of the patient's hip. [Fig. 4.7]

Step 7

Use your legs to push the patient's knee up, towards your monitoring finger. The tenderness and the hypertonicity will normalize.

Why are these three tender points important?

There will be occasions upon which a patient will present with neurological complaints down one leg, which include pain, paresthesias, and changes in cutaneous sensation. Upon examining the patient, you will find no abnormal reflexes or any other positive findings that support the symptoms. If, after spending time treating the patient, the symptoms still persist, I recommend looking for and treating any tender points found in these three areas. You will often find that these treatments relieve the patient's symptoms.

Iliopsoas Muscle Dysfunction

Technique 17
Diagnosis of a Chronic Iliopsoas Hypertonicity

Patient position

Ask the patient to lie in the supine position on the table.

Practitioner position

Stand at the bottom edge of the table, facing the patient's feet.

Procedure

Step 1

Ask the patient to slide down towards the end of the table until his buttocks reach the edge. He should bend his hips and knees as he slides down the table. Ask him to hug his knees tightly against his chest wall. At this point, his lumbar spine should be flat against the table.

Step 2

Ask the patient to release one leg down towards the table. Stop him from extending his leg if he develops any lordosis of the lumbar spine. [Fig. 1.28]

Step 3

Note the distance of the extended leg's popliteal space from the table.

Step 4

Ask the patient to bring his leg back to its starting position against his chest wall, and to extend his other leg.

Step 5

Note the distance between this extended leg's popliteal space and the table.

Interpreting the results

If the extended leg is approximately two inches or further from the table, there is a corresponding shortening of the involved iliopsoas muscle, which should be treated.

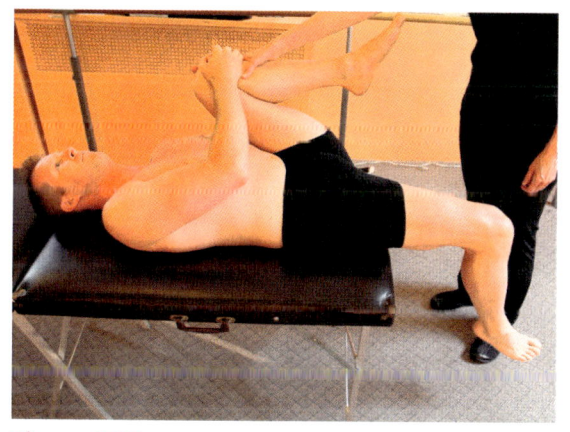

Figure 4.28
Ask the patient to release one leg towards the table.

Technique 18
Treatment of a Chronic Hypertonic Iliopsoas Muscle

To facilitate the treatment of a patient who has been diagnosed with a shortened iliopsoas muscle, you must determine the etiology of the shortening of the muscle.

1 Examine the lower thoracic and lumbar region for any chronic Somatic Dysfunctions.

2 Check for any anatomical short legs.

3 Take a complete history of the patient's work habits, sporting activities, and general posture. Make sure you pay particular attention to the ways in which the patient sits at home, at work, and in the car. It has been my experience that a patient's work habits and positions assumed while sitting are the usual causative factors.

Technique 19

A Stretching Exercise to Normalize Hypertonicity of the Iliopsoas Muscle

Step 1
Ask the patient to lie in the supine position on the table, with both legs extended.

Step 2
Stand next to the patient.

Step 3
Ask the patient to flex the involved hip and knee and to place the plantar surface of his foot flat on the table at the level of the other knee's patella.

Step 4
Place one hand on the patient's flexed knee and pivot his knee down towards the table, using his planted foot as the pivot point.

Step 5
Place your other hand on the patient's opposite anterior iliac crest. This hand will keep the patient's pelvis flat on the table throughout the treatment.

Step 6
Press the patient's knee down towards the table. Stop when you feel resistance. This is the point at which any more abduction would make the patient uncomfortable.
[Fig. 4.29]

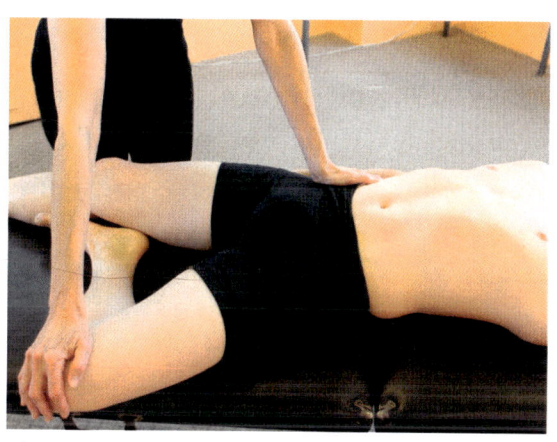

Figure 4.29
Press the patient's knee towards the table and stop when you feel any resistance.

Step 7
Maintaining this position, ask the patient to try to bring his knee back towards the midline while you resist this motion with your hand (isometric resistance). Hold this position for a slow count of four.

Step 8
Release the pressure, count to four, and then repeat Step 7. Abduction of the leg should increase with each contraction.

Step 9
Repeat Steps 7-8 four or five times. This will gradually create a stretching of the muscle involved and increase its function.

Diagnosis of the Acute Iliopsoas Dysfunction

Patients with acute iliopsoas dysfunction will exhibit some, or all, of the following signs and symptoms:

1 Pain, usually in the groin area, on the side of the dysfunction.

2 Inability to stand up straight.

3 While walking, the patient will be bent over and leaning towards the side of the dysfunction.

4 The foot on the affected side will be abducted.

5 Patients will usually have dysfunctions of the upper lumbar vertebrae. This might be difficult to diagnosis when the condition is very acute.

***Note:** It is important that a complete history and physical examination be performed to ensure that the etiology is localized to the lower thoracic and/or lumbar dysfunctions, and is not caused by pelvic disease, inflammation, hip disorders or a herniated disc.*

Technique 20
Treatment of an Acute Iliopsoas Dysfunction caused by Lumbar Dysfunction

Patients with this dysfunction are very uncomfortable, which may make it difficult for you to make a definitive diagnosis, or to treat any involved vertebra.

Example
The patient has acute Iliopsoas Dysfunction on the left side.

Patient position
Ask the patient to lie in the supine position on the table, with his left hip and knee flexed and slightly abducted. This position is usually relatively comfortable for the patient.

Practitioner position
Stand to the patient's left.

Procedure
Step 1
With your left hand, flex and adduct the patient's left hip and knee as far up towards the abdomen as possible. Make sure this maneuver does not cause any additional discomfort.

Step 2
Face your right palm up towards the ceiling and slide it under the patient's lower thoracic/upper lumbar spine. Stop when your fingers are under the right transverse processes, your thenar eminence is under the left transverse processes, and the spinous processes are lying in the middle of your hand. [Fig. 4.30]

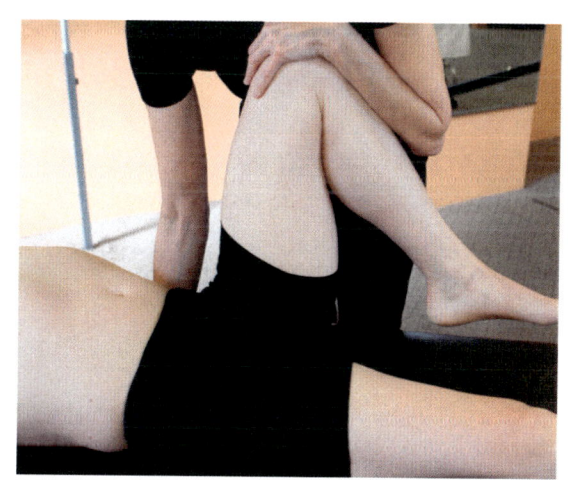

Figure 4.30
Place your hand under the patient's lower thoracic/upper lumbar region.

Step 3

Adjust the flexion and abduction of the patient's leg so that, when you lean on his left knee, you feel the compressive force at the crease of your right hand. You may need to adjust the flexion and/or abduction position of his hip to create a more direct vector force, without increasing the compressive force.

Step 4

While maintaining this compressive force, push your right thenar eminence up against the patient's left transverse processes. Hold for a slow count of four.

Step 5

Relax your hand, count to four, and then repeat this maneuver, maintaining compression on the patient's flexed knee.

Step 6

Repeat until you feel the patient's transverse processes rotating freely to the right.

Step 7

Move your right hand down the patient's lumbar spine and repeat the treatment.

Note: *Repeat Steps 1-7 until you feel free motion at the lower thoracic and lumbar vertebrae. The treatment should instantly relieve the patient's symptoms. To normalize the area, you may need to repeat these techniques over several sessions.*

A Quick Mobilization Technique for the Entire Thoracolumbar Area

This technique allows for normalization of the superficial muscles of the back, ribs, and shoulder girdle.

Procedure 1

Step 1

Ask the patient to lie on his left side on the table, with his knees bent.

Step 2

Stand facing the patient.

Step 3

Beginning at the patient's lower lumbar region, place both hands on the muscles on the patient's right side. Make sure that your fingers are pointing down towards the patient's spine, and that your hands are about two inches apart.

Step 4

Grasp the muscle, and move your hands towards each other. This will cause a shortening of the muscles. [Fig. 4.31]

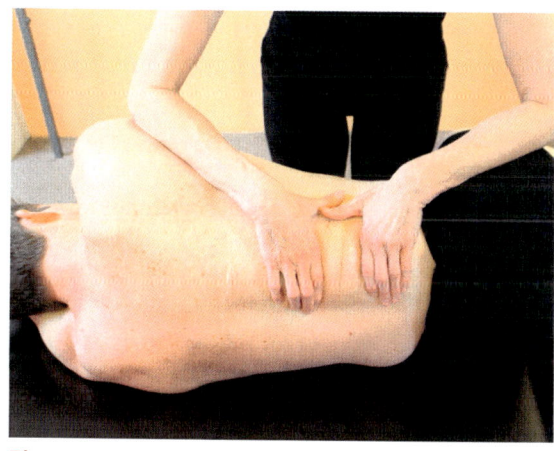

Figure 4.31
Move your hands towards each other.

Step 5

Move your hands in an upward direction, towards the ceiling. Next, move your hands away from each other and in a circular motion. Return your hands to their starting position.

Note: *All of these motions are done without releasing the muscles under your hands. You will feel the muscles soften and relax. You may also try placing your hands close together as you push your elbows down against the patient's hip and shoulder. While you are pushing down with your elbows lift the patient's thoracolumbar muscles up and then side to side.*
[Fig. 4.32]

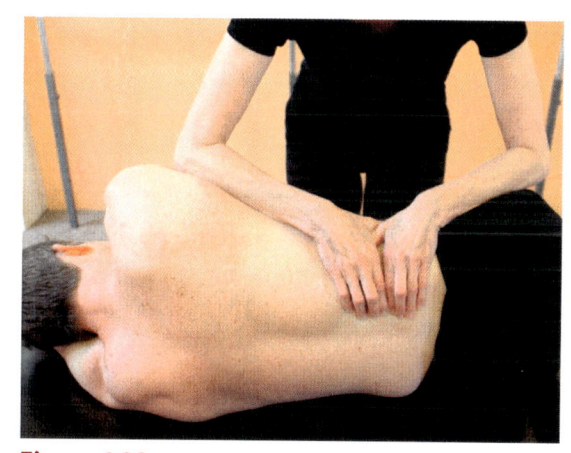

Figure 4.32
Use your elbows to push down against the patient's hip and shoulder.

Step 6

Move your hands two to three inches up the patient's back and repeat Steps 3-5.

Step 7

When you reach the patient's lower ribs, the procedure should be modified as follows: Place your hands close together, so that their lateral aspects are parallel. Lean down and put your weight on the patient's lateral chest wall. This mild compression will create a shortening and relaxation of the intercostal muscles.

Step 8

Move your hands, along with the patient's muscles, in a straight cephalic direction. Then, move them in the caudal direction. Repeat this step several times.

Step 9

Next, move your hands, with the patient's muscles still underneath them, up towards the patient's lateral rib cage, then medially towards his spine. Repeat several times. These maneuvers usually relax the superficial muscles of this section of the back.

Step 10

To move the patient's ribcage, push your hands gently against his ribs. Without moving your hands, rotate your body first in a clockwise, then a counter-clockwise, direction. Repeat this step several times. You will feel that the ribs are moving freely. Continue moving your hands up the back to engage the next group of ribs in the same manner.

*Note: *At this point, you may find a restriction of a rib due to a specific dysfunction. It is best to normalize the rib dysfunction at this time. Place one finger on the superior side of the involved rib, and a finger from your other hand on the inferior side of the rib. Maintaining pressure on the patient's chest wall, use your fingers to turn the rib in a clockwise and then a counter-clockwise direction. After one or two attempts, the rib will move and the motion will be normalized. Once motion is restored, continue to step 11.*

Step 11

When you reach the patient's scapula, lean down and compress it. This will push the patient's shoulder in a posterior direction, and will bring his scapula away from his back, allowing you to place your hands between the scapula and the posterior chest wall. [Fig. 4.33]

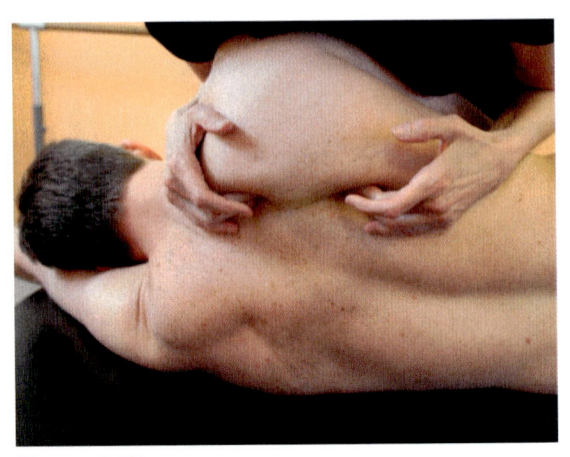

Figure 4.33
Lean down to bring the patient's scapula away from his back.

Step 12

Grasp the scapula and move it first in a cephalic, then in a caudal, direction, as well as in a lateral and medial direction. This will create freedom of motion of the scapula. Alternatively, you can place your right hand on his shoulder and push down while you use your left hand to move the scapula. [Fig. 4.34]

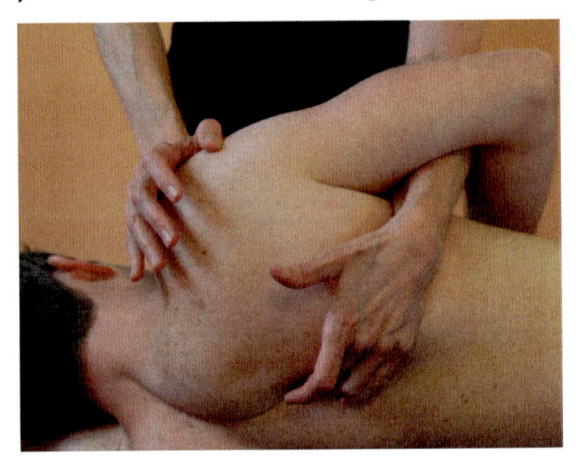

Figure 4.34
Grasp the scapula between your hands.

Step 13

If the patient is lying on his left side, place your right hand superior to his right shoulder. Place his right arm over your right arm. Place your left hand below the patient's right axilla, and push your right hand down and towards your left hand. This will add compression to the area. [Fig. 4.35]

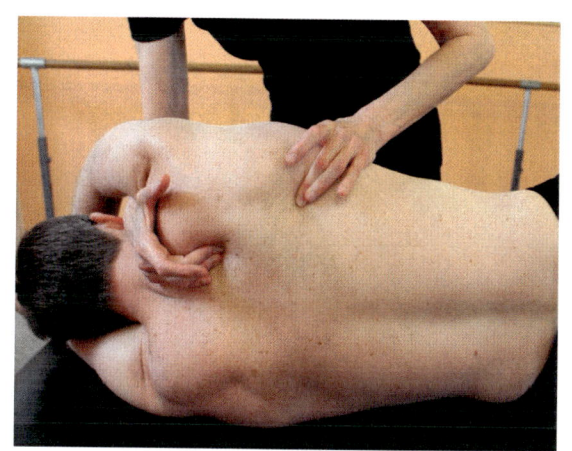

Figure 4.35
Hand position.

Step 14

Move the whole area in a cephalic and caudal direction, followed by a medial and lateral direction. This technique will add full motion to the patient's upper ribs, as well as relaxation of the shoulder girdle.

Step 15

To quickly relax the upper thoracic muscles, ask the patient to push his arm up against your hand, creating an isometric contraction, for a count of four and then relax. Reposition the patient's arm, to target different muscle groups, and have the patient repeat the isometric contraction against your hand. [Fig. 4.36]

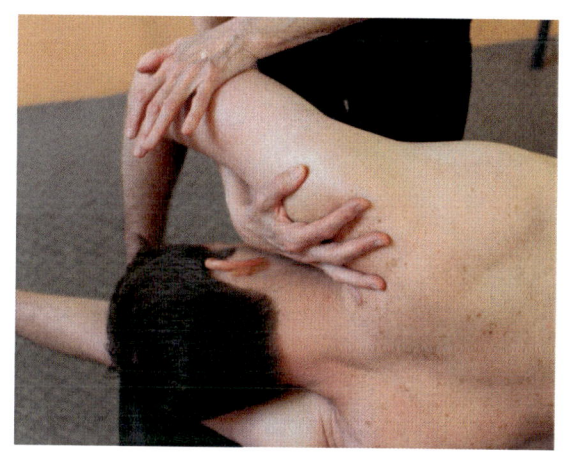

Figure 4.36
Have the patient push up against your left hand creating an isometric contraction.

Step 16

Turn the patient onto his other side and repeat Steps 1-15.

Procedure 2

After the superficial muscles have been normalized, you may want to add a quick method for diagnosing and treating Type II Somatic Dysfunctions of the lumbar region.

Step 1

Ask the patient to lie on his left side on the table, with his knees and hips bent to about ninety degrees. This should flatten his lordosis.

Step 2

Place a (monitoring) finger of your right hand on each of the transverse processes of L5, L4 and L3.

Step 3

With your left hand, grasp the patient's left ankle, and pivot his legs up to create a circular motion of his femurs and pelvis. Continue this motion until you feel movement at your monitoring fingers.

Step 4

If a Type II Somatic Dysfunction is present at any of these levels, you will feel the posterior transverse process increase its rotation (in this case, to the right side). It will press against your monitoring finger. Treat this dysfunction at this time.

Step 5

Maintain the patient in the position which created the rotation of the transverse process. Ask the patient to straighten out his left leg, but be sure that he does not straighten his leg into full extension. His right leg should be in its full circular position, so that his right foot is pointing upwards. [Fig. 4.37]

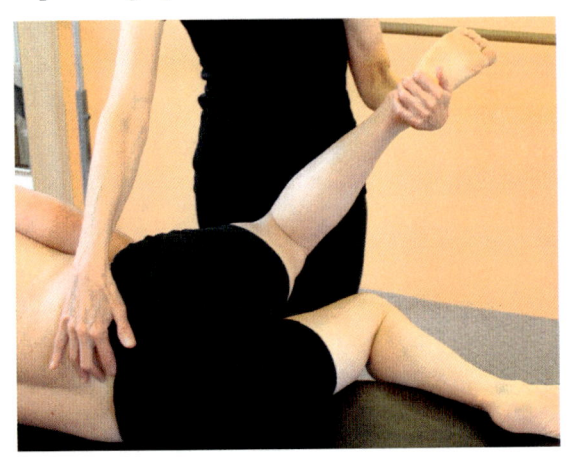

Figure 4.37
Position for treatment of a lumbar somatic dysfunction.

Step 6

Stabilize the patient's flexed right knee joint with your left thigh. Your thigh will also provide a resisting force.

Step 7

Ask the patient to press straight against your left thigh. This will create an isometric muscle contraction, which you should feel at your monitoring finger. If you do not feel the force at your finger, ask the patient to press slightly harder. If you still do not feel the force, then move the patient's right knee a few degrees downwards, towards the table. In this new position, ask the patient to press against your thigh again.

Step 8

Once you feel the force at your monitoring finger, increase the circular motion of the patient's right foot and hold it in its new position. Repeat Steps 7-8 several times.

Step 9

Recheck. The posterior rotation of the transverse process should be gone, and the Type II Somatic Dysfunction should be normalized.

Step 10

If, in Step 4, you do not feel any of the transverse processes rotated posteriorly, then move your fingers over the balance of the lumbar transverse processes and feel for any Somatic Dysfunctions at these levels.

Step 11

Repeat this entire procedure with the patient lying on his right side.

Chapter Five
APPROACH TO THE EXTREMITIES

APPROACH TO THE EXTREMITIES

Over my many years of practice, I found that the simplest and most efficient way of approaching extremity dysfunctions is to divide these dysfunctions into three categories:

Category 1 Hypertonic Muscles and/or Tender Points

Category 2 Motion Restrictions of the Large Joints

Category 3 Motion Restrictions of the Small Joints

Category 1
Hypertonic Muscles or Tender Points

Hypertonic muscles: Patients with hypertonic muscles will present with localized pain when trying to use or move an extremity. Palpation of the painful region will reveal an area of hypertonicity, either in the body of the muscle or at its tendon's attachment to the articulation.

Tender points: In this case, patients do not complain of pain while moving the extremity, but voice discomfort when a specific area in the body of the muscle is touched. I believe that these tender points are composed of very small groups of hypertonic muscles, and that, therefore, they can effectively be treated with FPR techniques.

An Overall Approach to Treatment of Hypertonic Muscle Dysfunctions in the Extremities

Treating hypertonic muscles of the extremities involves many of the general rules of FPR techniques. The muscle involved needs to be at rest and the articulation being treated must not be in a closed pack (locked) position. Compression should be introduced to the area before the muscle is put through its freedom of motion.

To determine the muscle's freedom of motion, imagine a line down the middle of the extremity. If the tender point or part of the muscle involved is lateral to the imaginary midline of the extremity, the ease of motion is abduction and external rotation. If the tender point or part of the muscle involved is medial to the imaginary midline, the ease of motion is adduction and internal rotation. This method is not foolproof, however; sometimes the muscle attachment or midline is not where you expect it to be. In such cases, you will need to adjust your treatment. It is important to remember to always obey and listen to your monitoring fingers - what I call thinking through your fingers. Once you start listening to your fingers, it will become easier to gauge the proper placement and direction of your treatments. [Fig. 5.1]

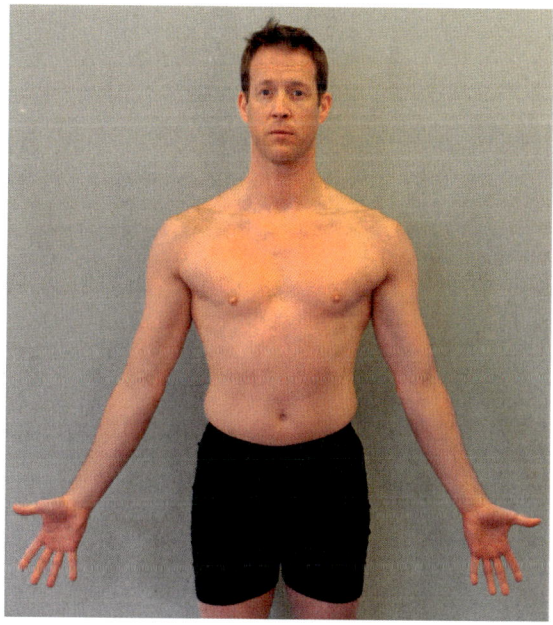

Figure 5.1
Determining the muscle's freedom of motion - Envision an imaginary line running down the midline of the extremity.

A Scanning Test for Upper Extremity Motion

Patient position
Ask the patient to stand with his back to you.

Practitioner position
Stand behind the patient at a distance that allows you to comfortably observe full arm motion.

Procedure

Step 1
Ask the patient to place his arms by his sides. Then, ask him to slowly abduct both arms, at the same time, up over his head until the dorsum (back part) of his hands meet.
[Fig. 5.2]

During this step, observe your patient's arm motion and try to answer these questions:

1 Do both the right and the left upper extremities move freely and equally?

2 Do the shoulders rise equally into abduction? If not, is there a shoulder joint dysfunction?

3 Are there changes in how smoothly the arms abduct? As the abduction motion occurs, does one arm move faster than the other? Does this indicate a shoulder dysfunction?

4 Do both scapulas rotate evenly? Does the reduction or failure of rotation of one scapula indicate dysfunction of the muscles which create rotation?

5 Are there any discrepancies in the angles of the shoulders, the elbows, or the hands?

6 If the angles created by the elbow joints are not equal, is this imbalance due to an elbow joint dysfunction?

7 Do the dorsal surfaces of the hands lie flat against each other? If not, is this a sign of wrist joint dysfunctions?

If there is any indication of a dysfunction, take a complete history and conduct a physical examination, with an emphasis on the regions involved.

Figure 5.2
Scanning test for upper extremity motion.

Technique 1
Treatment of Hypertonic Muscles or Tender Points at the Shoulder Joint and its Surrounding Region

Example
There is a tender point or hypertonic area near the insertion of the right biceps muscle.

Patient position
Ask the patient to lie in the supine position on the table.

Practitioner position
Stand by the right side of the patient.

Procedure

Step 1

Place your left (monitoring) finger on the hypertonic muscle or tender point.

Step 2

Use your right hand to grasp the patient's right arm right above the elbow joint. Tuck the patient's right hand under your right axilla. This will help keep the patient's hand out of the way.

Step 3

While using your monitoring finger to keep the patient's arm in a straight line, flex the patient's right upper arm to about ninety degrees.

Step 4

Compress the humerus towards your monitoring finger. To ensure proper placement of the force at your monitoring finger, you may need to move the patient's shoulder into more flexion or extension, or to move it more medially or laterally. Use no more than three to four ounces of force. [Fig. 5.3]

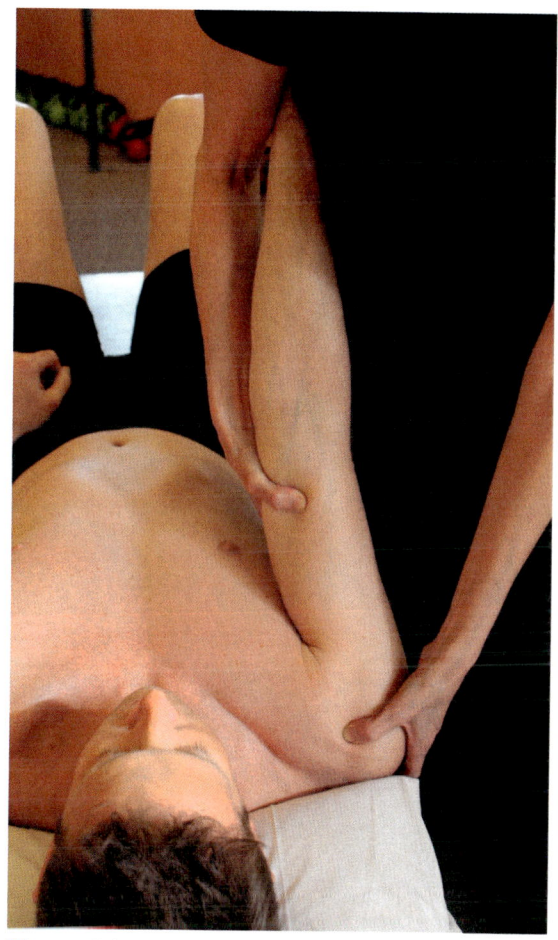

Figure 5.3
Treatment of hypertonic muscles by the shoulder region.

Step 5

If the monitoring finger is medial to the imaginary midline, move the humerus slightly into adduction and internal rotation. The monitoring finger will feel an instant release of the hypertonicity, and the patient will report that the point is no longer tender.

Note: When treating the patient's left side, switch hand positions.

Helpful Pointers

1 At times it may be difficult to find the location for the vector force which is needed for compression, because the shoulder joint has motion in three planes, as well as circumduction. To help localize the force at the articulation, try aiming the pressure from any direction: a posterior, superior, inferior, or anterior direction.

2 If you are having trouble localizing the hypertonic muscles involved, do not increase your compressive force. Instead, move the patient's shoulder up or down, medially or laterally, until you find the optimal position.

3 In some cases, the midline of an extremity may not be exactly where you think it is. If adduction and internal rotation fail, try abduction with external rotation.

4 Remember always to use SMALL movements. As soon as you feel normalization of the muscle hypertonicity, the treatment is completed.

Technique 2
Treatment of Hypertonic Muscles or Tender Points at the Elbow Joint and its Surrounding Region

Example
The patient requires treatment of a tender point or hypertonic area on the radial (outer) aspect of the right elbow.

Patient position
Ask the patient to lie supine, with his affected arm resting on the table.

Practitioner position
Stand by the patient's right side.

Procedure
Step 1
Place your left index (monitoring) finger on the hypertonic muscle or tender point.

Step 2
Flex the patient's elbow joint to ninety degrees.

Step 3
Use your right hand to grasp the patient's right forearm between the wrist and the elbow joint. Gently compress the forearm down towards the table until you feel the compressive force at the monitoring finger. To localize the force at your monitoring finger, you may need to adjust placement of the patient's elbow by introducing more flexion or extension.
[Fig. 5.4]

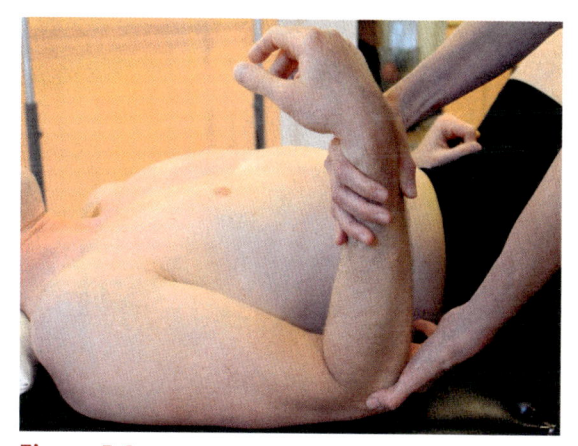

Figure 5.4
Treatment of hypertonic muscles at the elbow region.

Step 4
The area to be treated is lateral to the midline, so you will need to add small amounts of abduction and external rotation to the elbow joint. There will be an immediate resolution to the muscle hypertonicity or tender point, and the patient will report that the area is no longer tender to the touch.

Technique 3

Treatment of Hypertonic Muscles or Tender Points at the Wrist Joint and its Surrounding Region

Example

The patient requires treatment of a tender point or hypertonic area on the dorsal, mid-carpal region of the wrist.

Patient position

Ask the patient to sit facing you.

Practitioner position

Stand or sit by the patient's affected side.

Procedure

Step 1

Grasp the patient's forearm by the distal radius and ulna bones.

Step 2

With your free hand, hold the patient's hand, below the wrist and across the metacarpal region. One way of doing this is to grip the patient's hand as if you were about to shake his hand. [Fig. 5.5]

Step 3

Place one finger (monitoring finger) on the tender point or hypertonic area.

Step 4

Using your distal hand, compress the patient's hand towards his carpal bones until you feel the force at your monitoring finger.

Step 5

Maintain the compression and passively dorsiflex the wrist up to your monitoring finger.

Step 6

If the point to be treated is medial to the midline of the wrist, add a slight adduction and internal rotation motion. If the point is lateral to the midline, add abduction and external rotation to the patient's wrist. You should feel the hypertonicity normalize, and the tender point resolve.

***Note:** To achieve accurate positioning and results, remember to "think through your fingers." Your fingers will let you know in which direction to move your patient's hand.*

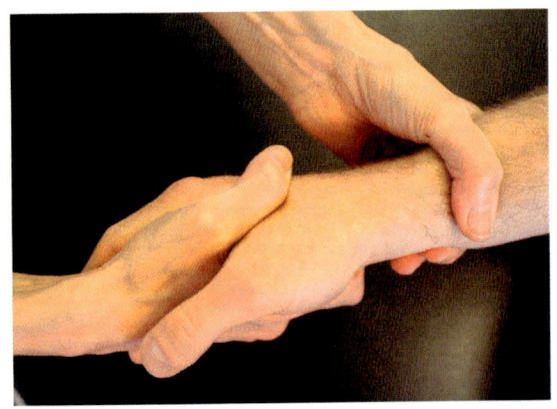

Figure 5.5
Treatment of hypertonic muscles by the wrist region.

Technique 4
Treatment of Hypertonic Muscles or Tender Points at the Hip Joint and its Surrounding Region

Example
The patient requires treatment of a tender point or hypertonic area on the lateral aspect of the right hip joint, by the greater trochanter.

Patient position
Ask the patient to lie in the supine position on the table.

Practitioner position
Stand by the right side of the patient.

Procedure
Step 1
Place your left (monitoring) finger on the tender point.

Step 2
Use your right hand to passively flex your patient's right hip and knee joint to ninety degrees.

Step 3
If the patient has no history of knee problems, lean on top of the patient's knee and direct a compressive force towards his hip joint and your monitoring finger. Do not use more than one pound of force.

*Note 1: *If the patient's knee is painful, bypass it. Instead, use your right hand to grasp his lower thigh. From this position, push the femur down towards the hip joint.*

*Note 2: *If the patient's thigh is too heavy or wide to grasp, place the leg over your shoulder and compress it downwards, towards the patient's hip joint.*
[Fig. 5.6]

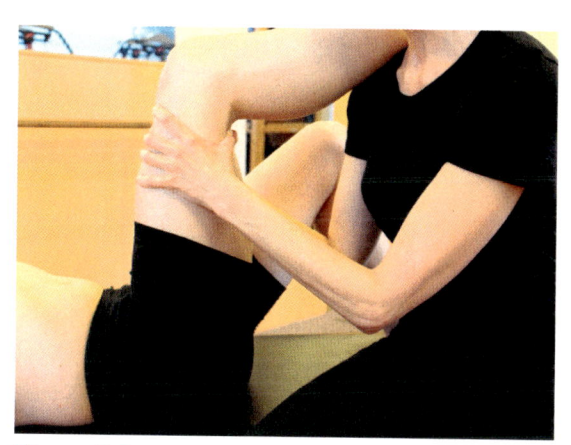

Figure 5.6
Alternative hand position.

Step 4
To obtain the most effective force at your monitoring finger, you may need to adjust the position of the thigh by adding either a little flexion or extension to the hip joint.

Step 5
In this example, the tender point is on the lateral aspect of the hip, so you will need to add slight abduction and external rotation to the hip. You should feel the hypertonicity normalize, and the patient should no longer be in pain.

*Note: *If the area to be treated is on the medial aspect of the hip joint or groin region, reverse the positioning of your hands and add adduction along with internal rotation.*

Technique 5

Treatment of Hypertonic Muscles or Tender Points at the Knee Joint and its Surrounding Region

Example
The patient requires treatment of a tender point or hypertonic area at the lateral aspect of his left knee.

Patient position
Ask the patient to lie in the prone position on the table

Practitioner position
Stand by the left side of the patient and face his head.

Procedure

Step 1
Place your left (monitoring) finger on the hypertonic muscle or tender point.

Step 2
Ask the patient to flex his knee to ninety degrees. Use your right hand to grasp the patient's left leg, between the ankle and the knee joint. [Fig. 5.7]

Step 3
Direct a compressive force down the patient's left leg, towards the table. Stop when you feel the mild compressive force at your monitoring finger. If needed, add a little flexion or extension to the knee joint to obtain the most effective compressive force at your monitoring finger.

Step 4
Move the leg into slight abduction and external rotation, until either the hypertonic muscle has normalized or the patient says that the point is no longer tender.

Note: *If the area to be treated is on the medial aspect of the knee joint, reverse the positioning of your hands and add adduction along with internal rotation.*

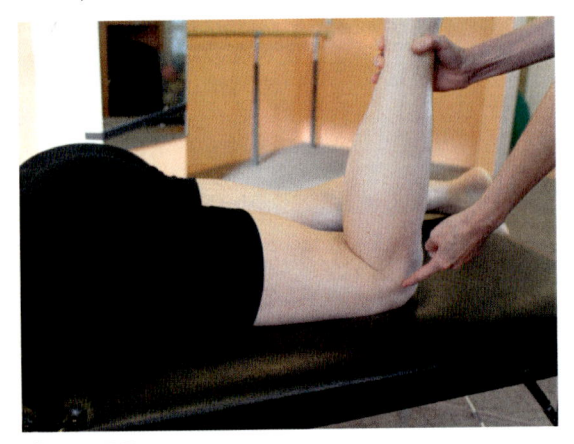

Figure 5.7
Treatment of a hypertonic muscle at the knee joint.

Technique 6
Treatment of Hypertonic Muscles or Tender Points at the Ankle Joint and its Surrounding Region

Example
The patient requires treatment of a tender point or hypertonic area at the lateral aspect of the left ankle joint.

Patient position
Ask the patient to lie prone with his left knee flexed to ninety degrees.

Practitioner position
Stand by the patient's left side and face his feet.

Procedure

Step 1
Grab the distal end of the tibia and fibula with your left hand.

Step 2
Cup your right hand over the plantar surface of the patient's heel and point your fingers down the lateral side of the ankle. Place one finger (monitoring finger) on the tender point.

Note: Make sure to maintain the patient's foot parallel to the table. Try placing your forearm over the patient's foot to maintain this position. [Fig. 5.8]

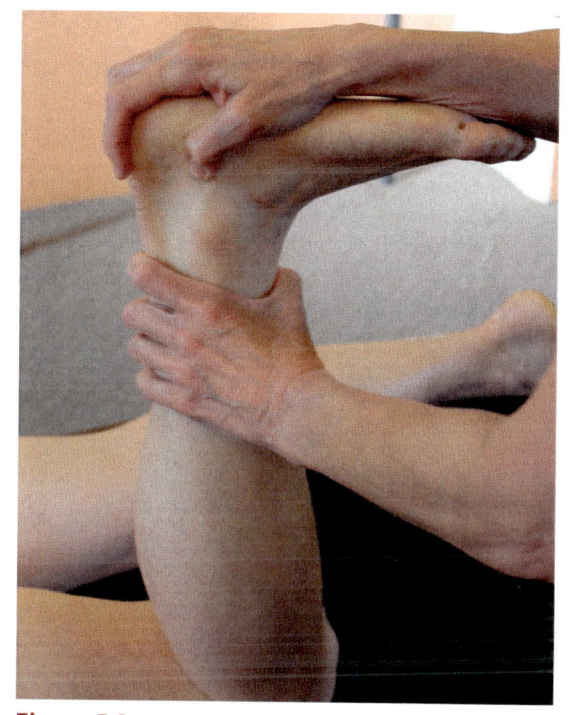

Figure 5.8
Treatment of hypertonic muscles at the ankle joint.

Step 3
Direct a compressive force straight down towards the table until you feel that force at your monitoring finger. You may need to lean your body weight over the leg.

Step 4
Sidebend the patient's foot and ankle laterally (eversion) until you feel motion at your monitoring finger.

Step 5
Depending on which motion produces normalization of the muscle and relief of the tender point, introduce either external or internal rotation of the ankle.

Note: If the hypertonic muscle or tender point is at the medial aspect of the ankle joint, reverse the positioning of your hands and treat as described above.

Technique 7
Treatment of Hypertonic Muscles or Tender Points at the Plantar Region of the Foot

Example
The patient requires treatment of a tender point or hypertonic area of the left foot, at the shaft of the fourth metatarsal.

Patient position
Ask the patient to lie prone, with his left knee flexed to ninety degrees.

Practitioner position
Stand by the patient's left side, facing his head.

Procedure
Step 1
Place your left hand posterior to the patient's left heel and grasp the heel.

Step 2
Put your right hand on the plantar aspect of the foot and grasp the metatarsal bones.

Step 3
Flex the ankle joint to ninety degrees, keeping the foot parallel to the table throughout.

Step 4
Extend your right (monitoring) finger onto the tender point. [Fig. 5.9]

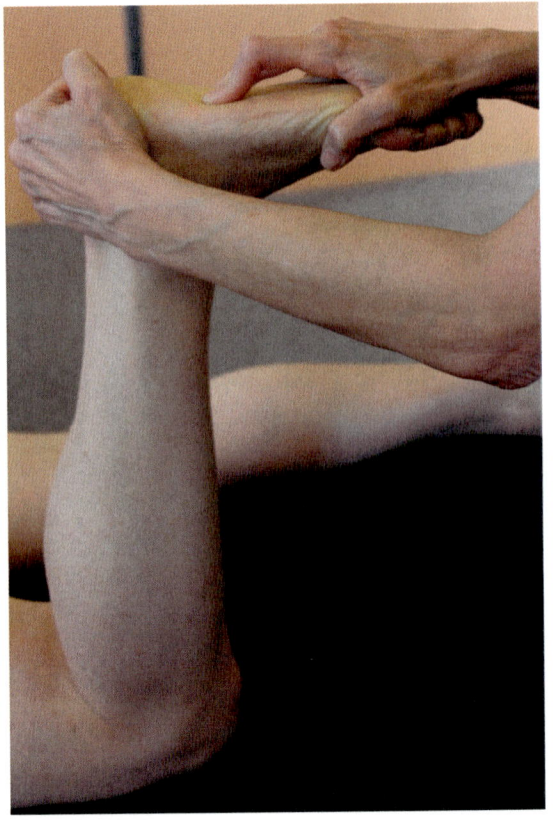

Figure 5.9
Treatment of hypertonic muscles at the foot.

Step 5
Bring both of your hands towards each other until you feel a compressive force at your monitoring finger.

Step 6
Keeping your left hand steady, use your right hand to dorsiflex the patient's metatarsals until you feel motion at your monitoring finger.

Step 7
Add adduction and rotation towards the midline of the foot until you feel motion at your monitoring finger.

*Note: If the tender point is located at the midline of the foot, then you may only need to add dorsiflexion to the foot.

Technique 8
Treatment of Hypertonic Muscles or Tender Points in the Middle of a Muscle

This technique can also be used to treat muscle hypertonicity at an articulation when the standard techniques do not work effectively.

Procedure

Step 1
Make sure the muscle involved is at rest and completely relaxed. With one hand, grasp the muscle fibers approximately one inch above the point of hypertonicity. With your other hand, grasp the muscle fibers one inch below the point of hypertonicity. [Fig. 5.10]

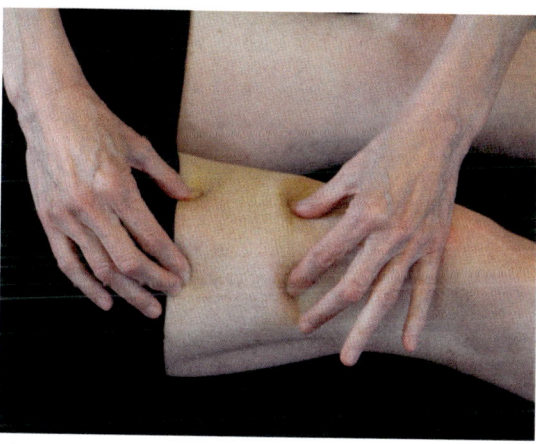

Figure 5.10
Treatment for hypertonic areas in the middle of a muscle.

Step 2
Extend a monitoring finger to the hypertonic muscle or tender point.

Step 3
Direct a compressive force by pushing your hands towards each other, until you feel a softening of the muscle fibers at the monitoring finger.

Step 4
Turn one hand into internal rotation, stopping when you feel motion at the monitoring finger. If normalization does not occur, turn the hand into external rotation until you feel motion at the monitoring finger. If the muscle fibers involved are directly at the midline of the muscle, rotation will not be necessary.

***Note:** With experience, it becomes easier to determine the direction in which your hands need to rotate to eliminate the tender point or hypertonicity. Remember always to "listen through your monitoring fingers."*

Category 2
Motion Restrictions of the Large Joint Articulations

Biomechanical Rules of Motion in the Extremities

Extremity articulations are either a "Convex-Concave" or "Sellar" (saddle) shape. They obey the following rules of motion:

1 When a convex articulatory surface rolls against a fixed concave surface of another bony articulation, it has a coupled sliding motion in the opposite direction of its rolling motion.

2 When a concave articulatory surface rolls against a fixed convex surface of another bony articulation, it has a coupled sliding motion in the same direction as its rolling motion.

In my experience, as a result of this biomechanical relationship, you should focus on increasing the coupled slide motion along with the rolling motion as you treat a restricted extremity articulation.

For example: If you find that the extension motion of the femur on the tibia is decreased, your treatment must include the restoration of normal anterior-posterior and medial-lateral sliding motions of the tibia on the femur.

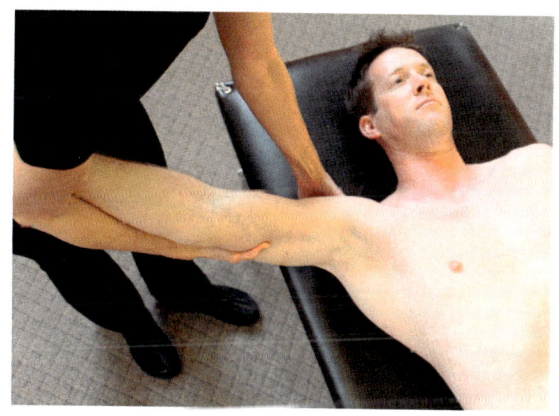

Technique 9
Treatment to Increase Motion at the Glenohumeral Articulation

Example
The patient is experiencing glenohumeral articulation motion restrictions of the right arm.

Patient position
Ask the patient to lie in the supine position.

Practitioner position
Stand by the patient's right side.

Procedure
Step 1
Place your left hand on top of the patient's right shoulder and firmly grasp the acromial process between your fingers.

Step 2
Use your right hand to grasp the patient's arm above the elbow joint. Place the patient's right hand under your right axilla. This position will keep the patient's hand out of the way throughout the procedure.

Step 3
Create a minimal compressive force of no more than two to three ounces by pushing the humerus towards the glenohumeral joint.

Step 4
Rotate the humerus into its full range of motion of internal, and then external, rotation. Repeat this step several times. This motion will help normalize the muscles attached to the articulation.

Step 5
Next, stabilize the scapula so that all movements introduced will be isolated to the humerus. Keeping your left thumb on top of the acromion process and your left index finger underneath it, continue to firmly grasp the acromion process.

Step 6
With your right hand, gently pull the patient's right humerus away from the glenohumeral articulation. This will create traction at the glenohumeral joint. Maintain this traction throughout the rest of the procedure.

Step 7
Move the right shoulder into a flexed position. Introduce a dorsal slide motion followed by a ventral slide motion of the humerus on the glenohumeral articulation.

Step 8
Next, move the patient's shoulder into abduction. Slide the humerus in a superior and then in an inferior direction. [Fig. 5.11]

*Note: Increasing these coupled slide motions will improve overall motion of the glenohumeral articulation.

Figure 5.11
Treatment to increase motion at the glenohumeral articulation.

Technique 10
Treatment to Increase Motion at the Elbow Articulation

Example

The patient is experiencing elbow articulation motion restriction of the right arm.

Patient position

Ask the patient to lie in the supine position.

Practitioner position

Stand by the patient's right side.

Procedure

Step 1

With your left hand, grasp the patient's humerus above the elbow joint. With your right hand, grasp the patient's forearm.
[Fig. 5.12]

Step 2

Push your hands together to create a minimal compressive force of two to three ounces at the elbow joint.

Step 3

Rotate the patient's forearm into full internal and external rotation.

Step 4

Next, use your right hand to pull the patient's forearm away from the elbow joint to create a traction force at the elbow articulation.

Step 5

Maintaining this traction, slide the forearm in a medial, then in a lateral, direction.

Note: Due to restriction of the bones involved, there is no ventral/dorsal slide at the elbow joint.

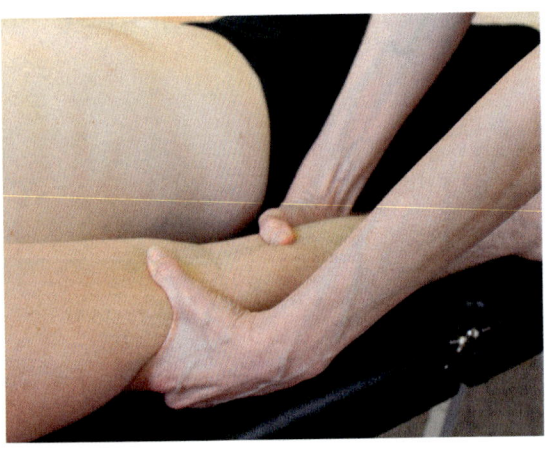

Figure 5.12
Treatment to increase motion at the elbow articulation.

Technique 11
Treatment to Increase Motion at the Femoroacetabular Articulation

Example
The patient is experiencing femoroacetabular articulation restriction of the right leg.

Patient position
Ask the patient to lie in the supine position.

Practitioner position
Stand by the patient's right side.

Procedure
Step 1
Flex the patient's knee and hip joint to ninety degrees.

Step 2
Grab the patient's upper thigh and compress it down towards the femoroacetabular articulation.

Step 3
Rotate the femur into internal, then external, rotation.

Step 4
Next, sit by the patient's right side and place his right knee over your right shoulder.

Step 5
Place your left hand on the lateral aspect of the patient's thigh, and your right hand, slightly lower than your left hand, on the medial side of the thigh.

Step 6
Maintaining your hand position, slowly stand up. This will create traction and separation of the patient's right hip joint.

Step 7
Move your hands towards each other. This will create a sliding motion of the femur on its joint.

Alternative Positioning for Technique 11:
To treat large patients, or patients who weigh more than you do, ask the patient to lie prone. Sit on a stool by the side that you are treating, and face the patient's head.

Step 1
Remove the patient's leg from the table, and flex the patient's hip and knee joint.

Step 2
Place the patient's leg between your legs and hold it tightly between your knees.

Step 3
Place one hand in the popliteal space of the knee and push down to create a traction force. [Fig. 5.13]

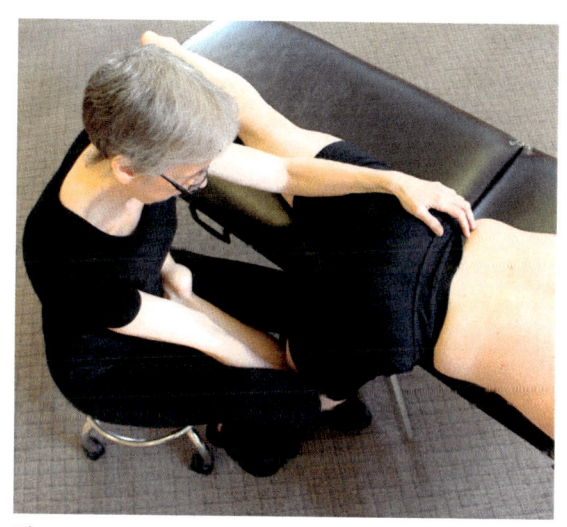

Figure 5.13
Treatment to increase motion at the femoroacetabular articulation.

Step 4
Position one knee slightly higher than the other and push your knees together. This will create a sliding motion of the femoroacetabular joint.

Technique 12
Treatment to Increase Motion at the Tibiofemoral Articulation

Example

The patient is experiencing tibiofemoral articulation restriction of the right leg.

Patient position

Ask the patient to lie in the supine position.

Practitioner position

Stand by the patient's right side and face his head.

Procedure

Step 1

Flex the patient's right hip and knee. Tuck his ankle joint under your axilla.

Step 2

Plant your feet on the ground, with one foot about two to three feet in front of the other.

Step 3

Place your thumbs on each side of the anterior aspect of the patient's tibia. Place your pinky and ring fingers behind the tibia. Position your middle and index fingers on each side of the patient's knee joint.
[Fig. 5.14]

Step 4

Firmly grasp the patient's tibia and slowly rock back and forth in a smooth rhythm. This movement will create a flexion motion, and then an extension motion of the patient's knee.

Step 5

With your pinky and ring fingers, pull the patient's tibia anteriorly as you flex his knee. Push the tibia backwards with your thumbs as you extend the knee. This motion will create an anterior-posterior slide of the tibia on the femur.

Step 6

Once you are comfortable with this technique, add a sliding motion from side to side by gently pushing your middle and index fingers against the medial and lateral sides of the tibia.

Step 7

Finally, combine all of these maneuvers to create a figure-eight motion of the knee joint. All of these motions will increase movement in the tibiofemoral articulation.

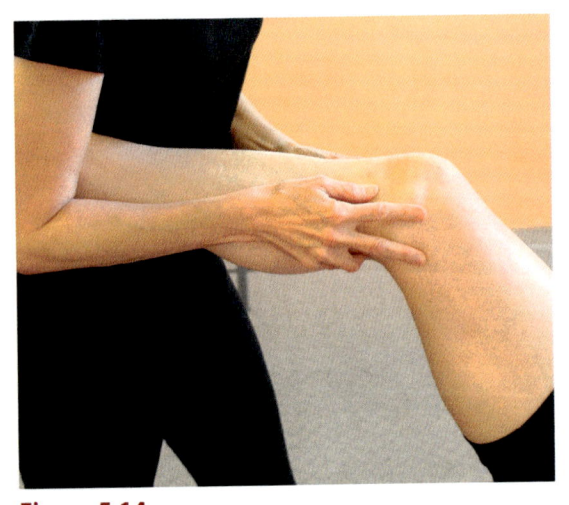

Figure 5.14
Treatment to increase motion at the tibiofemoral articulation.

Technique 13
Treatment to Increase Motion of the Ankle and Foot

Example
The patient is experiencing restriction of the right ankle and foot.

Patient position
Ask the patient to lie in the supine position.

Practitioner position
Stand by the patient's right side and face his feet.

Procedure

Step 1

Flex the patient's right hip and knee joints.

Step 2

Place your left elbow in the popliteal space of the patient's flexed right knee. Place your left arm against the medial (inside) surface of the patient's tibia. Grasp the patient's right foot, immediately below the distal end of the tibia.

Step 3

Grasp under and around the patient's right foot with your right hand. [Fig. 5.15]

Step 4

Lean back towards the patient's head. This motion will create traction and a separation of both the knee and the ankle joints.

Step 5

With your right hand, slide the talus up and down, then from side to side.

Step 6

To treat the rest of the foot, grasp the fifth metatarsal bone with your right hand. Introduce a traction force. Slide the fifth metatarsal in a dorsal and then in a plantar direction. Finally, slide it from side to side. Repeat these motions at each of the remaining metatarsal and phalangeal articulations.

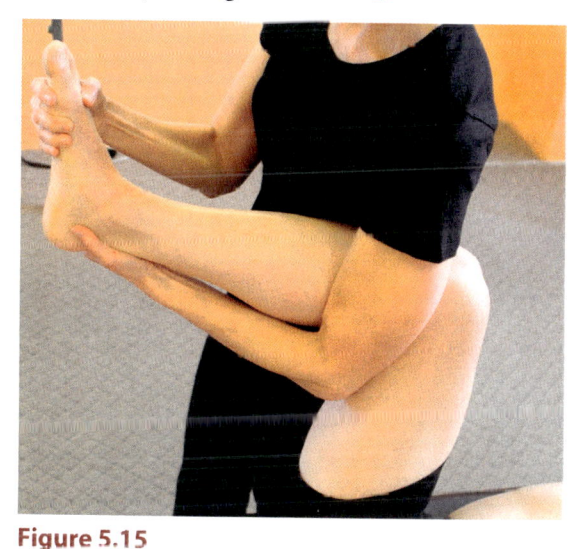

Figure 5.15
Treatment to increase motion at the ankle and foot.

Category 3
Motion Restrictions of the Small Joint Articulations

The prime objective when treating dysfunctions of the small joint articulations is to restore full motion to that articulation. I do not use designations such as an "anterior" or "posterior" restriction when labeling a dysfunction. Rather, I classify the dysfunction as a general restriction of that articulation. Treatment, therefore, will involve normalizing the articulation's motion.

Technique 14

Diagnosis and Treatment to Relieve Restrictions at the Humeral-Olecranon Articulation

The elbow articulation consists of the distal end of the humerus, the ulna, and the radial bone. Practitioners often treat only the humeral-radial articulation and overlook the humeral-ulna relationship. In my experience, restrictions of the ulna on the humerus cause many dysfunctions, and should not be ignored.

Example
The patient is experiencing restriction of the right arm's olecranon-humeral articulation.

Patient position
Ask the patient to sit and bend his right elbow into ninety degrees of flexion.

Practitioner position
Stand and face the patient.

Procedure

Step 1
Place your left hand under the patient's right elbow, so that your left thumb is on the radial side of the right olecranon and your left bent index finger is on the ulna side of the olecranon. Grasp the patient's olecranon process between your two fingers.

Step 2
With your right hand, fully pronate the patient's right forearm. Feel whether the tip of the olecranon process rolls and slides away from the pronated wrist and into abduction.
[Fig. 5.16]

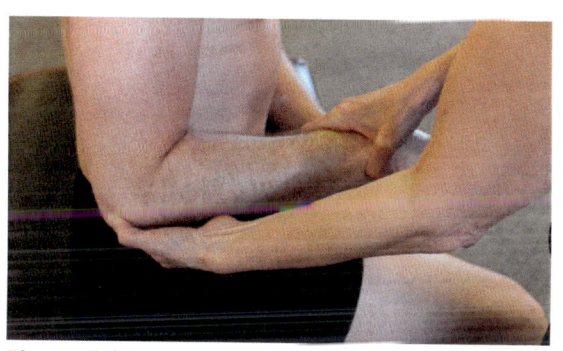

Step 3
Turn your patient's forearm into full supination. Note whether the tip of the olecranon process rolls and slides away from the supinated wrist and into adduction.

Step 4
If you detect any restriction of movement of the olecranon process, then fully supinate the patient's right forearm. Ask the patient to rotate his forearm into pronation while you resist any motion of the patient's forearm (isometric contraction). At the same time, push your thumb against the patient's olecranon process. You will feel his olecranon process trying to move against your left thumb.

Step 5
Hold for a count of four, then release for a count of four. Repeat several times.

Step 6
Next, have the patient try to supinate against your resistance as you push the olecranon process with your index finger. Repeat several times.

Figure 5.16
Treatment to relieve restrictions at the humeral-olecranon articulation.

Technique 15
Treatment to Relieve Restrictions of the Radial Head

Example
The patient is experiencing restriction of the right arm's radial head.

Patient position
Ask the patient to sit and bend his right elbow into ninety degrees of flexion.

Practitioner position
Sit by the patient's right side, facing him.

Procedure

Step 1
Use your left thumb and index finger to grasp the distal end of the humerus by the lateral epicondyle. Grasp the radial head with your right hand.

Step 2
Create a slight compressive force by pushing the radial head into the distal end of the humerus.

Step 3
Maintaining the compression, rotate the radial head on the humerus internally and externally. Repeat several times.

Step 4
Create traction and separation of the articulation by pulling the radial head away from the humerus.

Step 5
Slide the radial head in a ventral, then a dorsal direction. Repeat several times, until complete motion of the articulation is restored.

Technique 16
Treatment of Restriction of Motion at a Metacarpal Bone

Example
The patient is experiencing restriction of the right index finger at the metacarpal bone.

Patient position
Ask the patient to sit.

Practitioner position
Stand or sit by the patient.

Procedure

Step 1
With one hand, grab distal to the patient's right index finger metacarpal articulation. With your other hand, grasp the proximal end of the patient's right index finger's metacarpal bone. [Fig. 5.17]

Step 2
Push your hands together to create a compressive force. Rotate the patient's metacarpal internally and externally.

Step 3
Next, pull your hands apart to create a traction force.

Step 4
Maintaining the traction, move the metacarpal in every direction (dorsal, ventral, medial, and lateral).

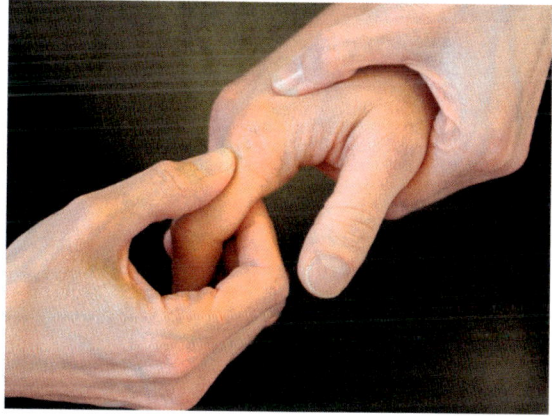

Figure 5.17
Treatment of restriction of motion at the metacarpals.

Technique 17
Treatment to Relieve Restrictions at the Fibula Head

Example
The patient is experiencing restriction at the left leg's fibula head.

Patient position
Ask the patient to lie supine. Place a small pillow under his left knee.

Practitioner position
Stand by the patient's left side, facing him.

Procedure

Step 1

Use your left hand to cup the plantar (bottom) aspect of the patient's left foot.

Step 2

Grasp the head of the patient's left fibula between your right thumb and index finger.

Step 3

Hyperdorsiflex the patient's left foot and ankle joints as far as they can comfortably go. You will feel the fibular head immediately disengage from its superior articulation with the femur. [Fig. 5.18]

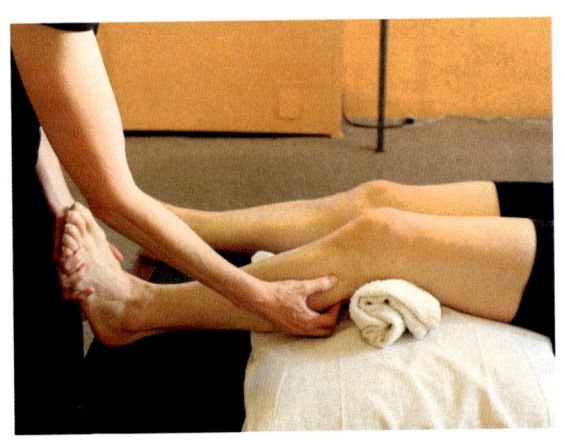

Figure 5.18
Treatment to relieve restrictions at the fibula head.

Step 4

With your right thumb and index finger, move the fibula head forwards and backwards until you have restored its normal motions.

Technique 18
Treatment to Relieve Restrictions of the Cuboid Bone

Example
The patient is experiencing restriction of the left foot's cuboid bone.

Patient position
Ask the patient to lie in the supine position.

Practitioner position
Sit at the end of the table.

Procedure

Step 1
Place the patient's left foot on your lap.

Step 2
Grasp the cuboid bone between the thumb and index fingers of your left hand.

Step 3
Grasp the fifth metatarsal bone with the thumb and index fingers of your right hand.
[Fig. 5.19]

Step 4
Bring your hands together to create a compressive force at the articulation. Rotate the bones internally and externally. Repeat several times.

Step 5
Pull the bones away from each other to create traction and separation of the articulation. Slide the cuboid bone in a plantar, then a dorsal, direction. Repeat several times, until complete motion of the articulation is restored.

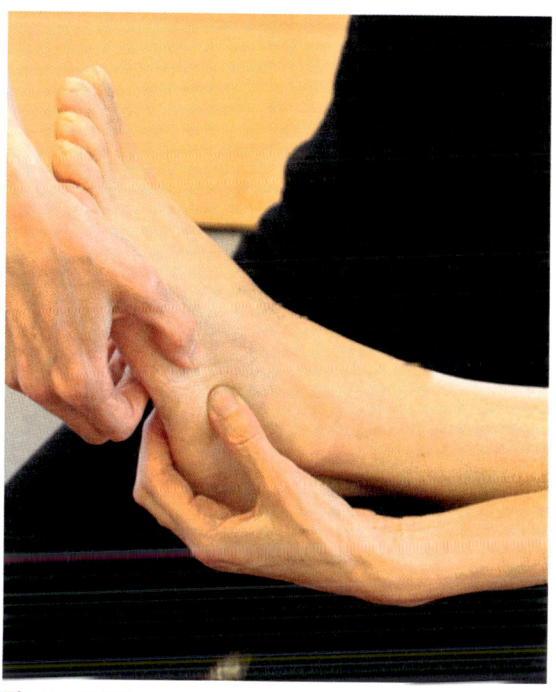

Figure 5.19
Treatment to relieve restrictions of the cuboid bone.

Technique 19

Outline for the General Treatment of an Extremity Articulation Somatic Dysfunction

The following technique is aimed at restoring normal physiological motions of any articulation.

Procedure

Step 1

With one hand, grasp the upper bone of the articulation. With the other hand, grasp the lower bone. Grasp as near to the articulation as you can. [Fig. 5.20]

Step 2

Push your hands together to create a compressive force at the articulation.

Step 3

Maintaining the compression, rotate the lower bone, internally and externally, on the upper bone. Repeat several times.

Step 4

Without changing your hand positions, pull the bones away from each other to create traction at the articulation.

Step 5

Add an anterior and posterior slide, followed by a side-to-side slide of one bone on the other.

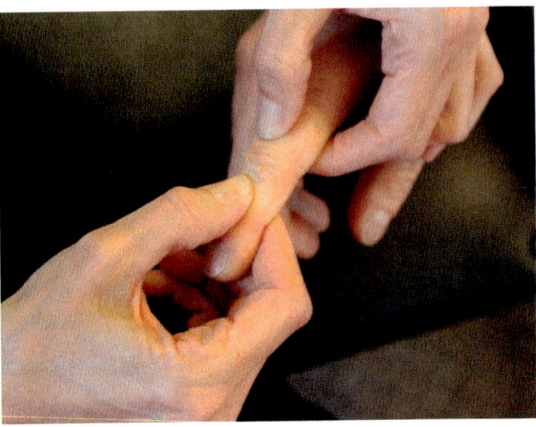

Figure 5.20
Treatment for a dysfunction at the phalanges articulation.

Commonly Found Syndromes and their Treatment

Syndrome 1
Carpal Tunnel Syndrome

Treatment for this condition requires normalizing several different areas and their articulations.

Part 1

First, loosen the interosseous membrane between the distal ends of the radius and ulna.

Step 1

Use your thumb and index finger to grasp the distal end of the patient's radius. Hold the distal end of the ulna with the thumb and index finger of the other hand. [Fig. 5.21]

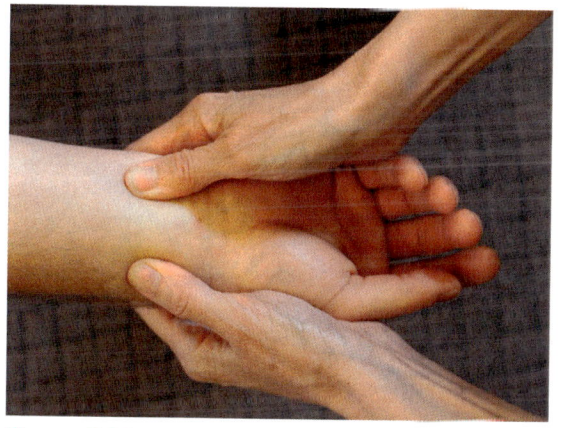

Figure 5.21
Carpal Tunnel Syndrome Step 1.

Step 2

Push the radius in a dorsal direction, while pushing the ulna in a ventral direction. Reverse directions. Repeat this step several times.

Step 3

Move your fingers up, one inch at a time, and repeat Step 2 at each spot.

Part 2

Use "Technique 19: Outline for the General Treatment of an Extremity Articulation Somatic Dysfunction" on the articulations of the radius, ulna, carpal, and metacarpal bones.

The numerous articulations involved are the distal end of the radius with the scaphoid and lunate bone, the distal end of the ulna and the triquetral bone, the scaphoid and the lunate, the lunate and the triquetral, the scaphoid and the trapezium, the scaphoid and the trapezoid, the lunate and the capitate, the triquetral and the hamate, the trapezium and the trapezoid, the trapezoid and the capitate, the capitate and the hamate, the trapezium and the proximal 1st metacarpal, the trapezoid and the 2nd metacarpal, the capitate and the 3rd and 4th metacarpals, the hamate and the proximal 5th metacarpal.

Repeat this treatment weekly, for at least three weeks.

Syndrome 2
Treatment for Restriction of Shoulder Motion

This condition is often caused by some form of inflammation to the shoulder joint, which leaves the patient with a Frozen Shoulder. Treatment objectives include lengthening/stretching the involved muscle fibers.

Example
The patient requires treatment for restricted abduction motion of the right shoulder.

Patient position
Ask the patient to lie in the supine position.

Practitioner position
Stand by the patient's right side.

Procedure

Step 1
Use your left hand to hold the patient's right acromion process throughout this procedure.

Step 2
Place your right hand above the patient's right elbow joint. Abduct the patient's arm. Stop when the arm can go no further, or if the patient has any pain.

Step 3
While the patient's arm is in abduction, compress the head of the humerus into the glenoid fossa.

Step 4
Turn the humerus into internal, then external, rotation. Repeat this step several times. The objective is to obtain as much motion as possible in both directions.
[Fig. 5.22]

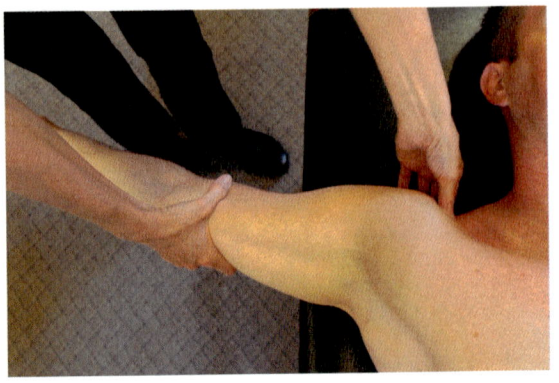

Figure 5.22
Treatment for restriction of shoulder motion.

Step 5
Next, create a traction force by pulling the humerus away from the glenoid fossa. To maximize efficiency, lean away from the patient, rather than relying on your arm, to create this force.

Step 6
Slide the humerus anteriorly and then posteriorly. Repeat this step several times.

Step 7
Ask the patient to adduct his arm while you resist the motion (isometric contraction). Hold the resistance for a slow count of four, then release. Repeat several times.

Step 8
Repeat Steps 3 through 7 several times. Stop earlier if the patient becomes fatigued. The patient should notice an increase in abduction.

> ***Note:*** *Repeat this treatment weekly, until you can no longer obtain further improvement of motion. Additionally, prescribe daily exercises that will increase motion at the shoulder joint.*

An Exercise to Increase Shoulder Joint Motion

Have the patient purchase an elastic band that can be anchored safely to a door.

Step 1

Instruct the patient to attach an elastic band firmly to a door, and then to sit facing the elastic band.

Step 2

Instruct the patient to grab one end of the band with the hand of the restricted shoulder, and to grasp the other end with the hand of the non-restricted shoulder.

Step 3

Instruct the patient to pull the band down towards the floor with the hand of his non-restricted shoulder. This will create abduction of the restricted arm. The patient should stop when he has reached his maximum pain-free point.

Step 4

Instruct the patient to increase the tension on the elastic band as his arm relaxes and stretches. This will increase abduction to the restricted arm.

Note: *For maximum efficacy, it is important to maintain pressure on the restricted arm. To ensure this, I instruct the patient to place the free end of the band under his foot.*

Syndrome 3
Thoracic Outlet Syndrome

The thoracic outlet is a space bordered by the clavicle, the first rib, the superior border of the scapula, and the manubrium. Within this space, the scalene muscles form a cone. The apex of the cone is formed by the attachment of the scalene muscles to the cervical area. The anterior section of the cone is formed by the anterior scalene muscle, the posterior section of the cone is formed by the middle scalene muscle, and the inferior section of the cone is formed by the first rib. The neurovascular bundle consisting of the brachial plexus and the subclavian artery descends through this cone. The bundle then passes behind the clavicle, and in front of the first rib.

As the bundle passes several points, disturbances to it may occur. These points include the muscular shaped cone, the bony space between the clavicle and the first rib, the coracoid process, the pectoralis minor, and the clavicopectoral fascia.

Symptoms, and their intensity, will vary. They may include pain, and/or paresthesias or anesthesia at the head, neck, chest, shoulder, or upper extremity. Some patients will complain of weakness, swelling, discoloration, or a Raynaud's-type reaction at the involved extremity.

If these symptoms derive from a congenital malformation, e.g., of the cervical rib or the scalene muscles, then surgery may be necessary.

Diagnosing Thoracic Outlet Syndrome

1 Without the patient realizing that you are studying him, note the position of his hands as he stands with them relaxed by his side. If one hand is internally rotated as compared to the other one, this may indicate changes in the postural relationship of the shoulder girdle.

2 While the patient is sitting, place a straight-edge ruler on the midpoint of the posterior aspect of his trapezius muscle between the spine and the shoulder. Drop the straight edge forward so that it rests anteriorly on the clavicle, and is directly aligned with its place on the posterior muscle. The ruler will have a downward slope between its posterior and its anterior positions. Repeat this procedure on the other side. There may be a problem if the angle of the downward slope is greater on the side of the internally rotated hand.

3 Stand behind the patient while he is sitting, and place your middle or index finger on the anterior aspect of his clavicle at its articulation with the sternum. Move your finger along the medial concave portion of the clavicle until you encounter the larger, lateral, convex portion of the clavicle. Slide your finger down and gently palpate the soft tissue at the inferior surface of the bone at the place right before the anterior concave region meets the convex portion. Normally, you will feel a hollow or depressed space at that site. If not, this may indicate a change in the normal relationship of the first rib and the clavicle. Compare your findings from both clavicles.

If these three signs are present, mechanical-postural dysfunctions are probably present, causing the thoracic outlet syndrome. Follow up by performing a thorough musculoskeletal examination. In many cases, you will find severe hypertonicity of the superficial muscles which radiate from C7 and T1 towards the acromion process, and restriction of motion of C7 on T1 and T1 on T2. In addition, you may find restriction of motion of the clavicle as it articulates with the sternum, and restriction of motion of the first rib at both its posterior and anterior articulations. Look for a flattening of the thoracic spine from T1 through T3, and note if the region moves as one fused unit. Raising the arm on the affected side into abduction may aggravate the symptoms.

Treatment for Thoracic Outlet Syndrome

Example

The patient is experiencing a dysfunction on the right side.

Patient position

Ask the patient to sit with his back to you.

Practitioner position

Ask the patient to lean against you as you stand behind him.

Part 1

Step 1

Place your left forearm under the patient's left axilla.

Step 2

Place your right thumb on the right transverse process of T1, and your right index finger on the right clavicle by the sternal articulation. Your right palm should be resting on top of the patient's right shoulder. [Fig. 5.23]

Step 3

Step to the left to create right sidebending of the patient's upper torso.

Step 4

Raise your left forearm straight up under the patient's axilla. This motion will lift the patient's left shoulder girdle, creating a lateral flexion motion of the entire left shoulder girdle. Stop when you feel motion at your right thumb and index finger. You will feel an immediate softening of the superficial muscles under the right hand.

Step 5

Use the web of your right hand to direct force medially and downwards towards the body of T1. Jiggle the body of T1. Repeat this step two or three times.

Step 6

Alternate pressing your right thumb anteriorly against the transverse process of T1 with pressing your right index finger against the clavicle and pushing it posteriorly.

Step 7

If the clavicle is still restricted, slide your right index finger down and hook it under the clavicle. Pull the clavicle in a superior, then a posterior, direction.

Step 8

If the rib motion is still restricted, laterally move your thumb to the point at which the rib meets the transverse process. Keep pressing until you feel a normalization of the involved structures.

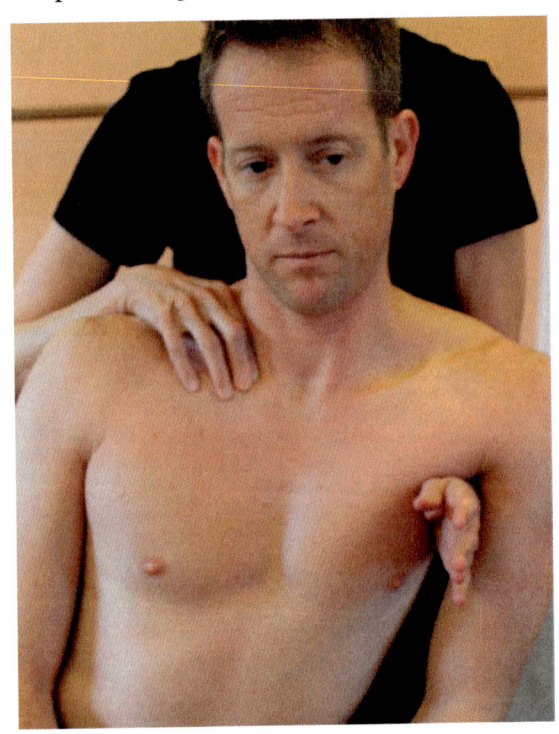

Figure 5.23
Treatment for Thoracic Outlet Syndrome - Step 2.

Part 2

Treatment of the flattening dysfunction of T1 on T2.

Patient position

Ask the patient to sit as far back on the treatment table as possible.

Practitioner position

Stand behind the patient.

Step 1

Ask the patient to cross his arms across his chest wall. Wrap your left arm around the patient's crossed elbows and raise the patient's arms to the level of T2. Press both of the patient's arms firmly against his chest.
[Fig. 3.11], [Fig. 3.12]

Step 2

Grasp the spinous process of T3 between your right thumb and index finger.

Step 3

Ask the patient to push his arms forward against your left hand (isometric resistance). Hold this position for a count of four, then release. Wait for a count of four before repeating. Repeat this step four to five times. The isometric resistance will cause T2 to slide backwards, and will normalize the anterior-posterior slide dysfunctions in this area. Repeat Steps 2 and 3 at the level of T2.

Part 3

Instruct the patient to perform the exercise described on the next page to improve his posture in the cervical and thoracic regions.

An Exercise to Improve Posture in the Cervical and Upper Thoracic Region

Step 1

Instruct the patient to sit in front of a mirror and to place an open tissue box atop his head, with the open side facing down.

Step 2

Instruct the patient to bring his chin straight back without flexing or extending his neck. Tell him to hold this position for ten to fifteen seconds, and then relax. If the head tilts, the tissue box will fall off. If done properly, this step will straighten the cervical lordosis and the upper thoracic kyphosis. The patient should repeat this step several times.

Step 3

Instruct the patient to repeat this exercise four to five times each day. With practice, the patient will no longer need to look into a mirror to keep the tissue box balanced on his head.

Note: *Please refer to Chapter One, Figures 1.5 and 1.6 for examples of these excercises.*

Chapter Six
THE FOOT

A number of musculoskeletal dysfunctions are directly attributable to problems with the foot. These problems are often overlooked, due to a lack of familiarity with the biomechanics of the foot, and with the treatment protocols available to address abnormalities in that area. This chapter introduces important basic biomechanical concepts, in addition to simple orthotic and shoe modifications which you can prescribe to help your patients.

Basic Structure and Biomechanics of the Foot

An arch is a curved structure which consists of two supports flanking a central keystone. The foot contains two longitudinal arches: the Lateral Longitudinal Arch, on the lateral side of the foot, and the Medial Longitudinal Arch, on the medial side.

The Lateral Longitudinal Arch, which is considered a true arch, has the cuboid bone as the keystone center, and the calcaneus and fifth metatarsal as the two supporting flanks. The Medial Longitudinal Arch has the talus bone as the keystone center, and the calcaneus and navicular bones as the supporting flanks. The Medial Longitudinal Arch is more accurately described as an arc, since its movement is similar to that of an arc (as defined as a portion of a curved line). As the ligaments and muscles which attach at the distal end of the medial arc tighten (contract) and loosen (relax), the Medial Longitudinal Arch changes shape, and the calcaneus changes position.

For example, when the foot moves into supination, the normal medial longitudinal arch lifts up. This is due to the calcaneal varus, which moves in such a way as to tighten the ligaments and muscles which support the Medial Longitudinal Arch. When the foot is placed in pronation, in contrast, a calcaneal valgus is produced: the ligaments and muscles of the Medial Longitudinal Arch loosen, drawing the arch down. These actions do not affect the Lateral Longitudinal Arch.

A Test for Medial Longitudinal Arch Function

Step 1

Ask the patient to stand with his feet about six inches apart. Measure the height of the Medial Longitudinal Arch. [Fig. 6.1]

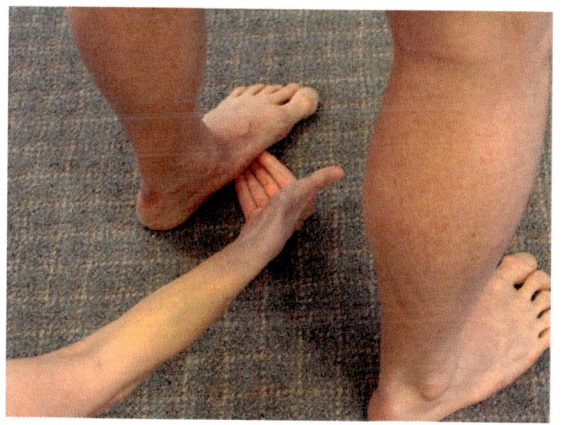

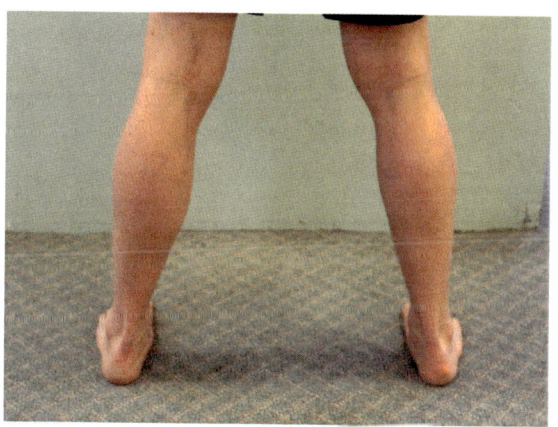

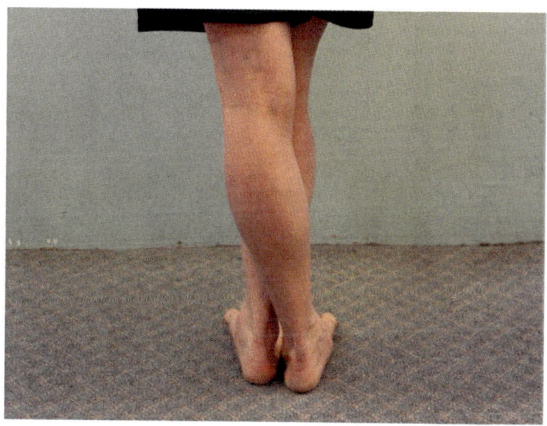

Figure 6.1
Measuring the Medial Longitudinal Arch.

Step 2

Next, ask the patient to stand with his feet fifteen to eighteen inches apart. Measure the height of the medial longitudinal arch. This stance should increase pronation of the foot and lower the medial arch. [Fig. 6.2]

Figure 6.2
Measuring the Medial Longitudinal Arch.

Step 3

Finally, ask the patient to cross one foot in front of the other and to stand so that the lateral sides of each ankle touch. Measure the height of the Medial Longitudinal Arch. This position should create an increase in supination of the foot and raise the Medial Longitudinal Arch. [Fig. 6.3]

Figure 6.3
Measuring the Medial Longitudinal Arch.

Patient Presentation

The patient has been diagnosed with flat feet, which result from fallen arches. Based on this diagnosis, he has been given a shoe orthotic to support his fallen arches.

As you test the patient's medial arches, you notice that, when the patient is standing, the Medial Longitudinal Arch is dropped. However, the arch elevates with supination and drops with pronation.

Interpreting the results

In true structural "flat feet," the foot is in a constant state of pronation, due to medial rotation and the dropping of the navicular bone. Regardless of the foot's placement, this position will not change. Your results show that the patient does not suffer from "flat feet," but, rather, an untwisting of the muscle and the ligamentous support which maintains the height of the Medial Longitudinal Arch. This problem often results from weakness of the supporting ligaments and muscles which rotate the calcaneal bone into a valgus position. Proper treatment entails strengthening the medial arch with exercise. The patient will probably not require a prescription for arch supports.

An Exercise for Strengthening of the Medial Longitudinal Arch

Step 1

Ask the patient to stand. Place several marbles on the floor next to one foot, and put an empty container about six inches lateral to the other foot. [Fig. 6.4]

Figure 6.4
Strengthening the Medial Longitudinal Arch.

Note: *If the patient is unable to perform this exercise while standing, have him try it while seated.*

Step 2

Instruct the patient to pick up a single marble with his toes, cross his foot over and in front of the other foot, and drop the marble into the can. Instruct him to repeat this step several times. [Fig. 6.5]

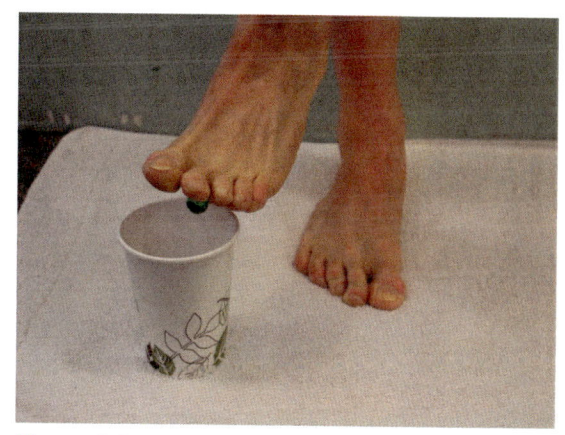

Figure 6.5
Strengthening the Medial Longitudinal Arch.

Step 3

Reverse the placement of the can and the marbles. Repeat the exercise with the other foot.

CALCANEAL VALGUS

A calcaneal valgus can cause several dysfunctions. These include pronation of the foot, which causes a dropped medial arch; an increased genu valgus, and a larger lumbosacral angle, which will accentuate the patient's lumbar lordosis; and thoracic kyphosis and cervical lordosis. If the calcaneal valgus is left untreated, it will eventually result in muscle imbalances, which will, in turn, cause back pain and disability.

A Test for Calcaneal Valgus

Step 1
Ask the patient to stand with his back to you and his feet approximately six inches apart. Make sure that his weight is evenly distributed.

Step 2
Observe the patient's achilles tendons, from the attachment at the calcaneus up to the attachment to the muscle body of the gastrocnemius muscle. [Fig. 6.6]

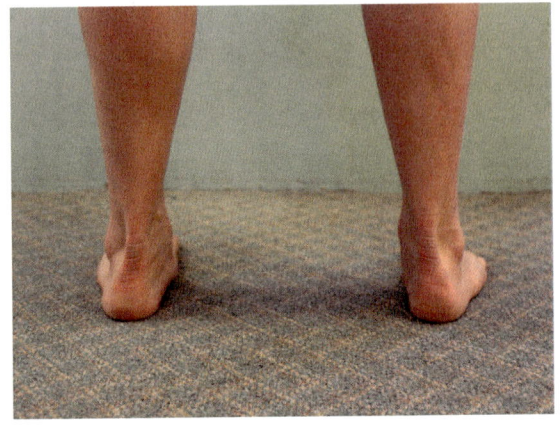

Figure 6.6
Test for Calcaneal Valgus.

Step 3
Normally, the tendons will be parallel to each other. If, instead, one or both of the tendons are bowed with a medially directed convexity, and the respective medial arch is lower on that side, a calcaneal valgus may be present.

A Test to Confirm the Presence of Calcaneal Valgus

Step 1
Purchase rubber heel wedges that are a quarter of an inch high on one side, and that gradually become even with the floor on the other side.

Step 2
Ask the patient to stand with his back to you and his feet approximately six inches apart. Make sure that his weight is evenly distributed.

Step 3
Place a wedge under the bowed calcaneal bone, so that the high part of the wedge rests under the medial aspect of the heel. The lower part of the wedge should be under the lateral part of the heel. [Fig. 6.7]

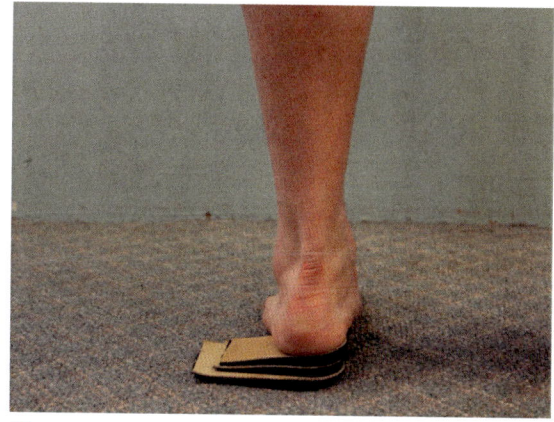

Figure 6.7
Confirm Calcaneal Valgus.

Interpreting the results
If the patient's dropped Medial Longitudinal Arch results from a calcaneal valgus, then the rubber wedge will create a varus movement of the heel. This will cause the achilles tendon to straighten and the Medial Longitudinal Arch to increase in height.

Treatment for Calcaneal Valgus

Use the techniques described in Chapter Five, *"The Extremities,"* to restore full motion to the calcaneus, talus, navicular, cuboid, cuneiforms and metatarsal bones. Prescribe an appropriately-sized medial heel wedge that can be placed in the patient's shoe. The wedge will diminish the pronation of the foot, and will straighten out the calcaneus and forefoot bones. Instruct the patient to perform the *"Exercise for Strengthening of the Medial Longitudinal Arch"* daily.

If appropriate, explain to the patient that high heels may be exaggerating the calcaneal valgus and increasing the symptoms. To decrease the calcaneal valgus, encourage the patient to wear low-heeled shoes, or even ones with a negative heel. If the patient is a runner, suggest building wedges into the heels of the running shoes. This may reduce the incidence of injuries and increase the patient's speed.

INTRODUCTION TO SHOES

Examining a patient's shoes and their wear patterns may uncover abnormalities in the patient's foot, gait pattern, and/or musculoskeletal system. It may also reveal that the shoes are ill-fitting, and that they may be directly causing problems to the foot or to other parts of the musculoskeletal system. Instruct the patient to bring in a pair of shoes that he wears daily. If he is an athlete, he should also bring in his running or training shoes.

Begin by examining the top portion of the shoe, looking for any bulging or distorted areas; foot deformity, which presses up against the shoe, or an ill-fitting shoe, may cause bulging. Examine the general pattern of wear on the heels of the shoes, paying special attention to excessive wear on one heel as compared to the other. In addition, compare the wear on the medial side of the heel to that on the lateral side and the back of the same heel. Look to see if any one of these areas is wearing out faster than the others. These heel patterns will help you determine where the patient places his weight while walking, and whether his weight is distributed evenly.

LAST

The "last" of a shoe is the solid shape or form around which the shoe is molded. Lasts are classified as outflare, inflare, and straight.

Determining the Shoe Last

1. Turn the shoe over to look at the bottom of the shoe.
2. Take a straight-edged object, such as a ruler. Starting at the heel, position it in a straight line that bisects the sole, thereby delineating a left and right side.
3. If the two sides at the tip of the sole are equal, the last is a straight last. If they are uneven and there is more sole on the medial side of the sole, then it is an inflare last. If there is more sole on the lateral side, it is an outflare last.

If you picture a line down the middle of the average person's foot, while the person is standing, you will notice that the medial portion of the foot is composed of the large toe and a portion of the second toe. The lateral side is made up of the lateral portion of the second toe and the three remaining toes. This suggests that most of us require a shoe with either an outflare last or a straight last in order to accommodate both the toes and the metatarsals comfortably. An improperly fitting last will squeeze the toes together, cause pain, affect the patient's gait, and if continually worn, will eventually deform the foot. There are a wide variety of shoes and sneakers available with different lasts, which are designed to accommodate a variety of foot shapes.

MEASURING SHOE SIZE

Measuring the shoe size is just as important as examining the last.

1. Ask the patient to stand with his shoes on. Push down on the top of the shoe at the point at which the first toe ends. A properly fitting shoe should have a space of about 3/8" to 1/2" between the end of the first toe and the front of the shoe.

2. Next, check the fit of the counter (the posterior enclosure in which the heel sits). With the patient still standing, slide a tongue depressor between the patient's calcaneus and the inner lining of the counter. There should be very little space between the foot and the inside of the counter. If you find 1/8" or more space available, the heel size is too large.

*Note: *Patients with narrow heels usually have difficulty finding shoes with small enough counters. If the counters are too large, the calcaneus will develop a valgus rotation and become imbalanced. When buying shoes, it is important to make sure not only that the shoe is the right length, but also that the heel counter fits properly and gives proper support to the foot.*

Anterior Transverse Arch of the Foot

Most authors agree that there are several transverse arches in the foot. For our purposes, we will limit our discussion to the Anterior Transverse Arch. The Anterior Transverse Arch is slightly posterior to the heads of the five metatarsal bones. It plays an important role during the stance phase of gait, which begins with the heel striking the ground. Next, the body's weight moves from the foot's Lateral Longitudinal Arch, medially across the Anterior Transverse Metatarsal Arch. The stance phase ends at the head of the first metatarsal. This complete act is referred to as the tripod action of the foot.

If, for any reason, the transverse arch drops, the weight of the body will be on the heads of the metatarsals, instead of on the arch. The patient will complain that he experiences pain and tenderness over the metatarsal heads while walking.

Several factors may increase the likelihood of the Anterior Transverse Arch dropping. Taking a complete history of a patient's employment and recreational activities may help reveal the causes. These may include:

1. Carrying excess body weight over a number of years.

2. Wearing improperly fitting shoes, which are either too tight or too wide over the arch.

3. Standing or walking on hard surfaces such as cement all day.

Treatment for a Dropped Anterior Transverse Metatarsal Arch

Treatment is multifaceted. Perform the techniques discussed in Chapter 5, *"The Extremities,"* to increase the motion of the bones in the foot, with particular attention to the metatarsals. Instruct the patient to perform the daily exercises described for a dropped Anterior Transverse Metatarsal Arch.

In addition, follow the instructions for examining your patient's foot and shoes. This will help you guide your patient on purchasing properly-fitting shoes. Some of your patients will benefit from having a shoe lift or bar inserted into the shoe, posterior to the heads of the metatarsals. This will take the weight off the metatarsals. Patients who are on their feet all day will need to modify their daily activities so as to reduce the wear and tear on their arches.

Exercises for a Dropped Anterior Transverse Metatarsal Arch

CAUTION

For these exercises, instruct your patient to lean one hand against a wall for stability.

Excercise 1

Step 1

Instruct the patient to stand. Ask him to rise up on his toes, and to hold for a count of five. The patient should then slowly return his feet to the floor. [Fig. 6.8]

Step 2

Next, instruct the patient to lean back on his heels and hold the front of each foot up for a count of five. He should then return his feet back to the floor slowly. He should repeat this exercise ten times. [Fig. 6.9]

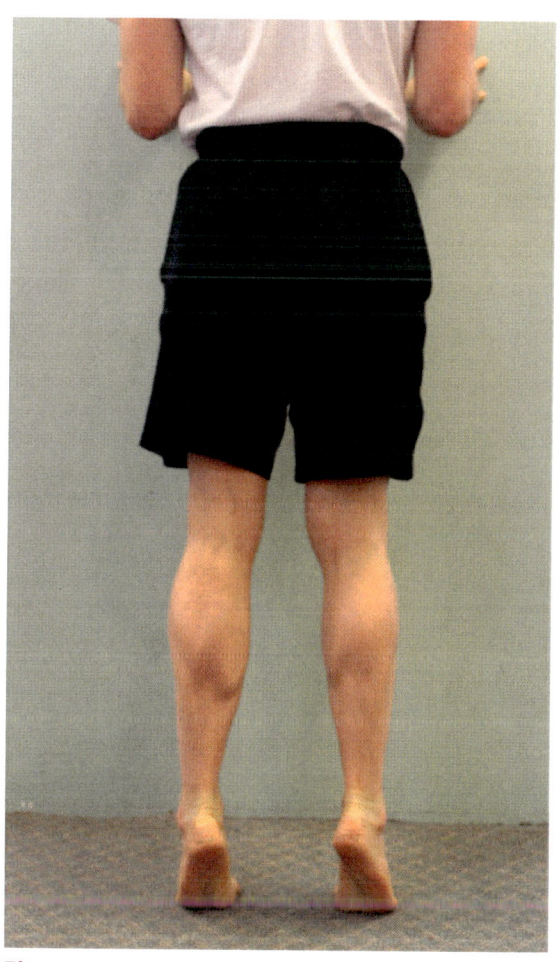

Figure 6.8
Anterior Transverse Arch Exercise 1.

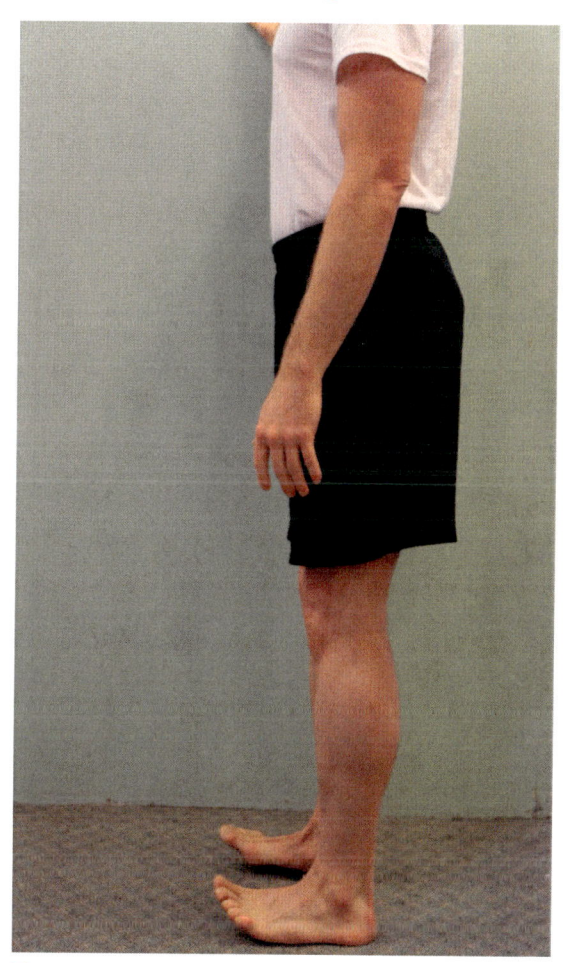

Figure 6.9
Anterior Transverse Arch Exercise 1.

Excercise 2

Step 1
Instruct the patient to stand on a book that is at least two inches thick. Tell him to let his toes hang slightly over the edge of the book.

Step 2
Instruct the patient to lift his toes up into dorsiflexion. He should hold for a count of five and then release.

Step 3
Next, instruct the patient to bend his toes down into full plantarflexion. He should hold for a count of five and then release. He should repeat the exercise ten times.

Excercise 3

Step 1
Instruct the patient to stand on a book, with his forefoot hanging over the edge of it.

Step 2
Once the patient is fully balanced on the book, he should plantarflex his forefeet down over the edge of the book, as far as is comfortable. He should hold for a count of five, and then release.

Step 3
Next, instruct the patient to dorsiflex his feet up towards the ceiling. He should hold for a count of five, and then release. He should repeat this exercise ten times. [Fig. 6.10]

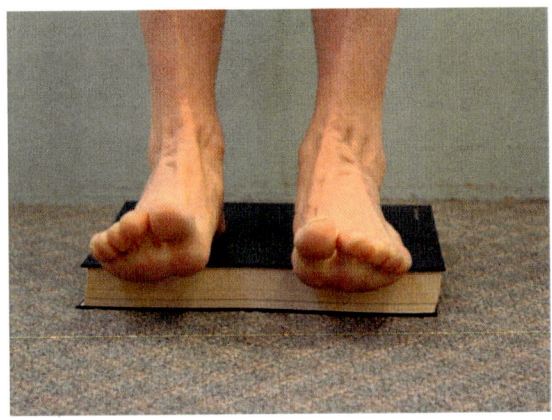

Figure 6.10
Anterior Transverse Arch Exercise 3.

Shotgun Technique to Restore Motion of the Metatarsals

I recommend performing this technique prior to prescribing any type of shoe correction or exercise.

Patient position

Ask the patient to lie in the supine position on the table.

Practitioner position

Sit on the table by the patient's feet, and face away from him.

Procedure

Step 1

Place the patient's foot on your lap.

Step 2

Wrap your fingers around the bottom of the patient's foot, and place your thumbs on top of the shaft of the second metatarsal.

[Fig. 6.11]

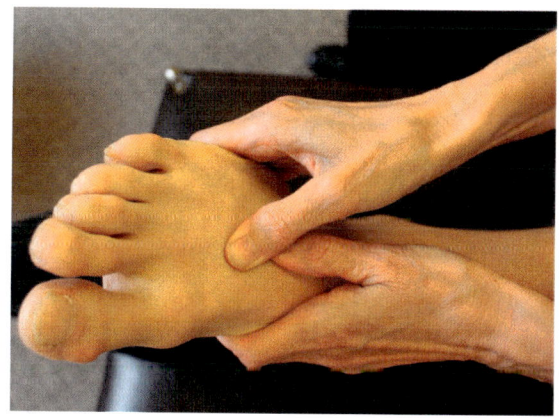

Step 3

With your fingers, lift up the metatarsals while pushing the second metatarsal down with your thumbs. This motion is similar to that of a hinge. The second metatarsal functions as the hinge; you are moving the metatarsals up and around it in a swinging motion.

Step 4

Use the same hinge motion that you used on the second metatarsal. This time, however, use the first and third metatarsal as the center of the hinge. Next, push down on the fourth metatarsal, then on the fifth metatarsal.

Step 5

Repeat these motions several times until you feel a free motion of all the metatarsals.

Figure 6.11
Shotgun technique to restore motion to the Metatarsals.

Shoe Modifications to Relieve Pain at the Metatarsals

1. To treat pain at the head of a metatarsal, instruct the patient to purchase a metatarsal pad from any drug store. These pads come in round or oval shapes, and can be glued inside the patient's shoe. Instruct the patient to place the pad in the shoe, posterior to the head of the painful metatarsal bone. Because the pad is slightly raised, it will take the pressure off the head of the metatarsal as the patient walks, thereby relieving the pain.

2. If the patient is experiencing pain over most or all of the metatarsal heads, then he should have a shoemaker place a 1/4" thick by 1/2" wide leather bar across the shoe, from the medial to lateral side, slightly posterior to the heads of the metatarsals. The bar should not be inserted into the shoe; instead, the sole of the shoe should be split and the bar placed between the layers. This bar will remove the weight from the metatarsal heads and relieve the pain while the patient walks.

Treatment of Pes Cavus (High Arch)

I recommend the following treatments for patients who were either born with, or have developed, a high medial arch from an orthopedic or neurological disorder:

1. Increase motion to all the articulations of the foot by following the techniques presented in Chapter 5, *"The Extremities."*

2. Instruct the patient to have a shoemaker insert a transverse metatarsal bar into the shoe, posterior to the metatarsal heads. This will help flatten the longitudinal arches.

3. Instruct the patient to perform the *"Exercises for Strengthening of the Medial Longitudinal Arch"* and the *"Exercises for a Dropped Anterior Transverse Metatarsal Arch"* daily.

4. Advise the patient to avoid high heels, and, if possible, to wear shoes with negative heels.

PLANTAR FASCIITIS

This disorder's symptoms include pain which is worse in the morning, and which is concentrated at the distal plantar surface of the calcaneus. Over time, the patient may develop a heel spur– a calcification where the plantar fascia attaches to the calcaneal bone. I recommend the following treatment:

1. First, perform the FPR techniques listed in Chapter 5, *"The Extremities,"* that treat hypertonicity and tender points in the foot. In addition, use the techniques that increase motion of the bones in the foot

2. Prescribe exercises that will stretch the muscles in the leg and the foot. Recommend strengthening exercises for the metatarsals and forefoot.

3. Instruct the patient to place a soft foam rubber pad in the shoe under the heel to relieve pressure as he walks. If this doesn't help, take a firm rubber or composite pad, and cut a hole in it, at the place at which the "heel spur" or concentrated pain is located. This will help to keep the weight off the painful area, and to distribute the weight more evenly over the heel.

4. If there are no contraindications to their use, prescribe non-steroidal anti-inflammatory drugs and ice treatments to relieve any inflammation.

CONDITIONS FOUND IN PEDIATRIC PATIENTS

Flat Feet

When children are born, they normally appear to have flat feet. Examination, however, reveals that the plantar area is soft. As the child begins to bear weight, he will develop longitudinal arches. If, as you examine a child's plantar aspect of the foot, you find solid bone-like structures, the child may be developing true "flat feet."

Pronation of the Foot

The child presents with a severely abducted forefoot. Sleeping on the belly as an infant may exacerbate this condition. Treatment includes recommending that infants sleep on their backs or their sides. Instruct the caregiver to stretch the baby's external rotator muscles by very gently grasping the ends of the child's femurs and rotating the child's legs internally. The caregiver should be made aware that this is a "stretching" exercise only, and that it should never be done with force, or in a way that will produce extreme motions.

Metatarsus Varus

In this condition, the child's forefeet are adducted. Treatment involves having the caretaker manually manipulate the forefoot into abduction, and applying specific stretching exercises to the foot. If the child's condition is very severe on first presentation, or if the child presents with a mild case that does not respond to stretching, then the child should be referred to a specialist, who may give him a splinting device. This will decrease the adduction over time.

Calcaneal Valgus

In this condition, the patient's feet are severely abducted, causing the patient to walk like a duck. This usually results from a severe calcaneal valgus. Placing medial wedges in the shoes will cause the child to walk with his toes pointed straight ahead

Calcaneal Varus

Another common complaint is that of a child whose toes are pointing in while walking, and who trips on his own toes. This usually results from a calcaneal varus. Placing lateral heel wedges in the child's shoes will cause the child to walk with his toes pointed straight ahead.

The simple treatment described above for mild cases of calcaneal valgus or varus can have very impressive results. The heel wedges can be removed after about two years of wear. If the condition is severe on presentation, or if it does not immediately respond to the wedge placement, then the patient should be referred to a specialist who may recommend a trial of splinting to the affected foot. This will straighten out the patient's structural abnormalities and improve his gait.

Chapter Seven

AN APPROACH TO GAIT ANALYSIS

Gait Analysis

Examining a patient's gait is a quick and easy way to uncover a number of neurological and musculoskeletal abnormalities. Unfortunately, this skill is frequently underemphasized. As a result, few practitioners learn how to analyze a patient's gait. I encourage every practitioner of manual medicine to quickly scan the patient's gait as part of the initial routine examination.

Biomechanics of Gait

It is important to understand the basic biomechanics of gait. The normal walking cycle consists of a stance phase and a swing phase. Although the two phases of gait are simultaneous, they occur on opposite legs; for example, if the left leg is in the stance phase, then the right leg is in the swing phase.

The Stance Phase is divided into four sections:

1 Heel strike

As the leg completes its swing phase and enters into its stance phase, its hip and knee gradually go into extension as the heel strikes the floor. [Fig. 7.1]

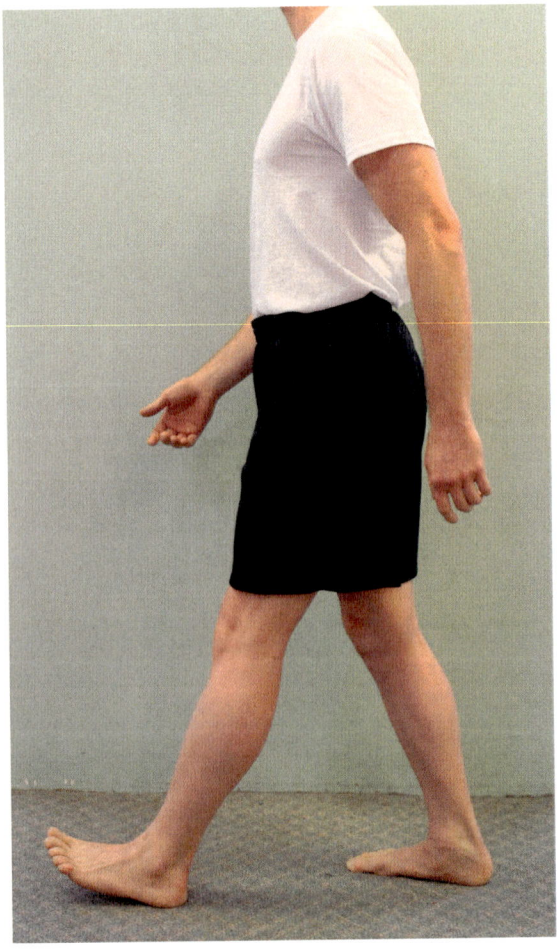

Figure 7.1
Left foot at Heel Strike.

2 Foot flat

Next, the complete foot makes contact with the floor, and the body begins to move forward. [Fig. 7.2]

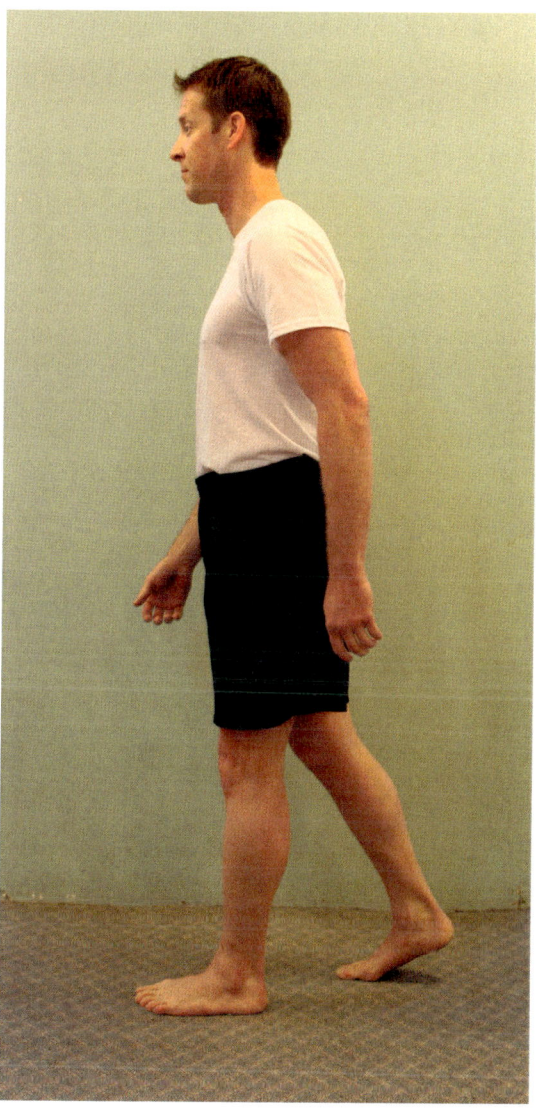

Figure 7.2
Foot Flat.

3 Mid-stance

The body's entire weight is now centered on the stance foot.

4 Push-off

The body's weight is transferred to the big toe, which, in turn, thrusts the body forward. The leg is in extension. [Fig. 7.3]

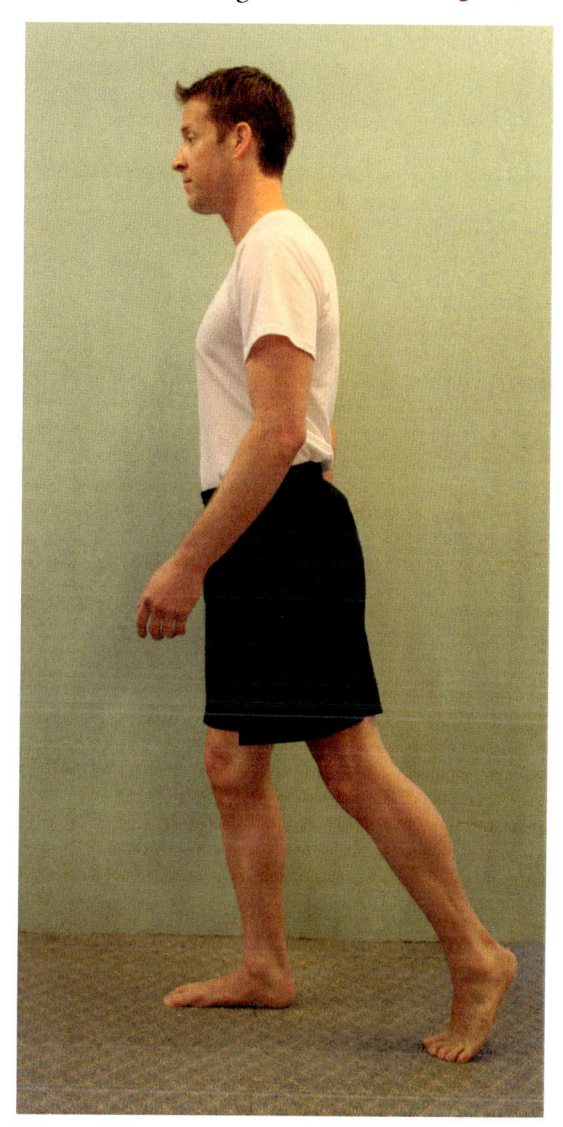

Figure 7.3
Left foot at Push-off.

The Swing Phase is divided into three sections:

1 Acceleration
As the leg pushes off from the stance phase and begins the swing phase, its hip and knee move from extension into flexion.

2 Mid-swing
The flexed leg reaches the midline of the body. [Fig. 7.4]

3 Deceleration
As the leg moves forward, its swing motion slows down, its hip and knee begin to extend, and it prepares itself for the onset of the stance phase heel strike.

The arm and shoulder move in the opposite direction of the corresponding leg. For instance, as the right leg goes forward, the right arm and shoulder swing backwards. At the same time, the left arm and shoulder swing forward as the left leg moves backwards. As the shoulder and arm swing forward, the upper thoracic vertebrae rotates in the opposite direction; for example, as the left shoulder swings forward, the thoracic vertebrae rotate to the right.

Furthermore, the body tries to control its vertical and horizontal displacement while walking. To achieve minimal displacement efficiently and effortlessly, the body follows six major determining principles.

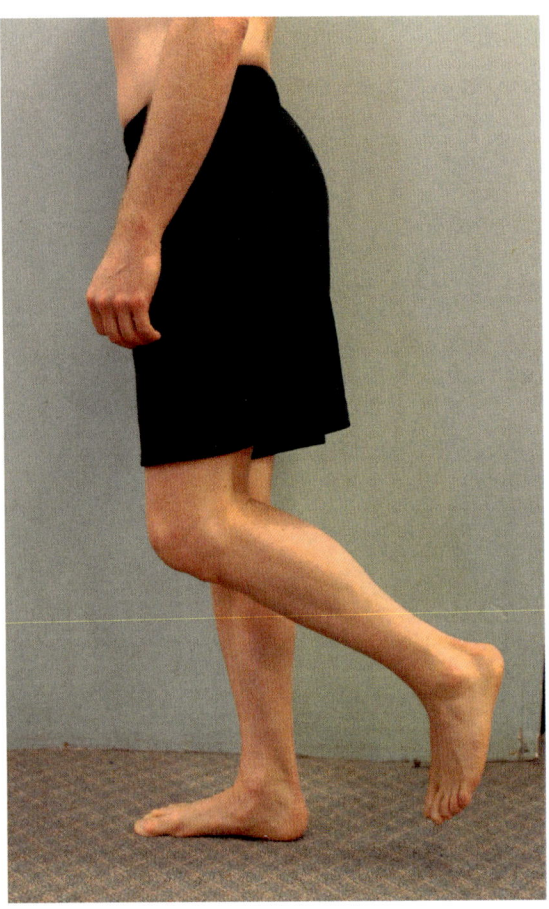

Figure 7.4
Left leg at Midswing.

Stance Leg Major Determining Factors

1 From heel strike to push off, the hip needs to be free to rotate from a posterior position to an anterior one.

2 The ankle joint needs to be free to rotate from extension into flexion.

3 The knee needs to be free to go from extension into flexion and back again into extension.

4 As the stance leg accommodates to the transfer of the individual's entire body weight, the pelvis must shift over the stance leg and be free to sway from side to side.

Swing Leg Major Determining Factors

5 As the leg goes from mid-swing to deceleration, the pelvis on the swing side will tilt down and rotate towards the stance leg. For example, if the right leg is in the swing phase, then the right side of the pelvis will tilt down and rotate towards the left side.

6 As the leg proceeds from a posterior to an anterior position, the knee joint needs to flex so that the foot does not strike the floor.

To Summarize:

On the stance side, you are looking for freedom of rotation of the hip, knee, and ankle joints, along with a shift of the pelvis as the body's center of gravity aligns over the stance leg. On the swing leg, you are looking for the knee's ability to flex, and the pelvis' ability to tilt downwards and rotate. You should also observe the patient's spine; as the pelvis drops down, the sacrum and lower back tilt down. This creates a lumbar scoliosis with its convexity towards the swing leg.

Observing the Patient's Gait

I recommend observing the patient's gait from several vantage points to ensure that you have a clear view of his spine and legs. Have your patient walk in the shoes he wears on a daily basis. Next, ask him to walk barefoot. Ask the patient to walk away from you for a distance of ten to fifteen feet. Then, ask him to turn around and walk back. Finally, ask the patient to walk past you while you observe him, first from his right side and then from his left.

As the patient walks away, ask yourself the following questions:

1. Do the iliac crests drop down equally?
2. Do the gluteal folds drop equally?
3. What is the effect on the lower lumbar vertebrae as each iliac crest drops?
4. Does an equal convexity pattern develop as each side of the pelvis drops?
5. Do the shoulder girdles swing equally as they go back? Is the effect upon the thoracic vertebrae equal from side to side?
6. Does the body shift to the stance leg for support? Is the shift equal from side to side?

As you view the patient from the side, ask yourself these questions:

1. Do the hip joints move freely? What about the knee and ankle joints?
2. At the beginning of the stance phase, does the heel strike the floor?
3. At the end of the stance phase, does the foot push off with the big toe?
4. Does the cervical area move freely?

Any noticeable abnormality of these patterns signals that the involved region requires further evaluation.

Differences between a Woman's Gait and a Man's Gait

Structurally, a woman's pelvis is wider than a man's. This may create an increased side-to-side motion of the pelvis as a woman walks. The wider pelvis may also create a tendency for genu valgus, which will, in turn, increase the pelvic rotation motions. A calcaneal valgus will also exaggerate the side-to-side motions. Women who wear high heels artificially create a calcaneal valgus and genu valgus, which increase the pelvis' shift from side to side.

Dysfunctional Gait Patterns

The Psoatic Gait

The patient's posture is slightly flexed toward the side of the affected psoas. He will have difficulty straightening up, and the foot on the involved side will be in abduction. Upon examination, you may find tender points at the insertion of the iliopsoas muscle at the lesser trochanter, and Somatic Dysfunctions along the lower thoracic vertebrae through the fifth lumbar vertebra. [Fig. 7.5]

Erector Spinae Gait

This patient walks with a very straight back, and has great difficulty moving the spine in any direction, especially into flexion. If the erector spinae are affected on one side only, then, in addition to the above, you will notice an extreme convexity in the lumbar region. This extreme convexity will be on the opposite side from the contracting muscles. You will find a raised iliac crest on the same side as the contracting muscles. Upon examination, you may find several Type II Extension Somatic Dysfunctions in the lower lumbar region. Some patients will complain of sciatic pain on the side of the muscle contraction, which may mimic the pain experienced by patients with herniated discs

Antalgic Gait

While observing the patient, you will notice that one side passes through the stance phase much more quickly than the other side. This is due to the pain he experiences on that side. The pain forces him to remove his weight from the painful leg as soon as possible. An antalgic gait has many causes, such as chronic musculoskeletal conditions or injuries.

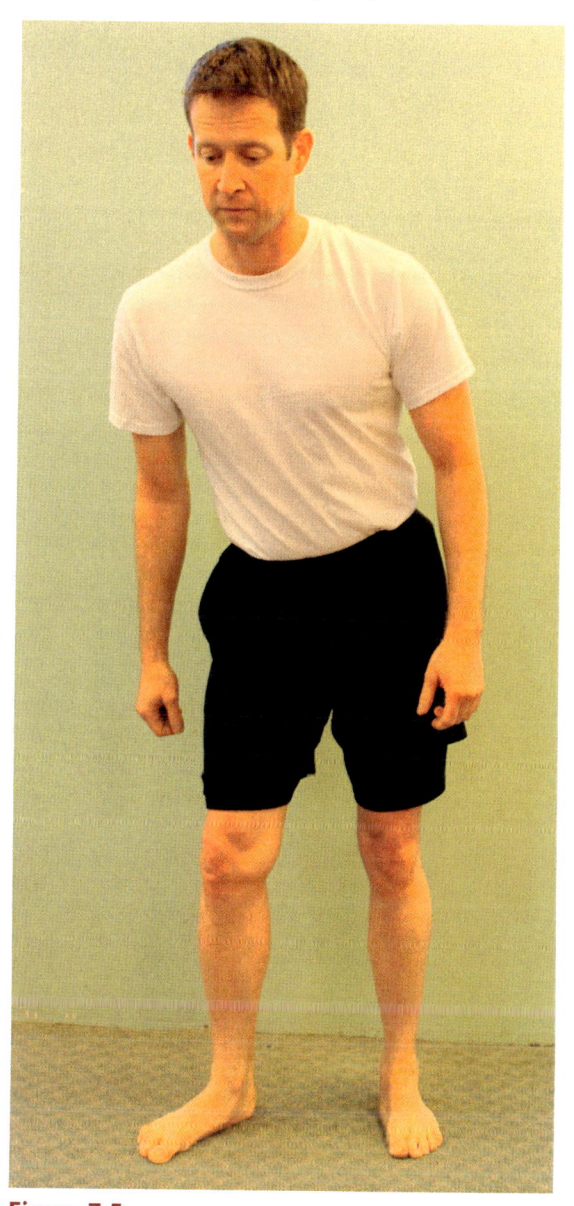

Figure 7.5
Psoatic Gait.

Gluteus Medius Gait

If there is weakness of the gluteus medius muscle, when the side with the weakened muscle is in the stance phase, the pelvis on the opposite side will drop excessively. Upon examination, the patient will have a positive Trendelenberg test. Ask the patient to stand with one leg raised. If the pelvis drops on the side of the elevated leg, then the test is positive. Weakness of the gluteus medius muscle on the opposite side cause the gluteus medius gait. [Fig. 7.6]

Gluteus Maximus Gait

The gluteus maximus muscle helps maintain the center of gravity in the sagittal plane (front-to-back). If there is weakness in the muscle, the patient will hyperextend the trunk and pelvis to stabilize the body.

Plantar Flexion Deficiency

In the case of a plantar flexion deficiency, the patient cannot use his toe to push off at the end of the stance phase. The many potential causes for this deficiency include restriction of the ankle joint or big toe, a painful big toe, plantar muscle weakness, or involvement of the L5 nerve root, which creates weakness of the muscles involved in push-off.

Hiking up of the Pelvis

Degenerative changes or fusion of the hip or knee articulations will limit the flexion of the hip or knee joint. This limitation will cause the patient to hike the entire pelvis up during the swing phase to avoid dragging the foot along the floor.

Dysfunction of the Foot Tripod Action

During the stance phase, the heel of the foot strikes the floor. The body weight then travels over the lateral longitudinal arch. Finally, the weight transfers to the metatarsal heads and ends at the big toe before push-off. The first three events are called the Foot Tripod Action. Dysfunctions may occur along any of the three strike points, and may result from a calcaneal valgus, a painful heel, a lateral longitudinal arch dysfunction, or metatarsal disorders.

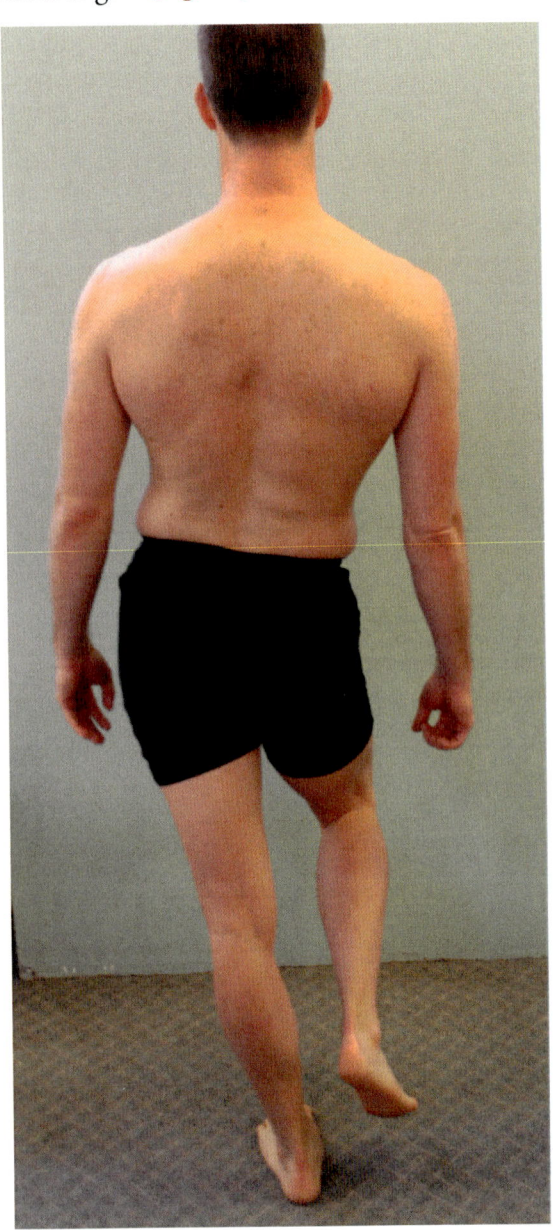

Figure 7.6
Gluteus Medius Weakness on the Left Side.

Gait Patterns of Some Common Neurological Problems

You may initially detect a neurological problem when the patient walks straight ahead towards a wall, stops, and then turns around. While attempting to turn, he will position one leg as a pivot, and take very small steps around the stationary (pivot) leg with the other leg. Alternatively, the patient may not lift his feet off the ground at all. These signs may appear in the early stages of Parkinson's disease or a diabetic neuritis.

1 Hemiplegic Gait
a The patient's affected leg will be stiff, with minimal hip and knee flexion. To walk, the patient will thrust the affected hip and leg forward and drag his shoe on the floor.

b The patient's torso will lean towards the affected side.

c If the arm is involved, it will remain fixed alongside the body, with the elbow flexed.

2 High Steppage Gait with the Toe Touching First (Foot Drop)
a The patient will hike up his hip and leg to avoid tripping on his foot. You will hear his foot slap on the floor as it drops straight down.

b This dysfunction may be caused by a herniated disc or a neuropathy, which causes paralysis of the pretibial or peroneal muscles.

3 High Steppage Gait with the Heel Touching First (Ataxic Gait)
a Due to a loss of the sense of position of the foot, the patient will reel from side to side while walking.

b You will notice bilateral loss of muscle coordination (ataxia).

c This gait may be caused by dysfunctions of the afferent portion of the peripheral nerves, or of the posterior roots of the spinal cord. Alternatively, it may result from medical conditions such as diabetic neuropathy, tabes dorsalis, and metal poisoning.

4 Shuffling Gait
a This patient takes small, flat-footed shuffling steps, which do not clear the floor.

b A typical example is a patient with Parkinson's disease. A very rigid cervical area is an early sign of Parkinson's. As the disease progresses, the patient will have difficulty starting to walk, stopping or turning. The patient will keep his extremities very rigid as he shuffles along.

5 Scissors Gait
a In this gait, the patient's limbs are spastic, and the legs adduct and cross in front of each other, like a pair of scissors.

b To compensate for this motion, the trunk and upper extremities swing with the legs.

c Potential causes include bilateral motor lesions, cervical spondylosis, multiple sclerosis, and severe osteoarthritis of the hip and knee joints.

6 Waddling Gait
a The patient with this gait will roll from side to side and is sometimes described as resembling a penguin as he walks.

b Potential causes include muscular dystrophy or bilateral hip dislocation.

Dr. Stanley Schiowitz
1922 - 2011

Made in the USA
Middletown, DE
22 November 2024